Robert Chambers

History of the rebellion of 1745-6

Robert Chambers

History of the rebellion of 1745-6

ISBN/EAN: 9783337208219

Printed in Europe, USA, Canada, Australia, Japan

Cover: Foto ©ninafisch / pixelio.de

More available books at **www.hansebooks.com**

REBELLION OF 1745-6
BY
ROBERT CHAMBERS.

NEW EDITION.

W. & R. CHAMBERS.
LONDON AND EDINBURGH.
1869.

TO

SIR PETER MURRAY THREIPLAND,

OF FINGASK, BARONET,

REPRESENTATIVE OF A FAMILY WHICH

CAN STILL VIEW WITH GENEROUS REGRET

THE CAUSE FOR WHICH FORMER GENERATIONS

GLADLY SUFFERED,

THIS

WORK IS RESPECTFULLY

AND AFFECTIONATELY INSCRIBED.

PREFACE TO THE FIFTH EDITION.

THE present work appeared originally in *Constable's Miscellany* in 1827. The principal sources of information which then existed for a history of the civil war of 1745, were the contemporary public journals, Mr Home's work (valuable at least for its reports of what the author himself witnessed), the Lockhart and Culloden Papers, the Chevalier Johnstone's *Memoirs*, and the still fresh traditions of the people. Since from these documents the author constructed the first edition of his narrative, a greater quantity of valuable materials has become accessible than during eighty preceding years. The personal narratives of two distinguished actors, Lord Elcho and Mr Maxwell of Kirkconnel, have been in part or wholly given to the world. In Dr James Browne's *History of the Highlands and Highland Clans*, there appeared extensive and very important excerpts from the great collection in the possession of the British sovereign, styled 'The Stuart Papers.' To this valuable set of excerpts, Lord Mahon has made additions in his *History of Great Britain between the Peace of Utrecht and that of Aix-la-Chapelle.* I was myself so fortunate, in 1832, as to become possessed of an extensive collection of papers which had been gathered, early in the present century, by the late Sir Henry Steuart of Allanton, with a view to his composing a History of the Efforts in behalf of the House of Stuart from the Revolution downwards. Amongst these was an assemblage of memoirs, notes, letters, and other memorabilia respecting the insurrection of 1745 and its actors, which had been formed with great labour, during the twenty years ensuing upon the event, by the Rev. Robert

Forbes, Episcopal minister at Leith, and ultimately (titular) Bishop of Orkney. From Sir Henry's collection, which eventually became mine, I published a selection in 1834, under the title of *Jacobite Memoirs of the Rebellion of* 1745-6; but by far the greater part of the more valuable documents still remained in manuscript.

In the present edition of my own narrative, advantage has been taken of the abundance of new materials thus placed at command. So ample were these, and so great were the changes consequently required in the fabric of the narrative, that the present might almost be described as a new work. That part, in particular, which records the singular adventures of the Prince after the battle of Culloden, is much more copious, and also more strictly correct, than it was before, chiefly in consequence of the special pains which Bishop Forbes took to ascertain all the particulars of those adventures from the gentlemen and others who had been concerned in them. The work is now submitted, in its extended and corrected form, not without a hope that it will be found to contain sufficient information to satisfy all reasonable curiosity upon the subject.

EDINBURGH, *February* 24, 1840.

PREFACE TO THE SEVENTH EDITION.

A FEW words as to the *feeling* manifested in this narrative.

It has been customary to call it a Jacobite history. To this let me demur. Of the whole attempt of 1745 I disapprove, as most men do. I think its authors were under a grave mistake in preferring a supposed right of One to the interest of the entire body of the people; and, undoubtedly, it was a crime to disturb with war, and to some extent with rapine, a nation enjoying internal peace under a settled government.

But, on the other hand, those who followed Charles Edward in his hazardous enterprise, acted according to their lights, with heroic self-devotion. They were not fairly liable to the vulgar ridicule and vituperations thrown upon them by those whose duty it was to resist and punish them. Even the sovereigns succeeding him whom Charles Edward strove to displace, came to feel for the exiled dynasty, and to wish for no better friends than it had had. Knowing how these men did all in honour, I deem it but just that their adventures should be detailed with impartiality, and their unavoidable misfortunes be spoken of with humane feeling.

There is no other Jacobitism in the book that I am aware of.

R. C.

EDINBURGH, 1869.

GENEALOGICAL AND HISTORICAL INTRODUCTION.

JAMES, sixth of Scotland and first of England, was the common progenitor of the two families whose contentions for the throne of Great Britain form the subject of this work. He was succeeded, at his death in 1625, by his eldest surviving son Charles.

Charles I., after a reign of twenty-three years, the latter portion of which had been spent in war with a party of his subjects, perished on the scaffold in 1649.

Charles II., eldest son of Charles I., lived in exile for eleven years after the death of his father, during which time the government was vested first in a Parliament, and afterwards in a Protectorate. He was at length placed upon the throne, May 1660. This event is known in British history by the title of 'the Restoration.' Charles died without legitimate issue in 1685, and was succeeded by his brother James, who had previously been entitled Duke of York.

James II. was fifty-three years of age when he mounted the throne. In his youth he had, as Admiral of England, shewn some talent for business, and considerable skill in naval affairs; but during his reign he manifested a want of judgment which would almost indicate premature dotage. Having been converted to the Roman Catholic faith, he entered into the spirit of it with the zeal natural to a weak mind, and ventured upon some steps which impressed his subjects with the conviction that he wished to place this religion on a par with Protestantism, if not to restore it to its ancient supremacy. Thus he alienated the affections of the people, but more especially of the clergy, who were otherwise disposed to have been his most zealous friends. The compliance of bad judges, and some imperfections of the British constitution, left it in his power to take the most arbitrary measures for the accomplishment of his designs; and he attempted to establish as a maxim, that he could do whatever he pleased by a proclamation of his own, without the consent of Parliament. Finally, his obstinacy and infatuation rendered it necessary for all parties of the state to seek his deposition. A secret coalition of Whigs and Tories resolved to call in the assistance of William, Prince of Orange, nephew and son-in-law to the king. William landed upon the south coast of England with an army of sixteen thousand men, partly his own native subjects, and partly English refugees, November 5, 1688. As he proceeded to London, James was deserted by his army, his friends, and even his own children; and in a confusion of mind, the result of fear and offended feelings, he retired to France. William, at the head of a powerful force, took possession of London. A Convention-Parliament then declared that James had abdicated the throne, and resolved to offer the crown to William and his consort Mary. In British history, this event is termed 'the Revolution.'

William III., son of Mary, eldest daughter of Charles I., and who had married his cousin Mary, eldest daughter of James II., thus assumed the crown, in company with his consort; while King James remained in exile in France. Mary died in 1695, and King William then became sole monarch. In consequence of a fall from his horse, he died in 1701, leaving no issue.

Anne, second daughter of King James II., was then placed upon the throne. James meanwhile died in France, leaving a son, James, born in England, June 10, 1688, the heir of his unhappy fortunes. This personage, known in history by the epithet of the Pretender, and less invidiously by his *incognito* title, the Chevalier St George, continued an exile in France, supported by his cousin Louis XIV., and by the subsidies of his English adherents. Anne, after a reign of thirteen years, distinguished by military and literary glory, died without surviving issue, August 1, 1714. During the life of this sovereign, the crown had been destined, by act of Parliament, to the nearest Protestant heir, Sophia, Electress of Hanover, daughter of Elizabeth, Queen of Bohemia, the daughter of King James VI. Sophia having predeceased Queen Anne, it descended of course to her son George, Elector of Hanover, who accordingly came over to England and assumed the sovereignty, to the exclusion of his cousin the Chevalier.

George I. was scarcely seated on the throne, when (1715) an insurrection was raised against him by the friends of his rival, now generally known as the Jacobite party. This rebellion was suppressed; and George I. continued to reign, almost without further disturbance, till his death in 1727.

George II. acceded to the crown on the death of his father. Meanwhile the Chevalier St George had married Clementina, grand-daughter of John Sobieski, the heroic king of Poland; by this lady he had two sons—1st, Charles Edward Lewis Casimir, born December 31, 1720, and, 2d, Henry Benedict, born 1725, afterwards well known by the name of Cardinal de York. James was himself a man of weak, though mild and virtuous character; but the blood of Sobieski seems to have descended to his eldest son, whose boldness, as displayed in 1745-6, did everything but retrieve the fortunes of his family.

CONTENTS.

	PAGE
Chapter I.—PRINCE CHARLES'S VOYAGE AND LANDING	13
„ II.—THE HIGHLANDERS	30
„ III.—THE GATHERING	40
„ IV.—PROCEEDINGS OF GOVERNMENT	49
„ V.—CHARLES'S DESCENT UPON THE LOWLANDS	59
„ VI.—ALARM OF EDINBURGH	72
„ VII.—CHARLES'S MARCH UPON EDINBURGH	78
„ VIII.—CAPTURE OF EDINBURGH	86
„ IX.—PRINCE CHARLES'S ENTRY INTO EDINBURGH	98
„ X.—COPE'S PREPARATIONS	106
„ XI.—THE PRINCE'S MARCH TO PRESTON	112
„ XII.—THE BATTLE OF PRESTON	120
„ XIII.—PRINCE CHARLES AT HOLYROOD	139
„ XIV.—GATHERING AT EDINBURGH	152
„ XV.—INVASION OF ENGLAND	170
„ XVI.—RETREAT TO SCOTLAND	193
„ XVII.—PRELIMINARIES OF THE BATTLE OF FALKIRK	212
„ XVIII.—THE BATTLE OF FALKIRK	230
„ XIX.—ARRIVAL OF THE DUKE OF CUMBERLAND	246
„ XX.—MARCH TO THE NORTH	255
„ XXI.—PROCEEDINGS IN THE NORTH	265
„ XXII.—PRELIMINARIES OF THE BATTLE OF CULLODEN	278

CONTENTS.

	PAGE
CHAPTER XXIII.—BATTLE OF CULLODEN	293
" XXIV.—TRANSACTIONS IMMEDIATELY AFTER THE BATTLE OF CULLODEN	302
" XXV.—SUPPRESSION OF THE INSURRECTION	313
" XXVI.—CHARLES'S WANDERINGS—THE LONG ISLAND	332
" XXVII.—CHARLES'S WANDERINGS—SKYE	348
" XXVIII.—CHARLES'S WANDERINGS—THE MAINLAND	388
" XXIX.—TRIALS AND EXECUTIONS	442
" XXX.—PRINCE CHARLES IN FRANCE	467
" XXXI.—MEASURES FOR PREVENTION OF FURTHER DISTURBANCES	481
" XXXII.—SUBSEQUENT LIFE OF PRINCE CHARLES	491
APPENDIX	515

HISTORY

OF THE

REBELLION OF 1745-6.

CHAPTER I.

PRINCE CHARLES'S VOYAGE AND LANDING.

'*Guard.* Qui est là?
Pucelle. Païsans, pauvres gens de France.'
King Henry VI.

THE idea of an insurrection in favour of the exiled house of Stuart, though, from the Revolution, it had never been for a moment out of the thoughts of the Jacobite party, remained, during the long peace which preceded 1739, in that state of dormancy which usually befalls the most deeply cherished schemes, when there is no hope of their being immediately carried into execution. When, however, Britain became engaged in war with Spain, and not long after mingled in the general conflict of European powers which took place in consequence of the exclusion of the house of Austria from the imperial dignity, the friends of the Stuarts eagerly embraced the belief that a fitting time had at length arrived for striking a blow in behalf of legitimacy. They had every reason to believe that France, in particular, if not also Spain, would grant them the assistance of an invading armament, under favour of which they might themselves take up arms. What made their prospects the more cheerful was, that a new promise had sprung up in the exiled family, in the person of the old Chevalier's eldest son, Charles Edward, whose character was understood to comprehend all that was graceful in a prince, united with the spirit of one destined to be a military hero. In this respect they stood in a better position than they had ever done before; for the two preceding generations of the dethroned family had possessed no personal qualities that could afford much aid to the cause.

So early, therefore, as 1740, associations had begun to be formed by the Scottish partisans of the Stuarts, engaging to rise in arms, provided that competent assistance should be sent from abroad.[1] At the end of 1743, the French court actually entered into the design of an invasion of Britain in behalf of the Stuarts, and sent to Rome for the young Chevalier, that he might be ready to accompany it, the chief command of the troops being designed for the celebrated Marshal Saxe. Charles instantly proceeded to Paris, and in the latter part of February 1744, a fleet was ready to sail, with an army of 15,000 men on board. The British government was thrown into great alarm, for their shores were comparatively unprotected, and the people were in a state of violent discontent. A small fleet was mustered under Sir John Norris, and sent to watch the French at Dunkirk. What this aged admiral could scarcely have done, was done by a storm, which drove the French vessels from their moorings, destroying some, and irretrievably damaging others. This, with the attacks of the British vessels, so far deranged the scheme, that the French ministry determined on abandoning it. The

[1] In the year 1740, seven persons of rank entered into an association of this kind—namely, the Earl of Traquair; his brother, John Stuart; Lord Lovat; James Drummond, commonly called Duke of Perth; Lord John Drummond, uncle of James Drummond; Sir James Campbell of Auchinbreck; and Cameron, younger of Locheil—most of these being persons possessing influence in the Highlands. Many others afterwards entered into similar engagements.

mortification of Charles was great; and with his characteristic boldness he actually proposed to his father's veteran partisan, Earl Marischal, to set sail in a herring-boat for Scotland, in order to put himself at the head of his friends—believing, apparently, that his own presence as their leader was alone wanting for success. The earl of course refused to sanction such a scheme; and Charles, after an ineffectual endeavour to be allowed by his father to serve in the French army, retired to an obscure part of France, to wait for better times.

At the end of the year, and in the early part of 1745, he used every exertion, by means of his emissaries, and by personal solicitations, to induce the French court to renew the enterprise; but without success. It appears that some of the Protestant powers in alliance with Louis had remonstrated against his giving aid to the Catholic party in Britain: every effort, they said, ought to be concentrated on the seat of war in Flanders.[1] Charles, therefore, found himself coldly treated in Paris. It is remarkable that he was not even introduced to the king—nor had he ever this honour until after his return from Scotland. Yet, for the sake of an object to which he had devoted his whole affections, he patiently endured this contumely, and all the other distresses of his situation, among which the low intrigues of some of his immediate followers were not the least. Writing to his father, January 3, 1745, when about to retire, for reasons of policy, to a dull place in the country, he says: 'This I do not regret in the least, as long as I think it of service to our cause. I would put myself in a tub, like Diogenes, if necessary.'[2] Afterwards (March 7), when contemplating some preparations for the expedition with his own means, he writes to the same person: 'I wish you would pawn all my jewels, for on *this* side of the water I should wear them with a very sore heart, thinking that there might be a better use for them; so that, in an urgent necessity, I may have a sum which can be of use for the cause.' Of another sum which he had obtained from his

---
[1] *Mémoires de Noailles*, vi. 22, quoted in Lord Mahon's *History of England*, iii. 335.
[2] Extracts from Stuart Papers, in Lord Mahon's *History*.

father, and expended in the purchase of broadswords, he says in the same letter: 'Rather than want it, I would have pawned my shirt: it is but for such uses that I shall ever trouble you with requests for money; *it will never be for plate or fine clothes, but for arms and ammunition, or other things which tend to what I am come about to this country.*'[1] It is generally believed that the victory, such as it was, gained by the French over the British army at Fontenoy in May, completed the resolution of France not to fit out a new armament for the young Chevalier, a diversion of the enemy by such means being now considered unnecessary.

When Charles was at length despairing of aid from this source, the very sense of resentment seems to have acted as an additional stimulus to throw him back upon the romantic design first propounded to Lord Marischal. He had great confidence in the enthusiasm of his British, and more particularly his Scottish partisans, some of whom had requested him to come to them, if he only could bring a sufficiency of arms and money. He thought if he could once raise his standard in Scotland, his friends would flock to it, and that at this particular juncture, when the British army had just sustained a notable defeat, and the country was drained of troops, he should be able at least to keep his ground until foreign aid should arrive, if not to do something which should make that aid more likely to come. The loud discontents expressed in Britain respecting the war and the existing ministry, held out additional encouragement. He therefore determined upon a secret voyage to Scotland, no matter how few might share in the danger, or how slenderly provided he might be with money or with military stores. Early in June, we find him at the Château de Navarre, near Evreux, writing a letter to his father, not to ask his sanction for the projected enterprise, but to inform him that, before the writing could be in his hands, that enterprise would be commenced. 'I am to tell you,' says he, 'what will be a great surprise to you.

---

[1] Extracts from Stuart Papers, in Lord Mahon's *History*.

I have been, above six months ago, invited by our friends to go to Scotland, and carry what money and arms I could conveniently get; this being, they are fully persuaded, the only way of restoring you to the crown, and them to their liberties. . . . . After such scandalous usage as I have received from the French court, even had I not given my word to do so, or got so many encouragements from time to time as I have had, I should have been obliged, in honour and for my own reputation, to have flung myself into the hands of my friends, and die with them, rather than live longer in such a miserable way here, or be obliged to return to Rome, which would be just giving up all hopes. I cannot but mention a parable here, which is: a horse that is to be sold, if [when] spurred, [he] does not skip, or shew some sign of life, nobody would care to have him even for nothing; just so my friends would care very little to have me, if, after such usage, which all the world is sensible of, I should not shew that I have life in me. Your majesty cannot disapprove a son's following the example of his father. You yourself did the like in the year 1715; but the circumstances now are indeed very different, by being much more encouraging. . . . . I have been obliged to steal off, without letting the king of France so much as suspect it; for which I make a proper excuse in my letter to him, by saying it was a great mortification to me never to be able to speak and open my heart to him; that this thing was of such a nature that it could not be communicated by any of the ministers, but to himself alone, in whom, after God Almighty, my resting lies, and that the least help would make my affair infallible. If I had let the French court know this beforehand, it might have had all these bad effects: *1st*, It is possible they might have stopped me, having a mind to keep measures with the elector;[1] and then, to cover it over, they would have made a merit of it to you, by saying they had hindered me from doing a wild and desperate thing: *2dly*, My being invited by my friends would not be believed, or

---

[1] The king of Great Britain was, by the Stuarts and their partisans, only allowed to be Elector of Hanover.

at least would have made little impression on the French court.

'I have,' he continues, 'sent Stafford to Spain, and appointed Sir Thomas Geraldine to demand succours in my name, to complete the work, to whom I sent letters for the king and queen, written in the most engaging terms to the same purpose. Let what will happen, the stroke is struck, and *I have taken a firm resolution to conquer or to die, and to stand my ground as long as I shall have a man remaining with me.* .... Whatever happens unfortunate to me, cannot but be the strongest engagement to the French court to pursue your cause. Now, if I were sure they were capable of any sensation of this kind, if I did not succeed, I would perish, as Curtius did, to save my country and make it happy; it being an indispensable duty on me as far as lies in my power. .... I write this from Navarre, but it will not be sent off till I am on shipboard. .... I should think it proper (if your majesty pleases) to put myself at his holiness's feet, asking his blessing on this occasion; but what I chiefly ask is your own, which I hope will procure me that of God Almighty, upon my endeavours to serve you, my family, and my country.'[1]

One Waters, a banker in Paris, had lent Charles 60,000 livres, which he had employed in paying off the debts he incurred at Paris during the past winter. The younger Waters, also a banker, now advanced to him 120,000 livres, with which he bought 1500 fusees, 1800 broadswords, and a considerable quantity of gunpowder, ball, flints, dirks, and other articles, including 20 small field-pieces. Mr Walsh, a merchant in Nantes, agreed to convey him to the coast of Scotland in a brig of 18 guns, which he had fitted out to cruise against the British trade; at the same time Mr Rutledge, a friend of Walsh, obtained from the French court the services of the *Elizabeth*, a vessel of 68 guns and 700 men, which was to cruise on the coast of Scotland. Some obscurity rests on the point; yet it is

---

[1] This remarkable letter is printed in the appendix to Lord Mahon's *History*, from the Stuart Papers.

clear that the Prince had the use of this latter vessel, to carry his stores, and convoy his own ship, without the knowledge of the French government. While the preparations were making at Nantes, the few gentlemen who had agreed to accompany the Prince lodged in different parts of the town, and when they met in public, took no notice of each other, the better to conceal their design.[1] They were seven in number; the most important being the Marquis of Tullibardine, who, having been concerned in the affair of 1715, was attainted, and thus prevented from succeeding to his father's title and estates as Duke of Athole, which were now enjoyed by his next younger brother. The rest were—Sir Thomas Sheridan, who had been the Prince's preceptor; Sir John Macdonald, an officer in the Spanish service; Mr Kelly, an English clergyman, who had been concerned in the Bishop of Rochester's plot in 1722; O'Sullivan, an Irish officer in the French service; Francis Strickland, an English gentleman; and Mr Æneas Macdonald, banker in Paris, a younger brother of Macdonald of Kinlochmoidart. Lord Mahon says very justly, 'that the charm of this romantic enterprise seems singularly heightened, when we find, from the secret papers now disclosed, that it was undertaken not only against the British government, but without, and in spite of, the French.'

At seven of the evening of the 22d of June, old style,[2] the Prince embarked at St Nazaire, in the mouth of the Loire, on board Walsh's little vessel, named the *Doutelle*, attended by his seven friends, besides one Buchanan, a messenger. Proceeding to Belleisle, he was there detained for some days, in expectation of the *Elizabeth*. Since the letter to his father before quoted, he had written again: 'I made my devotions,' he says, 'on Pentecost day, recommending myself particularly to the Almighty on this occasion to guide and direct me, and to continue to me always the same sentiments; which are, *rather to*

---

[1] *Jacobite Memoirs*, from the papers of Bishop Forbes, p. 2.
[2] Such was the day in British reckoning, old style being still used there. In France, the day was esteemed as the 3d of July. Old style is here preferred, as that used throughout the whole of the ensuing narrative.

suffer anything than fail in any of my duties.' He afterwards wrote to his father's secretary, Mr Edgar: 'I hope in God we shall soon meet, which I am resolved shall not be but at *home;'* meaning in the seat of his father's government.[1] His last words to the same gentleman in a postscript, dated the 12th July (N.S.), were: 'After having waited a week here, not without a little anxiety, we have at last got the escort I expected, which is just arrived—namely, a ship of 68 guns, and 700 men aboard. I am, thank God, in perfect health, but have been a little sea-sick, and expect to be more so; but it does not keep me much abed, for I find the more I struggle against it the better.' None of these letters were sent off till after he had finally quitted the shores of France. He had acted in like manner by his Scottish friends, sending Mr Murray of Broughton to apprise them of his intention of sailing, but too late to allow of their sending any answer that could be expected to reach him before he should have set sail. The Scottish gentlemen consequently met in great anxiety, to deliberate on the message, when it was agreed by all, excepting the Duke of Perth, that the scheme was the extreme of rashness, and Mr Murray was appointed by them to watch for the Prince in the West Highlands, and warn him off the coast. It would thus appear that Charles was, in some measure, under a false impression as to the eagerness of his Scottish friends for the undertaking. Probably only a very few had invited him to come, no matter how attended or provided. Murray actually waited during the whole month of June upon the west coast, when, finding that the Prince did not arrive, and conceiving that the scheme had been given up, he returned to his house in Peeblesshire. To the friends of the cause in England, it does not appear that any message was sent by the Prince before his voyage.

[1] After all that is here related of the Prince's proceedings, it seems scarcely necessary to allude to a letter of David Hume, in which that generally acute person relates an absurd story, communicated to him by Helvetius the philosopher, to the effect that Charles became faint-hearted at the point of commencing his enterprise, and had to be carried on board by his followers. The utter inconsistency of the tale with the above unquestionable facts, must be at once apparent.

All things being in readiness, the expedition sailed from Belleisle on the 2d July. Four days after, in latitude 47° 57′ north, and 39 leagues to the west of the Lizard Point, an English man-of-war appeared in sight. D'Eau, the captain of the *Elizabeth*, came on board the *Doutelle*, and asked Mr Walsh to aid in attacking this vessel, representing that an immediate engagement might be the best course, as the English ship, if joined by any other of the same nation, would become more than a match for both of theirs. Mr Walsh, feeling a great responsibility as to the Prince's person, declined this proposal. Captain D'Eau then resolved to make the attack singly. The British vessel proved to be the *Lion*, of 58 guns, commanded by Captain Brett, an officer who had distinguished himself in Anson's expedition by storming Paita. The engagement between the two vessels lasted five hours, during which the *Doutelle* looked on from a little distance. While the fight continued, the Prince several times represented to Mr Walsh what a small assistance would serve to give the *Elizabeth* the advantage, and importuned him to engage in the action; but Mr Walsh positively refused, and at last desired the Prince not to insist any more, otherwise he would order him down to his cabin.[1] At the close of the action, the *Lion* sheered off like a tub upon the water, but the *Elizabeth* was unable to give it any further annoyance. The vessel was much damaged in the rigging, and between thirty and forty of the officers and men were wounded or killed, the captain himself being amongst the former. It therefore returned to France to refit, carrying with it the Prince's too slender stores. Charles, nevertheless, continued his voyage, cheering himself up with the hopes he entertained from the ardour of his Scottish partisans.

In this voyage the Prince and his friends maintained a strict incognito, as may have been surmised from the liberty which Mr Walsh has just been represented as taking with one who

[1] *Jacobite Memoirs.*

considered himself as rightfully Prince Regent of the British dominions. Charles wore the dress of a student of the Scotch College at Paris, and, to conceal his person still more, he had allowed his beard to grow from the day he embarked. The vessel sailed by night without a light, the better to escape observation. On one occasion it was chased, and prepared for an action; but escaped by fast sailing. After some days' sailing, it approached that remotest range of the Hebrides which —comprehending Lewis, Uist, Barra, and many others—is commonly called the Long Island, from its appearing at a distance to form a single continent. A large Hebridean eagle came and hovered over the vessel. It was first observed by the Marquis of Tullibardine, who did not at first choose to make any remark upon it, lest his doing so might have been considered superstitious; but, some hours later, on returning upon deck after dinner, seeing the eagle still following their course, the marquis pointed it out to the Prince, saying: 'Sir, this is a happy omen: the king of birds is come to welcome your royal highness on your arrival in Scotland.'[1]

They now sailed into a strait between the islands of Eriska and South Uist, and, observing some doubtful sails at a distance, made haste to land on the former island, carrying on shore their money, arms, and ammunition. The Prince was conducted to the house of the *tacksman*, or tenant, and learned that Macdonald of Clanranald, chief of a branch of that great clan, and who held extensive possessions in the West Highlands and Hebrides, was upon South Uist, with his brother Boisdale,[2] while young Clanranald,[3] the son of the chief, and a person in whom he had great confidence, was at Moidart upon the mainland. A messenger was despatched to desire an interview with

---

[1] *Jacobite Memoirs*, p. 9.

[2] Throughout this narrative, the custom of the country has been conformed to, in designating the Scottish chiefs and landed proprietors by their family and territorial titles.

[3] The eldest son of a Highland chief always receives his father's title, with the additional epithet of *young;* thus, for instance, young Glengarry, young Locheil, &c. In the Lowlands, something like the same custom did lately, and perhaps still does exist, though it is more common to call him the *young laird*. Ludicrous instances sometimes occur of a man being called the young laird, when he is in reality far advanced in life.

Boisdale, and in the meantime Charles spent the night in the house of the tacksman.

He returned on board his vessel next morning, and Boisdale soon after came to visit him. This gentleman was supposed to have great influence over the mind of his elder brother the chief, who, on account of his advanced age and bad health, did not take an active part in the management of his own affairs.[1] Charles knew that, if Boisdale could be brought over to his views, the rising of the clan would be a matter of course. Here, however, he experienced a disappointment. Mr Macdonald seems to have been well affected to the cause, but strongly impressed with its hopelessness at the present moment. He spoke in a very discouraging manner, and advised the Prince to return home. 'I am *come* home, sir,' said Charles, 'and can entertain no notion of returning to the place whence I came. I am persuaded that my faithful Highlanders will stand by me.' Boisdale said he was afraid that the contrary would be found the case. Charles instanced Macleod of Macleod and Sir Alexander Macdonald of Sleat as chieftains upon whom he could depend. These were men who could bring twelve hundred broadswords to the field. Boisdale now gave him the unwelcome intelligence that these gentlemen had not only resolved to abandon his cause, but might be found to act against it. To prove this, he said a messenger might be sent to ask them to join the proposed expedition. As might be expected, Charles in vain exerted his eloquence to induce Boisdale to engage his brother's clan. He plainly told the Prince that he would rather use any influence he had with his brother and the clan to prevent them from taking arms.

Charles was greatly disconcerted at Boisdale's coldness, but he took care to shew no symptom of depression. He ordered his ship to be unmoored, and set sail for the mainland, expressing a resolution to pursue the enterprise he had commenced. He carried Boisdale along with him for several miles, and

---

[1] *Historical and Genealogical Account of the Clan or Family of Macdonald*, p. 159.

endeavoured, with all his eloquence, to make him relent and give a better answer. But Mr Macdonald continued to express the same unfavourable sentiments; and finally descending into his boat, which hung astern, he left the Prince to follow his own apparently hopeless course.[1]

Continuing his voyage to the mainland, it was with a still resolute heart that, on the 19th of July,[2] Charles cast anchor in Lochnanuagh, a small arm of the sea, partly dividing the countries of Moidart and Arisaig. The place which he thus chose for his disembarkation was as wild and desolate a scene as he could have found throughout the dominions of his fathers. Yet it was scarcely more unpromising than the reception he at first met with from its people.

The first thing he did, after casting anchor, was to send a boat ashore with a letter for young Clanranald, whom he knew to be inspired with the most enthusiastic affection to his cause. The young chief did not permit him to remain long in suspense. Next day (the 20th) he came to Forsy, a small village on the shore of the estuary in which the Prince's vessel lay, accompanied by his kinsmen, the Lairds of Glenaladale and Dalily, and by another gentleman of his clan, who has left an intelligent journal of the subsequent events.[3] 'Calling for the ship's boat,' says this writer, 'we were immediately carried on board, our hearts bounding at the idea of being at length so near our long-wished-for Prince. We found a large tent erected with poles upon the ship's deck, the interior of which was furnished with a variety of wines and spirits. On entering this pavilion, we were warmly welcomed by the Duke of Athole, to whom most of us had been known in the year 1715.[4] While we were conversing with the duke, Clanranald was called away to see the Prince, and we were given to understand that we should not

---

[1] *History of the Rebellion*, by the Rev. John Home; Home's Works, ii. 427.—*Jacobite Memoirs*, pp. 11, 12.
[2] Lockhart Papers, ii. 479.   [3] Printed in the Lockhart Papers.
[4] The person here meant was the Marquis of Tullibardine, whom the Jacobites considered as rightfully the Duke of Athole.

probably see his royal highness that evening.' Clanranald, being introduced into Charles's presence, proceeded to assure him that there was no possibility, under the circumstances, of taking up arms with any chance of success. In this he was joined by his relation, Macdonald of Kinlochmoidart, whom Mr Home has associated with him in the following romantic anecdote, though the journalist does not allude to his presence. Charles is said, by the historian, to have addressed the two Highlanders with great emotion; to have summed up, with much eloquence, all the reasons for now beginning the war; and, finally, to have conjured them, in the warmest terms, to assist their Prince, their friend, in this his utmost need. With eloquence scarcely less warm, the brave young men entreated him to desist from his enterprise for the present, representing to him that now to take up arms, without regular forces, without officers of credit, without concert, and almost without arms, would but draw down certain destruction upon the heads of all concerned. Charles persisted, argued, and implored; and they still as positively adhered to their opinion. During this conversation, the parties walked hurriedly backwards and forwards upon the deck, using all the gesticulations appropriate to their various arguments. A Highlander stood near them, armed at all points, as was then the fashion of his country. He was a younger brother of Kinlochmoidart, and had come off to the ship to inquire for news, not knowing who was on board. When he gathered from their discourse that the stranger was the heir of Britain, when he heard his chief and brother refuse to take up arms for their Prince, his colour went and came, his eyes sparkled, he shifted his place, and grasped his sword. Charles observed his demeanour, and turning suddenly round, appealed to him: 'Will *you* not assist me?' 'I will! I will!' exclaimed Ranald, 'though not another man in the Highlands should draw a sword; I am ready to die for you!' With tears and thanks Charles acknowledged the loyalty of the youth, and said he wished that all the Highlanders were like him. The two obdurate chieftains were overpowered by this incident, and no longer expressed any reluctance to make an appearance in the cause.¹

The Prince's interview with Clanranald, according to the journalist, who was on board at the same time, occupied no less than three hours. The young chief then returned to his friends, who had spent that space of time in the pavilion. 'About half an hour after,' says the journalist, 'there entered the tent a TALL YOUTH of a most agreeable aspect, dressed in a plain black coat, with a plain shirt, a cambric stock fixed with a plain silver buckle, a fair round wig out of the buckle, a plain hat with a canvas string, one end of which was fixed to one of his coat-buttons, black stockings, and brass buckles in his shoes. At the first appearance of this pleasing youth I felt my heart swell to my throat. But one O'Brien, a churchman, immediately told us that he was only an English clergyman, who had long been possessed with a desire to see and converse with the Highlanders.'

'At his entry,' continues the same writer, 'O'Brien forbade any of those who were sitting to rise; he saluted none of us, and we only made a low bow at a distance. I chanced to be one of those who were standing when he came in, and he took his seat near me; but he immediately started up again, and desired me to sit down by him upon a chest. Taking him at this time for only a passenger and a clergyman, I presumed to speak to him with perfect familiarity, though I could not suppress a suspicion that he might turn out some greater man. One of the questions which he put to me, in the course of conversation, regarded my Highland dress. He inquired if I did not feel cold in that habit, to which I answered that I believed I should only feel cold in any other.² At this he laughed heartily; and he next desired to know how I lay with it at night. I replied

---

¹ Home's Works, ii. 427.
² This is a common Highlandman's answer to a very common question. The fact is, that the philabeg, while exposing the knees, invests the haunches and middle with such dense folds, as to give great general warmth. I believe it has been found that the private men of the Highland regiments have nowhere complained of their dress so much as in the West Indies.

that the plaid served me for a blanket when sleeping, and I shewed him how I wrapped it about my person for that purpose. At this he remarked that I must be unprepared for defence in case of a sudden surprise; but I informed him that, during war or any time of danger, we arranged the garment in such a way as to enable us to start at once to our feet, with a drawn sword in one hand and a cocked pistol in the other. After a little more conversation of this sort, the mysterious youth rose from his seat and called for a dram, when O'Brien whispered to me to pledge the stranger, but not to drink to him, which confirmed me in my suspicions as to his real quality. Having taken a glass of wine in his hand, he drank to us all round, and soon after left the tent.'[1]

During this and the succeeding day, Clanranald remained close in council with Charles, the Marquis of Tullibardine, and Sir Thomas Sheridan, devising means for raising the rest of the well-affected clans, who were at this time reckoned to number 12,000 men. On the 22d (July), young Clanranald proceeded with Allan Macdonald, a younger brother of Kinlochmoidart, on an embassy to Sir Alexander Macdonald of Sleat and the Laird of Macleod, whom Charles was most unwilling to suppose unfaithful to his cause. During the absence of these emissaries, Mr Hugh Macdonald, a younger brother of the Laird of Morar, was brought on board the *Doutelle* to visit the Prince. This gentleman, after a short complimentary conversation, took leave to caution him as to the necessity of keeping strictly incognito for the present, as the garrison of Fort William was not far off, and the neighbouring clan Campbell might be very glad to obtain possession of his person. Charles answered: 'I have no fear about that at all.' With reference to the proposed expedition, Mr Macdonald said he had great fears of the event, and, like Boisdale, he recommended the Prince to return to France. Charles said 'he did not choose to owe his restoration to foreigners, but to his own friends, to whom he was now come

[1] Lockhart Papers, ii. 480.

to put it into their power to have the glory of that event. And as to returning to France, foreigners should never have it to say that he had thrown himself upon his friends, that they turned their backs upon him, and that he had been forced to return from them to foreign parts. In a word, if he could get but six trusty men to join him, *he would choose far rather to skulk with them among the mountains of Scotland, than to return to France.*

On the 25th he came on shore from the *Doutelle*, accompanied by only the seven gentlemen formerly mentioned. He first set his foot upon Scottish ground at Borodale, a farm belonging to Clanranald, close by the south shore of Lochnanuagh. Borodale is a wild piece of country, forming a mountainous tongue of land betwixt two bays. It was a place suitable above all others for the circumstances and designs of the Prince, being remote and difficult of access, and in the centre of that country where Charles's surest friends resided. It belongs to a tract of stern mountain land, serrated by deep narrow firths, forming the western coast of Inverness-shire. Although in the very centre of the Highland territory, it is not above one hundred and eighty miles from the capital. The Macdonalds and the Stuarts, who possessed the adjacent territories, had been, since the time of Montrose, inviolably attached to the elder line of the royal family; had proved themselves irresistible at Kilsyth, Killiecrankie, and Sheriffmuir; and were now, from their resistance to the Disarming Act, perhaps the fittest of all the clans to take the field.

During the absence of young Clanranald, into whose arms Charles had thus thrown himself, several gentlemen of the family collected a guard for his person, and he remained a welcome and honoured guest in the house of Borodale.[1] Considering that no other chief had yet declared for him, and that, indeed, the enterprise might never advance another step, it must be acknowledged that the Clanranald family acted with no small share of gallantry; for there can be little doubt that if he

---

[1] Lockhart Papers, ii. 482.

had retired, they must have been exposed to the vengeance of government. 'We encountered this hazard,' says the journalist, 'with the greatest cheerfulness, determined to risk everything, life itself, in behalf of our beloved Prince.' Charles, his company, and about one hundred men constituting his guard, were entertained with the best cheer which it was in the power of Mr Macdonald, tenant of Borodale, to purvey. He sat in a large room, where he could see all his adherents at once, and where the multitudes of people who flocked from the country around, 'without distinction of age or sex,'[1] to see him, might also have an opportunity of gratifying their curiosity. At the first meal which took place under these circumstances, Charles drank the *grace*-drink in English, a language which all the gentlemen present understood; but for a toast of more extensive application, our friend the journalist rose and gave the king's[2] health in Gaelic—'*Deoch slaint an Righ.*' This of course produced universal satisfaction; and Charles desired to know what was meant. On its being explained to him, he requested to hear the words pronounced again, that he might learn them himself. He then gave the king's health in Gaelic, uttering the words as correctly and distinctly as he could. 'The company,' adds the journalist, 'then mentioning my skill in Gaelic, his royal highness said I should be his master in that language; and I was then desired to ask the healths of the prince and duke.'[3] It may be scarcely possible to conceive the effect which Charles's flattering attention to their language had upon the hearts of this brave and simple people.

---

[1] Lockhart Papers, ii. 482.   [2] Charles's father.
[3] Charles's younger brother, styled the Duke of York.

CHAPTER II.

THE HIGHLANDERS.

> '*Belarius.* 'Tis wonderful,
> That an invisible instinct should frame them
> To loyalty unlearned; honour untaught;
> Civility not seen from other; valour,
> That wildly grows in them, but yields a crop
> As if it had been sowed.'
> *Cymbeline.*

THE people amidst whom Charles Stuart had cast his fate, were then regarded as the rudest and least civilised portion of the nation of which he conceived himself the rightful ruler. Occupying the most remote and mountainous section of Britain, and holding little intercourse with the rest of the community, they were distinguished by peculiar language, dress, and manners; had as yet yielded a very imperfect obedience to government; and formed a society not only distinct from their immediate neighbours, but which had probably no exact parallel in Europe.

The country possessed by this people, forming the north-west portion of Scotland, comprehends a large surface; but being of a mountainous and rugged character, it has never maintained a large population. In numbers, the Highlanders did not now exceed 100,000, or a twelfth of the whole population of Scotland. The community was divided into about forty different tribes, denominated *clans*, each of which dwelt upon its own portion of the territory.

At the period of this history, the Highlanders displayed, in a state almost entire, what has been called the patriarchal form of society. This extreme corner of Europe had the fortune to shelter nearly the last unmixed remnants of the Celts, that early race of people whom the dawn of history shews in possession of the ancient continent, but who were gradually dispelled to the extremities by others which we are now accustomed to call ancient. As they retained their primitive manners with almost unmixed purity, there was to be seen in the Highlanders of Scotland nearly a distinct picture of a state of society compared with which that of Rome might be considered as modern.

Owing to the circumstances of their country, the Highlanders were, however, by no means that simple and quiescent people who are described as content to dwell each under his own vine and fig-tree, any more than their land was one flowing with milk and honey. A perpetual state of war with the neighbours who had driven them to their northern fastnesses, and their disinclination to submit to the laws of the country in which they nominally lived, caused them, on the contrary, to make arms a sort of profession, and even to despise in some measure all peaceful modes of acquiring a subsistence. Entertaining, moreover, a belief that the Lowlands had been originally theirs, many of them, even at this period, practised a regular system of reprisal upon the frontier of that civilised region, for which of course the use of arms was indispensably necessary. What still more tended to induce military habits, many of the tribes maintained a sort of hereditary enmity against each other, and therefore required to be in perpetual readiness, either to seize or repel opportunities of vengeance.

The Highlanders, in the earlier periods of history, appear to have possessed no superiority over the Lowlanders in the use of arms. At the battle of the Harlaw in 1410 (till which period they had been quite independent of the kings of Scotland), the largest army that ever left the Highlands was checked by an inferior number of Lowlanders. They proved not more invincible at the battles of Corrichie, Glenlivat, and others, fought during the sixteenth century.

But the lapse of half a century after this last period, during which the Border spear had been converted into a shepherd's crook, and the patriot steel of Lothian and Clydesdale into penknives and weavers' shears, permitted the mountaineers at length to assert a decided superiority in arms. When they were called into action, therefore, by Montrose, they proved invariably victorious in that short but brilliant campaign, which almost retrieved a kingdom for their unfortunate monarch. Amidst the exploits of that time, the victory of Kilsyth (1645) was attended with some circumstances displaying their superiority in a remarkable degree. The army arrayed against them, almost doubling theirs in number, consisted chiefly of the townsmen of Fife, which county has been described, in a publication of the time,[1] as remarkable for the enthusiasm of its inhabitants in regard to the cause of this quarrel—the National Covenant. Religious fervour proved nothing in this case when opposed to the more exalted enthusiasm of 'loyalty unlearned,' and the hardihood of an education among the hills. The Whig militia scarcely stood a minute before the impetuous charge of the Highlanders, but running off in a shameful rout, were killed in great numbers by their pursuers.[2]

Though the Highlanders were nominally subjugated by Cromwell, they regained at the Restoration their former privileges and vigour. They were kept in arms, during the reigns of the last two Stuarts, by their occasional employment as a militia, for the harassment of the west-country Presbyterians. At the Revolution, therefore, when roused by the voice of Dundee, they were equally ready to take the field in behalf of King James, as they had been fifty years before to rise up for his father. The patriarchal system of laws upon which Highland society was constituted, disposed them to look upon these unfortunate princes as the general fathers or *chiefs* of the nation, whose natural and unquestionable power had been

---

[1] *Montrose Redivivus*, 1650.

[2] Sir John Sinclair of Longformacus reported to the late Bishop Low, his having in early life met an aged Highlander who had been at the battle of Kilsyth. The man spoke with savage glee of his performances amongst the hen-hearted Fife men. 'It was a braw day Kilsyth; at every stroke of my sword I cut an ell o' breeks!' The people of Fife are said to have consequently got a distaste for the army, which had not ceased at the close of the ensuing century. See *Statistical Account of Scotland*, xii. 86.

rebelliously disputed by their children; and there can be little doubt that, both on these occasions and the subsequent attempts in behalf of the Stuart family, they fought with precisely the same ardour which would induce a man of humanity to ward off the blow which an unnatural son had aimed at a parent. On the field of Killiecrankie, where they were chiefly opposed by regular and even veteran troops, they fought with signal bravery.[1] Their victory was, however, unavailing, owing to the death of their favourite leader, *Ian Dhu nan Cath*, as they descriptively termed him—Dark John of the Battles—without whose commanding genius their energies could not be directed, nor even their bands kept together.

The submission which was nominally paid throughout Britain to the '*parliamentary*' sovereigns, William and Anne, was in no degree participated by the children of the mountains, whose simple ideas of government did not comprehend either a second or a third estate, and who could perceive no reasons for preferring a sovereign on account of any peculiarity in his religion. In the meantime, moreover, the progress of civilisation, encouraged in the low countries by the Union, affected but slightly the warlike habits of the clans. Their military ardour is said to have been, if possible, increased during this period, by the injudicious policy of King William, who, in distributing £20,000 amongst them to bribe their forbearance, only inspired an idea that arms were their best means of acquiring wealth and importance. The call, therefore, which was made upon them by the exiled Prince in 1715, found them as willing and ready as ever to commence a civil war.

---

[1] The battle of Killiecrankie was fought upon a field immediately beyond a narrow and difficult pass into the Highlands. The royal troops, under General Mackay, on emerging from this pass, found Dundee's army, which was not half so numerous, posted in columns or clusters upon the face of an opposite hill. Both lay upon their arms, looking at each other, till sunset, when the Highland troops came down with their customary impetuosity, and, charging through Mackay's lines, soon put them to the rout. Mackay retreated in the utmost disorder, and reached Stirling next day with only two hundred men. His whole army must have been cut to pieces in retreating through the pass, but for the death of Dundee, and the greater eagerness of the Highlanders to secure the baggage than to pursue their enemies.

The accession of the house of Hanover was at this period so recent, and the rival candidate shared so largely in the affections of the people, that very little was wanting to achieve the restoration of the house of Stuart. That little *was* wanting—a general of military talent, with some degree of resolution on the part of the candidate. The expedition was commanded in Scotland by the Earl of Mar, who had signalised himself by some dexterity in the slippery politics of the time, but possessed no other abilities to fit him for the important station he held. In England, the reigning sovereign had even less to dread, in the ill-concerted proceedings of a band of debauched young noblemen, who displayed this remarkable difference from the Scottish insurgents—that they could not fight at all. Mar permitted himself to be cooped up on the north of the Forth, with an army of 8000 or 9000 men, by the Duke of Argyll, who occupied Stirling with a force not half so numerous. An action at length took place on Sheriffmuir, in which it is impossible to say whether the bravery of the Highlanders, the pusillanimity of their leader, or the military genius of Argyll, was most signally distinguished.

The Duke of Argyll learning, on the 11th of November, that Mar had at length formed the resolution to fight him, and was marching for that purpose from Perth, set forward from Stirling; and next day the armies came within sight of each other upon the plain of Sheriffmuir, a mile north-east from Dumblane. They both lay upon their arms all night; and a stone is still shewn upon the site of the Highlanders' bivouac, indented all round with marks occasioned by the broadswords of these warriors, who here sharpened their weapons for the next day's conflict. The battle commenced on Sunday morning, when Argyll himself, leading his dragoons over a morass which had frozen during the night, and which the insurgents expected to protect them, almost immediately routed their whole left wing, consisting of the Lowland cavaliers, and drove them to the river Allan, two or three miles from the field. His left wing, which was beyond the scope of his command, did not meet the same success against the right of the insurgents, which consisted entirely of Highlanders.

Those warriors had come down from their fastnesses with a resolution to fight as their ancestors had fought at Kilsyth and Killiecrankie. They appeared before the Lowlanders of Perthshire, who had not seen them since the days of Montrose, in the wild Irish shirt or plaid, which, covering only the body and haunches, leaves the arms and most of the limbs exposed in all their shaggy strength.[1] Their enthusiasm may be guessed from a simple anecdote. A Lowland gentleman, observing amongst their bands a man of ninety, from the upper part of Aberdeenshire, had the curiosity to ask how so aged a creature as he, and one who seemed so extremely feeble, had thought of joining their enterprise. 'I have sons here, sir,' replied the man, 'and I have grandsons; if they fail to do their duty, cannot I shoot them?'—laying his hand upon a pistol which he carried in his bosom.[2]

The attack of these resolute soldiers upon the left wing of the royal army was, to use language similar to their own, like the storm which strews a lee-shore with wrecks. The chief of Clanranald was killed as they were advancing; but that circumstance, which might have been expected to damp their ardour, only served to inspire them with greater fury. 'To-morrow for lamentation!' cried the young chieftain of Glengarry; 'to-day for revenge!' and the Macdonalds rushed on the foe with irresistible force. Instantly put to rout, this portion of the royal army retired to Stirling, leaving hundreds a prey to the Highland broadsword. Thus each of the two armies was partially successful and partially defeated.

The battle was by no means indecisive in its results. Mar, as he deserved none of the credit of his partial victory, reaped no profit from it, but was obliged to retire to Perth. Argyll remained upon the field, in possession of the enemy's cannon and many of his standards. The conduct of this celebrated

---

[1] Preface to Pinkerton's *Select Old Scottish Poems*.
[2] 'Can I no *sheet* them?'—these were the exact words.

warrior and patriot was in every respect the reverse of that of Mar. He had won a victory, so far as it could be won, by his own personal exertions, and that with every advantage of numbers against him. The humanity he displayed was also such as seldom marks the details of a civil war. He offered quarter to all he met, in the very hottest of the fight, and he granted it to all who desired it. With his own sword he parried three different blows which one of his dragoons aimed at a wounded cavalier who had refused to ask his life.[1]

In January, James himself, the weak though amiable man for whom all this blood was shed, landed at Peterhead, and immediately proceeded *incognito* to join the Earl of Mar at Perth. His presence might inspire some enthusiasm, but it could not give strength or consistency to the army. Some preparations were made for his coronation in the great hall of Scoon, where his ancestors had been invested with the emblems of sovereignty so many centuries ago. But the total ruin of his English adherents conspired with his own imbecility and that of his officers to prevent the ceremony from taking place. In February, he retired before the advance of the royal army. The Tay was frozen at the time, and thus he and all his army were fortunately enabled to cross without the difficulty which must otherwise have attended so sudden a retreat; directing their march towards the seaports of Aberdeenshire and Angus. I have heard that, as the good-natured prince was passing over, the misery or his circumstances prompted a slight sally of wit, as a dark evening will sometimes produce lightning; and he remarked to his lieutenant-general, in allusion to the delusive prospects by which he had been induced to come over: 'Ah, John, you see how you have brought me on the ice.'[2]

The Chevalier embarked with Mar and other officers at Montrose; and the body of the army dispersed with so much

---

[1] Printed *broadside* of the battle.   [2] Information by Bishop Low.

rapidity, that Argyll, who traversed the country only a day's march behind, reached Aberdeen without ever getting a glimpse of it. We may safely suppose that the humanity of this general, if not the secret leaning to Jacobitism of which he was suspected, induced him to favour the dispersion and escape of the unfortunate cavaliers. The Lowland gentlemen and noblemen who had been concerned in the campaign suffered attainder, proscription, and in some cases death; but the Highlanders returned to their mountains unconquered and unchanged.

In 1719, a plan of invasion and insurrection in favour of the Stuarts was formed by Spain. A fleet of ten ships of the line, with several frigates, having on board 6000 troops and 12,000 stand of arms, sailed from Cadiz to England; and while this fleet was preparing, the Earl Marischal left St Sebastian with two Spanish frigates, having on board 300 Spanish soldiers, ammunition, arms, and money, and landed in the island of Lewis. The Spanish fleet was completely dispersed by a storm off Cape Finisterre; and as everything remained quiet in England, very few Highlanders rose. General Wightman came up with the Spanish and Highland force in Glenshiel, a wild vale in the west of Ross-shire. The Highlanders, favoured by the ground, withdrew to the hills without having suffered much; and the Spaniards laid down their arms, and were made prisoners.

During the ensuing twenty years, the state of the Highlands was often under the consideration of government, and some steps were taken with a view to render the people less dangerous, but none with the design of making them more friendly. Three forts—one at Inverness; a second, named Fort Augustus, at Killiewhimmen; and a third, named Fort William, at Inverlochy, in Lochaber—were kept in full garrison, as a means of overawing the disaffected clans. Under the care of General Wade, the soldiers were employed in forming lines of road, for the purpose of connecting these forts with the low country. An act was also passed to deprive the people of their arms. It was obeyed to some extent by such clans as the Campbells, Sutherlands, and Mackays, whose superiors were, from whatever cause, well affected to the government; but was generally evaded by the Macdonalds, Stuarts, Camerons, and others, who maintained their zeal for the house of Stuart. Thus the measure was rather favourable to the Jacobite cause in the Highlands than otherwise.

Such had been the history, and such was the warlike condition of the Scottish mountaineers at the time when Prince Charles landed amongst them in July 1745. If anything else were required to make the reader understand the motives of the subsequent insurrection, it might be said that Charles's father and himself had always maintained, from their residence in Italy, a correspondence with the chiefs who were friendly to them. For the service of these unhappy princes, their unlimited power over their clans gave them an advantage which the richest English partisans did not possess. At the same time, as sufficiently appears from the preceding and following chapter, the idea of taking the field for the Stuarts without foreign assistance was not agreeable to the Jacobite chiefs, though, in most instances, their ardour of character ultimately overcame their scruples on that point.

The constitution of Highland society, as already remarked, was strictly and simply patriarchal. The clans were families, each of which, bearing one name, occupied a well-defined tract of country, the property of which had been acquired long before the introduction of writs. Every clan was governed by its chief, whose native designation—*Kean-Kinnhe* ('The Head of the Family')—sufficiently indicated the grounds and nature of his power. In almost every clan there were some subordinate chiefs called chieftains, being cadets of the principal family, who had acquired a distinct territory, and founded separate septs. In every clan, moreover, there were two ranks of people—the *Doaine-uailse*, or gentlemen, persons who could clearly trace their derivation from the chiefs of former times, and assert their kinsmanship to the present; and a race of commoners, who could not tell how they came to belong to the clan, and who always acted in inferior offices.

There is a very common notion among the Lowlanders that their northern neighbours, with, perhaps, the exception of the chiefs, were all alike barbarians, and distinguished by no shades of comparative worth. Nothing could be further from the truth. The *Doaine-uailse* were, in every sense of the word, gentlemen—*poor* gentlemen, perhaps, but yet fully entitled, by their feelings and acquirements, to that appellation. On the contrary, the commoners, who yet generally believed themselves related to the chiefs, were a race of mere serfs, having no certain idea of a noble ancestry to nerve their exertions or elevate their conduct. The *Doaine-uailse* invariably formed the body upon which the chief depended in war; for they were inspired with notions of the most exalted heroism by the well-remembered deeds of their forefathers, and always acted upon the supposition that their honour was a precious gift, which it was incumbent upon them to deliver down unsullied to posterity. The commoners, on the contrary, were often left behind to perform the humble duties of agriculture and cow-driving; or, if admitted into the array of the clan, were put into the rear rank, and armed in an inferior manner.

With such a sentiment of heroism, the Highland gentleman of the year 1745 must have been a person of no mean order. His mind was further exalted, if possible, by a devoted attachment to his chief, for whose interests he was at all times ready to fight, and for whose life he was even prepared to lay down his own. His politics were of the same abstract and disinterested sort. Despising the commercial Presbyterians of the low country, and regarding with a better-founded disgust the dark system of parliamentary corruption which characterised the government of the *de facto* sovereign of England, he at once threw himself into the opposite scale, and espoused the cause of an exiled and injured prince, whom he looked upon as in some measure a general and higher sort of chief. Charles's cause was the cause of justice, of filial affection, and even, in his estimation, of *patriotism;* and with all his prepossessions, it was scarcely possible that he should fail to espouse it.[1]

CHAPTER III.

THE GATHERING.

'Oh, high-minded Murray, the exiled, the dear,
In the blush of the dawning the standard uprear;
Wide, wide on the winds of the north let it fy,
Like the sun's latest flash when the tempest is nigh!'
Waverley.

AT Borodale, the Prince received a reply to the message which he had sent to Sir Alexander Macdonald and the Laird of Macleod. What Boisdale had said of these chiefs proved exactly true. Originally well affected to the Stuart family, they had recently been tampered with by Duncan Forbes, president of the Court of Session, so distinguished as a virtuous and enlightened friend of the Hanover succession, as well as by the genuine love he bore for his native country. Being now disposed to remain on good terms with the government, the two insular chiefs returned for answer, that although they had promised to support his royal highness if he came with a foreign force, they did not conceive themselves to be under any obligation since he came so ill provided. They likewise offered the advice, that he should immediately return to France. It was

---

[1] In this chapter notice might also have been taken of the effect which their popular native poetry had upon the minds of the Highlanders. Throughout nearly the whole country, but especially in Athole and the adjacent territories, *there were innumerable songs and ballads tending to advance the cause of the Stuarts, while there was not one to depreciate them.* A Lowlander and a modern cannot easily comprehend, nor can he set forth, the power of this simple but energetic engine. It has been described to me as something overpowering. Most of the ballads were founded upon the wars of Montrose and Dundee, and aimed at rousing the audience to imitate the actions of their ancestors in these glorious campaigns.

not known at the time, but has since been made manifest, that these chiefs at this crisis did active service for the government, in sending intelligence of the Prince's arrival. Their answer to Charles was so disheartening, that now even those who had come with him joined with his Highland friends in counselling him to give up the enterprise.[1] The example of the two Skye chiefs would, they said, be fatal, as many others would follow it. Nevertheless, Charles adhered to his design, repeating, in reply to all their representations, the same words he had used to Mr Hugh Macdonald. With six good trusty followers, he said, he would skulk in Scotland rather than return to France.

From Borodale, where he lived in the manner described for several days, he despatched messengers to all the chiefs from whom he had any expectation of assistance. The first that came to see him was Donald Cameron, younger of Locheil; a man in middle age, of great bravery, and universally respected character. Young Locheil, as he was generally called, was the son of the chief of the clan Cameron, one of the most numerous and warlike of all the Highland tribes. His father had been engaged in the insurrection of 1715, for which he was attainted and in exile; and his grandfather, Sir Evan Cameron, the fellow-soldier of Montrose and Dundee, had died in 1719, after three-fourths of a century of military partisanship in behalf of the house of Stuart. Young Locheil had been much in confidence with the exiled family, whose chief agent in the north of Scotland he might be considered; an office for which he was peculiarly well qualified, on account of his talents, his integrity, and the veneration in which he was held by his countrymen. He was one of the seven gentlemen who, in 1740, entered into an association to procure the restoration of King James; and he

---

[1] Young Clanranald was himself shaken in his resolution of arming for the Prince by the conversation he had with Sir Alexander Macdonald, and returned to his own country with a decided disinclination to the enterprise. But when he arrived, he found his clan determined to go out at all hazards, *whether he should head them or not*, having probably been much gained upon in the interval by the Prince's address. The young chieftain was thus ultimately brought back to his former resolution. These facts are stated by Bishop Forbes (*Lyon in Mourning*, MS. in my possession), on the concurring testimony of Ranald Macdonald, a son of Borodale, and Mr Macdonald of Bellfinlay.

had long wished for the concerted time when he should bring the Highlands to aid an invading party in that cause. When he now learned that Charles had landed without troops and arms, and with only seven followers, he determined to abstain from the enterprise; but thought himself bound, as a friend, to visit the Prince in person, and endeavour to make him withdraw from the country.

In passing from his own house to Borodale, Locheil called at Fassefern, the residence of his brother, John Cameron, who, in some surprise at the earliness of his visit, hastily inquired its reason. Locheil informed his relative that the Prince of Wales had landed at Borodale, and sent for him. Fassefern asked what troops his royal highness had brought with him?—what money?—what arms? Locheil answered that he believed the Prince had brought with him neither troops, nor money, nor arms; and that, resolved not to be concerned in the affair, he designed to do his utmost to prevent it from going any further. Fassefern approved of his brother's sentiments, and applauded his resolution, advising him at the same time not to go any farther on the way to Borodale, but to come into the house, and impart his mind to the Prince by a letter. 'No,' said Locheil; 'although my reasons admit of no reply, I ought at least to wait upon his royal highness.' 'Brother,' said Fassefern, 'I know you better than you know yourself; if this Prince once sets his eyes upon you, he will make you do whatever he pleases.'[1]

On arriving at Borodale, Locheil had a private interview with the Prince, in which the probabilities of the enterprise were anxiously debated. Charles used every argument to excite the loyalty of Locheil, and the chief exerted all his eloquence to persuade the Prince to withdraw till a better opportunity. Charles represented the present as the best possible opportunity, seeing that the French general kept the British army completely engaged abroad, while at home there were no troops but one or two newly raised regiments. He expressed his confidence that a small body of Highlanders would be sufficient to gain a victory

[1] Home's Works, iii. 7.

over all the force that could now be brought against him; and he was equally sure that such an advantage was all that was required to make his friends at home declare in his favour, and cause those abroad to send assistance. All he wanted was, that the Highlanders should begin the war. Locheil still resisted, entreating Charles to be more temperate, and consent to remain concealed where he was, till his friends should meet together, and concert what was best to be done. Charles, whose mind was wound up to the utmost pitch of impatience, paid no regard to this proposal, but answered that he was determined to put all to the hazard. 'In a few days,' said he, 'with the few friends I have, I will raise the royal standard, and proclaim to the people of Britain that Charles Stuart is come over to claim the crown of his ancestors—to win it, or to perish in the attempt! Locheil, who my father has often told me was our firmest friend, may stay at home, and learn from the newspapers the fate of his Prince!' 'No!' said Locheil, stung by so poignant a reproach, and hurried away by the enthusiasm of the moment; 'I will share the fate of my Prince; and so shall every man over whom nature or fortune has given me any power.' Such was the juncture upon which depended the civil war of 1745; for it is a point agreed, says Mr Home, who narrates this conversation, that if Locheil had persisted in his refusal to take arms, no other chief would have joined the standard, and 'the spark of rebellion must have been instantly extinguished.'[1]

Locheil immediately returned home, and proceeded to raise

---

[1] Mr Home's account of this affair harmonises with all besides that we know of the reckless ardour of the young Prince, and the cautious reluctance of the principal chiefs. We may therefore receive it as in the main true. Perhaps, however, the ultimate consent of Locheil was less sudden than is here represented. In the volume entitled *Jacobite Memoirs*, compiled by the present author from the papers of Bishop Forbes (p. 22, note), it is stated that Locheil, before agreeing to *come out*, took full security for the value of his estates from the Prince, and that it was to fulfil this engagement that Charles, after the unfortunate conclusion of the enterprise, obtained a French regiment for Locheil. It is scarcely necessary to remark, that the presence of generous feelings does not necessarily forbid that some attention should be paid to the dictates of prudence and caution. Locheil might feel that he had a right to peril his life and connection with his country, but not the fortune on which the comfort of others besides himself depended, especially in an enterprise of which he had a bad opinion, and which he only acceded to from a romantic deference to the wishes of another person.

his clan, as did some other gentlemen whom Charles then prevailed upon to join him. It being now settled that he was to erect his standard at Glenfinnin on the 19th of August, he despatched letters on the 6th of the month to all the friendly chiefs, informing them of his resolution, and desiring them to meet him at the time and place mentioned. In the meantime Clanranald, returned from his unsuccessful mission to Skye, actively set about raising his own clan.

Charles removed, about the 11th of August, from the farmhouse of Borodale to the mansion of Kinlochmoidart, situated seven miles off. While he and his company went by sea, with the baggage and artillery, the guard of Clanranald Macdonalds, which had been already appointed about his person, marched by the more circuitous route along the shore of the intervening bays. At Kinlochmoidart[1] he was joined by Mr John Murray of Broughton, who has already been mentioned as an emissary of the Prince to his Scottish friends, and who, after waiting during June to warn him from the west coast, had afterwards returned to his house in Peeblesshire. Mr Murray, who was a man of good talents and education, had now once more come to the Highlands, in order to join an enterprise which it was too late to think of stopping. From this time he acted throughout the campaign as the Prince's secretary. Charles remained at Kinlochmoidart till the 18th, when he went by water to Glenaladale, the seat of another chieftain of the clan Macdonald, upon the brink of Loch Shiel. He was here joined by Gordon of Glenbucket, a veteran partisan, who had figured in the affair of 1715, and who brought with him a prisoner of the opposite party, in the person of Captain Sweetenham, of Guise's regiment, who had been taken by the Keppoch Macdonalds, while travelling from Ruthven barracks, in Badenoch, to Fort William.

[1] 'As the Prince was setting out for Glenfinnin, I was detached to Ardnamurchan to recruit, and soon returned with fifty clever fellows, who pleased the Prince; and upon review, his royal highness was pleased to honour me with the command of them, telling me I was *the first officer he had made in Scotland*. This compliment delighted me exceedingly, and we all vowed to the Almighty that we should live and die with our noble Prince, though all Britain should forsake him but our little regiment alone.'—*Macdonald's Journal; Lockhart Papers*, ii. 483.

From Glenaladale the Prince proceeded next morning, with a company of about five-and-twenty persons, in three boats, to the eastern extremity of Loch Shiel, near which was the place where he designed to raise his standard.

Meanwhile an incident had occurred which tended not a little to foment the rising flame of insurrection. The governor of Fort Augustus (a military post, at the distance of forty or fifty miles from Charles's landing-place) concluding, from reports he heard, that the Moidart people were hatching some mischief, thought proper, on the 16th of August, to despatch two companies of the Scots Royals to Fort William, as a reinforcement to awe that rebellious district. The distance between the two forts is twenty-eight miles, and the road runs chiefly along the edge of a mountain, which forms one side of the Great Glen, having the sheer height of the hill on one side, and the long narrow lakes, out of which the Caledonian Canal has since been formed, on the other. The men were newly raised, and, besides being inexperienced in military affairs, were unused to the alarming circumstances of an expedition in the Highlands. When they had travelled twenty out of the eight-and-twenty miles, and were approaching High Bridge, a lofty arch over a mountain torrent, they were surprised to hear the sound of a bagpipe, and to discover the appearance of a large party of Highlanders, who were already in possession of the bridge. The object of their alarm was in reality a band of only ten or twelve Macdonalds of Keppoch's clan; but by skipping and leaping about, displaying their swords and firelocks, and by holding out their plaids between each other, they contrived to make a very formidable appearance. Captain (afterwards General) Scott, who commanded the two companies, ordered an immediate halt, and sent forward a sergeant with his own servant to reconnoitre. These two persons no sooner approached the bridge, than two nimble Highlanders darted out and seized them. Ignorant of the number of the Highlanders, and knowing he was in a disaffected part of the country, Captain Scott thought it would be better to retreat than enter into hostilities.

Accordingly, he ordered his men to face about, and march back again. The Highlanders did not follow immediately, lest they should expose the smallness of their number, but permitted the soldiers to get two miles away (the ground being so far plain and open) before leaving their post. As soon as the retreating party had passed the west end of Loch Lochy, and were entering upon the narrow road between the lake and the hill, out darted the mountaineers, and ascending the rocky precipices above the road, where there was shelter from both bush and stone, began to fire down upon the soldiers, who only retreated with the greater expedition.

The party of Macdonalds who attempted this daring exploit was commanded by Macdonald of Tiendrish, who, having early observed the march of the soldiers, had sent expresses to Locheil and Keppoch, whose houses were only a few miles distant on both sides of High Bridge, for supplies of men. They did not arrive in time, but he resolved to attack the party with the few men he had; and he had thus far succeeded, when the noise of his pieces causing friends in all quarters to fly to arms, he now found himself at the head of a party almost sufficient to encounter the two companies in the open field.

When Captain Scott reached the east end of Loch Lochy, he perceived some Highlanders near the west end of Loch Oich, directly in the way before him; and not liking their appearance, he crossed the isthmus between the lakes, intending to take possession of Invergarry Castle, the seat of Macdonell of Glengarry. This movement only increased his difficulties. He had not marched far, when he discovered the Macdonells of Glengarry coming down the opposite hill in full force against him. He formed the hollow square, however, and marched on. Presently after, his pursuers were reinforced by the Macdonalds of Keppoch, and increased their pace to such a degree as almost to overtake him. Keppoch himself then advanced alone towards the distressed party, and offered good terms of surrender; assuring them that any attempt at resistance, in the midst of so many enemies, would only be the signal for their being cut in pieces. The soldiers, by this time fatigued with a march of thirty miles, had no alternative but to surrender. They had scarcely laid down their arms, when Locheil came up with a body of Camerons from another quarter, and took them under his charge. Two soldiers were slain, and Captain Scott himself was wounded in this scuffle, which had no small effect in raising the spirits of the Highlanders, and encouraging them to commence the war.[1]

The *gathering of the clans* was therefore proceeding with great activity, and armed bodies were seen everywhere crossing the country to Glenfinnin, at the time when Charles landed at that place to erect his standard. Glenfinnin is a narrow vale, surrounded on both sides by lofty and craggy mountains, about twenty miles north from Fort William, and as far east from Borodale, forming, in fact, the outlet from Moidart into Lochaber. The place gets its name from the little river Finnin, which runs through it, and falls into Loch Shiel at its extremity. Charles disembarked with his company from the three boats which had brought them from Glenaladale, at the place where the river discharges itself into the lake. It was eleven in the forenoon, and he expected to find the whole vale alive with the assembled bands which he had appointed to meet him. In this he was disappointed. Only a few natives, the inhabitants of a little village, were there to say ' *God save him !*' Some accident, it was concluded, had prevented the arrival of the clans, and he went into one of the neighbouring hovels to spend the anxious hours which should intervene before they appeared.

At length, about an hour after noon, the sound of a pibroch was heard over the top of an opposite hill, and immediately after the adventurer was cheered by the sight of a large band of Highlanders in full march down the slope. It was the Camerons, to the amount of 700 or 800,

'All plaided and plumed in their tartan array,'

coming forward in two columns of three men abreast, to the

[1] Home's Works, iii. 12.

spirit-stirring notes of the bagpipe, and enclosing the party of soldiers whom they had just taken prisoners. Elevated by the fine appearance of this clan, and by the auspicious result of the little action just described, Charles set about the business of declaring open war against the Elector of Hanover.

The spot selected for the rearing of the standard was a little eminence in the centre of the vale. The Marquis of Tullibardine, whose rank entitled him to the honour, pitched himself upon the top of this knoll, supported by two men, on account of his weak state of health. He then flung upon the mountain breeze that flag which, shooting like a streamer from the north, was soon to spread such omens of woe and terror over the peaceful vales of Britain. It was a large banner of red silk, with a white space in the centre, but without the motto of 'TANDEM TRIUMPHANS,' which has been so often assigned to it —as also the significant emblems of a crown and coffin, with which the terror of England at one time adorned it. The appearance of the standard was hailed by a storm of pipe-music, a cloud of skimmering bonnets, and a loud and enduring shout. Tullibardine then read several documents of an important nature, with which the Prince had provided himself. The first was a declaration, or manifesto, in the name of James VIII., dated at Rome, December 23, 1743; containing a view of the public grievances of Britain, and expressing an earnest desire to do the utmost to redress them; calling for this purpose on all his loyal subjects to join his standard as soon as it should be set up; and promising, in the event of his restoration, to respect all existing institutions, rights, and privileges. The second was a commission of the same date, in which James appointed his son Charles to be prince regent. The third was a manifesto by the Prince, dated at Paris, May 16, 1745, declaring that he was now come to execute the will of his father by setting up the royal standard, and asserting his undoubted right to the throne of his ancestors; offering pardon for all treasons to those who should now take up arms in his behalf, or at the least abjure allegiance to the usurper; calling on the officers of the army and navy to come over to his service, in which case he should pay all their arrears, and reappointing as his servants all public officers whatever who should henceforth act in his name; commanding payment of all public moneys to officers authorised by him; promising the same respect to existing institutions and privileges as his father; and, finally, calling on all his father's subjects 'to be assisting to him in the recovery of his just rights and of their own liberties.' The standard was carried back to the Prince's quarters by a guard of fifty Camerons.[1]

About two hours after this solemnity was concluded, Macdonald of Keppoch arrived with 300 of his hardy and warlike clan; and in the evening, some gentlemen of the name of Macleod came to offer their services, expressing great indignation at the defection of their chief, and proposing to return to Skye and raise all the men they could. The army, amounting to about 1200 men, was encamped that evening in Glenfinnin, Sullivan being appointed quartermaster-general.

The insurrection was thus fairly commenced; and it will now be necessary to advert to the means taken by government for its suppression, as well as to the state of the country upon which Charles was about to descend.

CHAPTER IV.

PROCEEDINGS OF GOVERNMENT.

'*Duke Frederick.* Come on; since the youth will not be entreated, his own peril on his forwardness.' *As You Like It.*

At the time when the insurrection broke out, George II. was absent in Hanover, on one of those frequent visits to his paternal dominions which, with great appearance of truth,

---

[1] Amongst the spectators on this occasion was a lady named Miss Jeany Cameron, who afterwards became the subject of many unfounded popular rumours. She was, in reality, a middle-aged lady, of perfect propriety of deportment, and after this occasion did not see the Prince any more, except when she met him in public during his stay in Edinburgh.

caused his British subjects to accuse him of being more devoted to the interests of his electorate, than he was to those of the more important empire over which his family had been called to reign. The government was intrusted, during his absence, to a regency composed of his principal ministers. So far as the northern section of the island was concerned in the affairs of government, it was then managed by a minister called Secretary of State for Scotland; and the Marquis of Tweeddale held the office in 1745.

The negotiations which the exiled family had constantly carried on with their adherents in Britain, and their incessant menaces of invasion, rendered the event which had now taken place by no means unexpected on the part of government, and indeed scarcely alarming. During the whole summer, a report had been flying about the Highlands that Prince Charles was to come over before the end of the season; but the king's servants at Edinburgh heard nothing of it till the 2d of July, when the President of the Court of Session came to Sir John Cope, commander-in-chief of the forces in Scotland, and shewed him a letter which he had just received from a Highland gentleman, informing him of the rumour, though affecting to give it little credit. Cope instantly sent notice of what he heard to the Marquis of Tweeddale, expressing disbelief in the report, but yet advising that arms should be transmitted to the forts in Scotland, for the use of the well-affected clans, in anticipation of any attempt which might be made. The marquis answered General Cope upon the 9th, ordering him to keep a vigilant eye upon the north, but mentioning that the lords of the regency seemed to decline so alarming a measure as sending arms. Cope replied immediately that he would take all the measures which seemed necessary for his majesty's service, avoiding as much as possible the raising of unnecessary alarm. Some further correspondence took place before the end of the month, in which the zeal and promptitude of this much-ridiculed general appear very conspicuous, while the supineness and security of the regency are just as remarkable.

Sir John Cope, whose fortune it was to be Charles's first opponent, and who was regarded by President Forbes as a good officer of his standing, had at present under his command in Scotland two regiments of dragoons,[1] three full regiments of infantry,[2] and fourteen odd companies,[3] together with the standing garrisons of invalids in the various castles and forts. The most of these troops were newly raised, being, indeed, intended for immediate transportation to Flanders; and it was impossible to place much confidence in them, especially as forming an entire army, without the support of more experienced troops.

With this little army, nevertheless, Cope found himself obliged to undertake a campaign against the formidable bands of the north. He received a letter from the Scottish secretary on the 3d of August, announcing that the young Chevalier, as Charles was called, had really left France in order to invade Scotland, and was even said to have already landed there; commanding him to make such a disposition of his forces as to be ready at a moment's notice; and promising immediately to send him down the supply of arms he formerly requested. On the 8th, he received a letter from the Lord Justice-clerk (Milton), then residing at Roseneath, enclosing another letter, dated the 5th instant, which had just been transmitted to Mr Campbell of Stonefield, sheriff of Argyle, by Mr Campbell of Aird (factor in Mull to the Duke of Argyll); which letter gave him almost certain intelligence of the Prince's landing. Next morning, the 9th, Cope was shewn by the Lord President another letter, confirming the news; and he sent all these papers to London, as the best means of rousing the slumbering energies of government.

[1] Gardiner's, lying at Stirling, Linlithgow, Musselburgh, Kelso, and Dunse; and Hamilton's, quartered at Haddington, Dunse, and adjacent places. Their horses, as was then the custom, were placed at grass in the parks near the quarters of the men.
[2] Guise's regiment of foot at Aberdeen, Murray's in the Highland forts, and Lascelles's at Edinburgh and Leith.
[3] Five of Lees's at Dumfries, Stranraer, Glasgow, and Stirling; two of the Scots Royals (taken by Keppoch's men); two of the Scots Fusiliers at Glasgow; two of Lord Semple's at Cupar, in Fife; and three of Lord John Murray's at Crieff.

Without waiting for this communication, the Lords Regent published on the 6th of August a proclamation, offering £30,000 for the person of the young Chevalier, whom they announced to have sailed from France for the purpose of invading Britain. This proclamation proceeded upon an act of George I., by which the blood of James Stuart and of his children was attainted, and themselves outlawed. Charles, on learning the price offered for his life, issued from his camp at Kinlocheil (August 20) a proclamation expressing great indignation at ' so insolent an attempt,' and offering a like sum for the *person* of the Elector of Hanover. Charles's first idea is said to have been to propose only £30 for the latter object; but ultimately he was induced to offer the same sum which the government had placed upon his own head.

It is amusing to observe, in the newspapers of the period, the various reports which agitated the public mind, and, above all, the uncertainty and meagreness of the intelligence which reached Edinburgh regarding Charles's transactions in Lochaber. On the 5th of August, it is mentioned in the *Edinburgh Courant* that the Prince had left France. Next day, it is reported, as a quotation from some foreign journal, that he had actually landed in the Highlands, and was sure of 30,000 men and ten ships of war. No other intelligence of note is observable till the 22d, when it is stated that two Glasgow vessels, in their way home from Virginia, had touched somewhere in the north-west Highlands, and learned that the dreaded Pretender was actually there, with 10,000 men, and had sent word to the governor of Fort William ' *that he would give him his breakfast that morning.*' The uncertainty which long prevailed in Edinburgh regarding the proceedings in Lochaber, shews, in a striking manner, how difficult it was to obtain correct intelligence in those days from a district which now would be considered as distant little more than a day's journey.

In projecting measures against the threatened insurrection, Sir John Cope had all along held council with those civil officers who, ever since the Union, have exercised influence over the affairs of Scotland—the Lord President of the Court of Session, the Lord Justice-clerk, the Lord Advocate, and the Solicitor-general. The gentlemen who held the first two of these offices —Duncan Forbes and Andrew Fletcher—were men of not only the purest patriotism and loyalty, but of good understanding and attainments. Duncan Forbes, in particular, from his intimate acquaintance with the Highlanders, of whom he had previously converted many to government, seemed well qualified to direct the operations of a campaign against that people.

The advice of all these gentlemen tended to this effect—that Sir John Cope should march as fast as possible into the Highlands, in order to crush the insurrection before it reached any height. It is very probable[1] that this advice was dictated by a feeling of humanity towards the insurgents, many of whom were the intimate friends and associates of the advisers. Forbes seems to have wished, by this means, at once to repress those who *had* risen, before government should become exasperated against them, and to prevent as many as possible from joining, who, he was sure, would soon do so if the enterprise was not immediately checked. The counsel was more honourable in its motive than prudent in policy. The royal army was not only inferior in numbers to that which Charles was believed to have drawn together, but had to contend with all the disadvantages of a campaign in an enemy's country, and on ground unsuitable for its evolutions: would first have to drag its way slowly over rugged wildernesses, with a clog of baggage and provisions behind it, and then perhaps fight in a defile, where it would be gradually cut to pieces, or, what was as bad, permit the enemy to slip past and descend upon the low country, which it ought to have protected. The advice was even given in defiance of experience. The Duke of Argyll, in 1715, by guarding the pass into the Lowlands at Stirling, prevented the much superior army of Mar from disturbing the valuable part of the kingdom, and eventually was able to paralyse and confound the whole of that enterprise.

[1] Probable from the tenor of their letters.—See Culloden Papers.

Cope is conjectured by Mr Home,[1] though the fact is not so obvious, to have been confirmed in his desire of prompt measures by a piece of address on the part of the Jacobites. These gentlemen, who were very numerous in Edinburgh, remembering perhaps the precedent alluded to, and knowing that Charles, with a small supply of money, would not be able to keep the Highlanders long together in their own country, conceived it to be their best policy to precipitate a meeting between the two armies. They therefore contrived, it is said, that Sir John Cope, who seemed to have no opinions of his own, but consulted everybody he met, should be urged to perform the march he proposed, as the measure most likely to quell the insurrection, which, it was hinted by these insidious advisers, wanted nothing but a little time to become formidable.

Thus advised, and thus perhaps deluded, Sir John Cope rendezvoused his raw troops at Stirling, and sent off a letter to the Scottish secretary, requesting permission to march immediately against the rebels. The reasons which he gave for his proposal seemed so strong in the eyes of the Lords Regent, that they not only agreed to it, but expressly ordered him to march to the north and engage the enemy, whatever might be his strength, or wherever he might be found. This order reached Sir John at Edinburgh on the 19th of August, the very day when Charles reared his standard; and Cope set out that day for Stirling, to put himself at the head of his little army.

Next day, the commander-in-chief commenced his fatal march. His force consisted of twenty-five companies of foot, amounting in all to 1400 men; for he had left the two regiments of dragoons behind, on account of their presumed unfitness for a Highland campaign. He carried with him four pieces of cannon (one-and-a-half pounders), as many cohorns, and a thousand stand of arms, to be given to the native troops which he expected to join him as he went along. Besides a

---

[1] Works, iii. 28. Mr Home adds, that he was assured of the fact by the Jacobites themselves.

large quantity of baggage, he was followed by a train of black-cattle, with butchers to kill them as required; and he had as much bread and biscuit as would serve for twenty-one days; for the production of which, all the bakers in Edinburgh, Leith, and Stirling had been working for a week.[1]

It was Sir John's intention to march to Fort Augustus, the central fort of the three which are pitched along the Great Glen. He considered this the most advantageous post that could be occupied by the king's army, because it was in the centre of the disaffected country, and admitted of a ready communication with the adjacent places of strength. He accordingly adopted that military road through the middle of the Highlands, which, stretching athwart the Grampians, is so remarkable in the memory of all travellers for its lonely desolation in summer, and its dangerous character when the ground is covered with snow. His first day's march was to Crieff, where he was obliged to halt till he should be overtaken by 100 *horse-loads* of bread that had been left at Stirling. He had previously written to the Duke of Athole, Lord Glenorchy (son of the Earl of Breadalbane), and other loyal chiefs, desiring them to raise their men, and the first of these noblemen here visited him; but the chief of Athole, though disposed to preserve his estate by keeping on good terms with the government, was by no means so ardently loyal as to take arms in its defence. Cope was then, for the first time, shaken in his hope of gaining accessions of strength as he went along—the hope which had mainly induced him to go north with so small an army; and he would have gladly returned to Stirling, had not the orders of government, as he afterwards acknowledged,[2] been so peremptory for a contrary course. Lord Glenorchy waited upon the disconcerted general on the afternoon of the same day, and gave him additional pain by the intelligence that he could not gather his men in proper time. He then saw fit to send back 700 of his spare arms to Stirling.

Advancing on the 22d to Amulree, on the 23d to Tay Bridge,

[1] Report of Cope's Trial.   [2] Ibid. 17.

on the 24th to Trinifuir, and on the 25th to Dalnacardoch, the difficulties of a Highland campaign became gradually more and more apparent to the unhappy general, whose eyes were at the same time daily opened wider and wider to the secret disaffection of the Highlanders. His baggage-horses were stolen in the night from their pastures, so that he was obliged to leave hundreds of his bread-bags behind him. Those who took charge of this important deposit, though they promised to send it after him, contrived that it should never reach its destination, or at least not until it was useless. He was also played upon and distracted by all sorts of false intelligence; so that he at last could not trust to the word of a single native, gentleman or commoner.

When at the lonely inn of Dalnacardoch, he was met by Captain Sweetenham, the officer already mentioned as having been taken by the insurgents; who, after witnessing the erection of the standard, had been discharged upon his parole, and now brought Cope the first certain intelligence he had received regarding the real state of the enemy. Sweetenham had left them when their numbers were 1400; he had since met many more who were marching to the rendezvous; and as he passed Dalwhinnie, the last stage, he had been informed by Macintosh of Borlum that they were now 3000 strong, and were marching to take possession of Corriearrack. Cope soon after received a letter from President Forbes (now at his house of Culloden, near Inverness), confirming the latter part of Captain Sweetenham's intelligence.

Corriearrack, of which the insurgents were about to take possession, is a lofty and wide-spreading mountain, interposed betwixt Cope's present position and Fort Augustus, and over which lay the road he was designing to take. This road, which had recently been formed under the care of General Wade, ascends the steep sides of the mountain by seventeen *traverses*, each of which leads the traveller but a small way forward in the actual course of his journey. It was the most dangerous peculiarity of the hill, in the present case, that the deep ditch or water-course along the side of the road afforded many positions in which an enemy could be intrenched to the teeth, so as to annoy the approaching army without the risk of being annoyed in return; and that, indeed, a very small body of resolute men could thus entirely cut off and destroy an army, of whatever numbers or appointments, acting upon the offensive. It was reported to Sir John Cope that a party of the Highlanders was to wait for him at the bridge of Snugborough, one of the most dangerous passes in the mountain, and that, while he was there actively opposed, another body, marching round by a path to the west, and coming in behind, should completely enclose him, as between two fires, and in all probability accomplish his destruction.[1]

The royal army had advanced to Dalwhinnie, about twenty miles distant from the summit of Corriearrack, when the general received this intelligence; and so pressing had his dilemma then become, that he conceived it improper to move farther without calling a council of war. It was on the morning of the 27th of August that this meeting took place, at which various proposals were made and considered for the further conduct of the army. All agreed, in the first place, that their original design of marching over Corriearrack was impracticable. To remain where they were was needless, as the insurgents could slip down into the Lowlands by other roads. Two objections lay against the measure which seemed most obvious, that of *marching back again*—namely, the orders of government, so express in favour of a northward march, and an immediate encounter with the enemy; and the likelihood of the Highlanders intercepting them in their retreat by breaking down the bridges and destroying the roads. The only other course was to turn aside towards Inverness, where they had a prospect of being joined by some loyal clans, and in which case they might expect that the insurgents would scarcely dare to descend upon the Lowlands, as such a course would necessarily leave their own country exposed to the vengeance of an enemy.

[1] Report of Cope's Trial, 24.

In reality, as the event shewed, the proper course on this occasion would have been to fall back on some convenient post near the frontier of the low country, there to make a determined stand against the clans, as the Duke of Argyll had done in 1715. Yet this expedient was supported by only one voice in the council. It was at last *unanimously agreed* to turn aside to Inverness—thus leaving the valuable part of the country completely exposed, and sacrificing a real object for the mere sake of obeying the letter of an order given, probably, in the contemplation of totally different circumstances. Sir John, having taken care to get the seals-manual of his companions to the resolution, issued orders to alter the route of the army. The van had reached Blairobeg, three and a half miles south of Garvamore Inn, and ten miles from Corriearrack, and the rear was at Catlaig, four miles behind, when the troops were ordered to halt, face about, and, retracing their steps, turn off by the road which parts to the east at the last-mentioned place, and proceeds by Ruthven to Inverness.[1] In order to deceive the enemy, who lay upon the top of Corriearrack expecting his approach, the general caused a small portion of his army to advance, with the camp-colours flying, towards the hill, under the semblance of an advanced guard, with orders to overtake the main body with all speed, when they had allowed time for it to get half a day's march upon its new route. He arrived, by forced marches, at Inverness upon the 29th, without having rested a single day since he left Crieff.

[1] 'Two rowan-trees (mountain-ashes) mark the place where Sir John Cope's army faced about, and avoided an action with the rebels.'—HOME.

CHAPTER V.

CHARLES'S DESCENT UPON THE LOWLANDS.

'Rouse, rouse, ye kilted warriors!
Rouse, ye heroes of the north!
Rouse, and join your chieftains' banners;
'Tis your Prince that leads you forth.'
Jacobite Song.

AT Glenfinnin, where the standard had been raised on the 19th, the Prince spent two happy days. So at least we are assured they were by Major Macdonald of Tiendrish, who, when confined in the castle of Edinburgh, told Bishop Forbes 'that he had never seen the Prince more cheerful at any time, and in higher spirits, than when he had got together four or five hundred men about the standard.' He then removed to Kinlocheil —that is, the head of Loch Eil—in the country of the chief of the Camerons. The retaliatory proclamation, offering £30,000 for the person of the reigning king, was 'given in our camp at Kinlocheil, August the 22d.' He lodged on the night of Friday the 23d at Fassefern, on the side of Loch Eil, the residence of the young chief's brother. Loch Eil is a branch of Loch Linnhe, the arm of the sea on which Fort William is situated: it was therefore liable to a hostile inroad from the nautical craft of the enemy. A war-vessel having actually appeared at Fort William, the Chevalier removed across a hill to Moy, a village on the river Lochy, belonging to the Camerons. He was now daily receiving intelligence of Cope's northern progress from deserters who nightly left the camp of that general, in order to join their respective clans. On the 26th he crossed the Lochy, and advanced to Letterfinlay, a lonely inn on the brink of Loch Lochy; he was joined on the way (at Low Bridge) by the Stuarts of Appin, 260 in number, under the command of

Stuart of Ardshiel. About midnight, an express arrived from Gordon of Glenbucket, informing him that Cope had advanced into Badenoch, and was designing to cross Corriearrack; immediately on which, though the night was extremely stormy, he gave orders for his men to go forward and take possession of the hill, and went himself to Invergarry Castle, where he spent the remainder of the night.

At Invergarry he was visited by Fraser of Gortuleg, on a secret embassy from Lord Lovat. This nobleman, now advanced to the seventy-eighth year of his age, was chief of the clan Fraser, and possessed large estates in Inverness-shire: he was able to bring several hundred men into the field. Discontented with the government, and well inclined to the Stuart family, he was yet disposed to act with great caution. Gortuleg therefore excused the personal presence of the chief on account of his age, but recommended Charles to march into his country of Stratherrick, and raise the Frasers; at the same time he asked for a patent which had been promised by the old Chevalier, creating Lovat a duke, and begged to have an order for seizing the President Forbes *dead or alive*. The patent chanced to be left behind with the baggage, and was therefore not forthcoming: the Prince so far complied with the other request as to give an order for seizing the person of the Lord President. With this Gortuleg returned to his chief. He is found, two days after, writing a friendly letter to the President, in which he only adverts to his having seen some of the insurgent chiefs at Invergarry, and seems anxious to serve the government by communicating the information he had thus acquired. We shall see more of the crooked policy of Lovat in the sequel.

Next day, the 27th, while the royal officers were determining upon their evasive march to Inverness, Charles and his army, now augmented by the Macdonells of Glengarry and Grants of Glenmorriston to 1800 men, proceeded to the foot of Corriearrack, the summit of which was already in possession of the party which had been sent forward the night before. The Prince, always the most eager man of the whole army, is said by

Fraser of Gortulcg, in his letter to the Lord President, to have 'called that morning for his Highland clothes, and, tying the latchets of his shoes, solemnly declared that he would be up with Mr Cope before they were unloosed.' The insurgents were informed of Cope's evasive movement by a soldier of the clan Cameron, who deserted in order to convey the intelligence, as soon as he perceived the army turn off at Catlaig. They hailed the news with a loud shout of exultation; and the Prince, calling for a glass of brandy, and ordering every man one of usquebaugh, drank: 'To the health of good Mr Cope, and may every general in the usurper's service prove himself as much our friend as he has done!'[1] They then descended the steep traverses upon the south side of Corriearrack, with the rapid steps and eager countenances of men who give chase.

It was the first wish of the Highland army on this occasion that Johnny Cope, as they called him, should be pursued, and he and his men cut to pieces. However, when they reached Garvamore, the first stage from the bottom of the hill, it was determined, by a council of war, that the unfortunate general should be left to the consequences of his own false step at Inverness, and that they should proceed in the meantime to take advantage of his desertion of the Lowlands. They were confirmed in this resolution by Mr Murray of Broughton, who represented that, by the influence of the Jacobites in Edinburgh, they would gain easy possession of that capital, and thus give as much *éclat* to their arms as might be expected from the achievement of a victory. It also appeared that, by this course, if they left the Frasers, the Macintoshes, and other northern clans, whom they expected to join them, the Marquis of Tullibardine would raise the men of Athole before the duke his brother had time to interest them in the cause of government.

It was more particularly at this juncture that Charles's enterprise assumed that bold and romantic character for which it was destined to be so remarkable. Having once made the resolution

[1] Henderson's *History of the Rebellion*, 34.

to descend upon the low countries, he did so with spirit and rapidity. Two days sufficed to carry him through the alpine region of Badenoch; another to open up to his view the pleasant vale of Athole, which might be considered as the avenue into the fertile country he was invading. He seems to have acted entirely like a man who has undertaken a high and hazardous affair, which he is resolved to carry through with all his spirit and address. Nature and education had alike qualified him for such an enterprise. Originally gifted with a healthy and robust constitution, he had taken care to inure himself to a hardy and temperate mode of life; had instructed himself in all kinds of manly exercises; and, in particular, had made himself a first-rate pedestrian by hunting afoot over the plains of Italy.[1] The Highlanders were astonished to find themselves overmatched at running, wrestling, leaping, and even at their favourite exercise of the broadsword, by the slender stranger of the distant lands; but their astonishment gave place to admiration and affection, when they discovered that Charles had adopted all these exercises out of compliment to them, and that he might some day shew himself, as he said, a true Highlander. By walking, moreover, every day's march alongside one or other of their corps, inquiring into their family histories, songs, and legends, he succeeded in completely fascinating the hearts of this simple people, who could conceive no greater merit upon earth than accomplishment in the use of arms, accompanied by a taste for tales of ancient glory. The enthusiastic and devoted attachment with which he succeeded in inspiring them, was such as no subsequent events could ever altogether extinguish. Half a century after, when age might have been supposed to deaden their early feelings, his surviving fellow-adventurers rarely spoke of him without a sigh or a tear.

At Dalwhinnie, where the army cheerfully bivouacked, along

---

[1] Boswell's *Tour to the Hebrides* (2d ed.), 231. In his march through the Highlands to meet Cope, he walked sixteen Scottish miles one day, in boots, fatiguing the hardiest of his companions. The men, hearing that one of his boots had lost a heel, said they were glad of it, as he would now be obliged to walk more at leisure.—*Donald Cameron's Narrative, Lyon in Mourning.*

with their young leader, on the open moor, a party who had gone upon an unsuccessful expedition against the small government fort of Ruthven,[1] brought in Macpherson of Cluny, chief of that clan, and son-in-law of Lord Lovat—a man of vigorous character, and one whose accession to the cause at such a moment would have been of considerable importance. He had accepted a command under government, and only the day before attended Sir John Cope at Dalwhinnie, and received orders to embody his clan, in which there were about 300 fighting men; but he was in reality a partisan of the Stuart family, though, under the present circumstances, not decided to take up arms in its behalf. He was conducted to Charles as a kind of honourable prisoner, and carried along with the army to Perth, whence he returned to raise his clan for the Chevalier. The same cautious policy which has been attributed to Locheil, is said to have been followed by Cluny. Before consenting to join the Prince, he demanded and obtained from him security for the full value of his estate, lest the expedition should prove unsuccessful.[2] Let not this policy be regarded as detracting too much from any merit of self-sacrifice hitherto attributed to these men. It might appear to them as not only justified, but demanded, in consequence of the failure of the Prince to bring foreign aid. And, after all, the purchase-money of a Highland gentleman's estate was but a small part of what he risked on this occasion, seeing that, in the first place, he took the common hazards of war; in the second, risked the pains of treason; and, after these, the loss of his home and country, in which was included all that was enviable in the state and circumstance of one who enjoyed the veneration, and could control the actions, of perhaps a thousand of his fellow-creatures.

[1] 'In this route, Lochgary, Dr Cameron, and O'Sullivan, were sent to Ruthven, in Badenoch, to take the barracks. Neither side had any cannon. The Highland party endeavoured to set fire to the door; but the soldiers fired through holes in the door, killed one man, and mortally wounded two more; and then the party retired. This garrison consisted only of twelve men, commanded by Sergeant Molloy.'—*Journal of Æneas Macdonald, Forbes Papers, in possession of the author.*

[2] Young Glengarry communicated this fact, which he said he had from Cluny's own mouth, to Bishop Forbes in April 1752.—*Jacobite Memoirs*, p. 22.

As the mountain host descended upon the plain, they were joined, like one of their own rivers, by accessions of strength at the mouths of all the little glens which they passed. But while many of the people joined, and prepared to join them, a very considerable number of the landed proprietors fled at their approach; among the rest, the Duke of Athole. In the absence of this nobleman from his house at Blair, his brother, the Marquis of Tullibardine, took possession of it as his own; and here Charles spent the night of the 30th of August. Along with Charles, the marquis undertook on this occasion to entertain all the Highland chiefs; and the supper which he gave was suitable to the distinguished character of the guests. During the evening, it is said, the Prince exerted himself to appear cheerful, though the anxiety arising from his circumstances occasionally drew a shade of thoughtfulness over his otherwise sprightly features. He partook only of the dishes which are supposed to be peculiar to Scotland; and, in pursuance of the same line of policy which induced him to walk in tartan at the head of his troops, attempted to drink the healths of the chiefs in the few words of Gaelic which he had already picked up. To the Marquis of Tullibardine, who, as a gentleman of the old school, always talked in broad Scotch, he addressed himself in similar language; and in all his deportment, he shewed an evident anxiety to conciliate and please those among whom his lot was cast.[1] Observing the guard which his host had placed in the lobby to be constantly peeping in, he affected a desire of enjoying the open air; and walking out into the lobby, gratified the poor Highlanders with a view of his person, which they had not previously seen, on account of their recent arrival at the house.[2]

The morning after his arrival at Blair, he reviewed his troops. Some whom he had lately seen around him being now wanting, he despatched a few of his officers to bring them forward to Blair, when it was found that their only reason for lingering behind was, that they had been denied the satisfaction of

---

[1] Henderson's *History of the Rebellion*, 36. [2] Tradition in Athole.

pursuing General Cope! At Blair he spent two days, during which he was joined by Lord Nairn, a cadet of the great house of Athole, and by several gentlemen of the country. At Lude, the seat of a chieftain of the clan Robertson, to which he next proceeded, he was very cheerful, and took his share in several dances, including minuets and Highland reels. A faithful chronicler informs us that the first tune he called for was the well-known Jacobite one, 'This is no my ain house'—referring to the alien character of all political arrangements since 1688.[1] Proceeding down the Blair or Plain of Athole, he arrived on the 3d at Dunkeld, and next day he dined at Nairn House, between that town and Perth. Here 'some of the company happened to observe what a thoughtful state his father would now be in, from the consideration of those dangers and difficulties he had to encounter, and that upon this account he was much to be pitied. The Prince replied that he did not half so much pity his father as his brother; "for," said he, "the king has been inured to disappointments and distresses, and has learned to bear up easily under the burdens of life; but poor Harry! his young and tender years make him much to be pitied, for few brothers love as we do."'[2]

This evening he entered Perth, where a party of his troops had already proclaimed his father and himself as respectively king and regent. He rode on this occasion the horse which had been given to him by Major Macdonald of Tiendrish, and was attended by a cavalcade of gentlemen, amongst whom were the Duke of Perth, Oliphant of Gask, and Mercer of Aldie, who had joined him as he passed through their estates. Well mounted, and attired in a handsome suit of tartan trimmed with gold-lace, he made a very good appearance. The people, dazzled by the novelty of the spectacle, hailed him with acclamations, and conducted him in a kind of triumph to the lodgings which had been prepared for him in the house of a Jacobite nobleman. This was the first town of consequence

---

[1] Duncan Cameron's Narrative, *Jacobite Memoirs*. [2] The same.

which Charles had yet arrived at, and he had every reason to be satisfied with his reception; although the magistrates had thought proper to leave their charge, and disappear on the preceding evening. A fair being held at the time in Perth, there were many strangers present, to join in the novel and agitated feelings with which this singular scene was contemplated.

The house appropriated for Charles's residence was that of the Viscount Stormont,[1] elder brother to the elegant William Murray, who afterwards became Chief-justice of the King's Bench and Earl of Mansfield. Stormont, like his brother and all the rest of the family, was a Jacobite at heart, but one who did not feel inclined to risk life and property in the cause. He did not choose to be present on this occasion to entertain the Prince; but no attentions were wanting on the part of his household; and one of his sisters is said to have spread down a bed for Prince Charlie with her own fair hands.[2]

The neighbouring seaport of Dundee, though not in the Prince's line of march, was of too much importance to escape notice on this occasion. That very evening Charles despatched Keppoch and Clanranald with a party of Macdonalds, who, entering the town about daybreak next morning, captured two vessels in the harbour, containing arms and ammunition, which they immediately sent to Perth for the use of the army.

The 'Duke of Perth,' who had joined the Prince before he reached that town, was, strictly speaking, only James

---

[1] It was an antique house with a wooden front, standing upon the site of the present Perth Union Bank, near the bottom of the High Street.

[2] Information from the late John Young, Esq., W.S., Castle Street, Edinburgh. Mr Young, as the son of a non-jurant clergyman in Fife, was likely to be correctly informed on such matters. The Stormont family relaxed in their Jacobitism as the great man of their family advanced in legal and state honours; for which, it may be supposed, the more faithful of the remnants of the party did not like them the better. One day, early in the reign of George III., Hamilton of Kilbrachmont, in Fife, a most determined old partisan, and a good deal soured in his temper, calling upon the Misses Murray, was much annoyed at the ostentation with which the good ladies paraded a few portraits of members of the royal family, which had been sent to them by their brother. The irritation was completed by their speaking of the great personages represented as 'the people above.' 'People above!' exclaimed old Hamilton—'fient nor they were up the lum!' Lum being *chimney* in English. And, thus saying, he flung out of the house.

Drummond, proprietor of large estates in Perthshire, and representative of the Drummonds, Earls of Perth, one of the most distinguished of the noble families of Scotland. His grandfather, James, fourth Earl of Perth, had followed the fortunes of James II., and been created a duke at St Germain. The son of this nobleman, joining the insurrection in 1715, was attainted, so that, at his father's death in 1716, the titles became dormant. But the estates having been previously transferred to his infant son, were preserved for the benefit of that person, who now lived upon them, boldly assuming the title which had been conferred by James II. upon his grandfather. The so-called duke was thirty-two years of age, brave, frank, and liberal, but disliked by many on account of his profession of the Catholic faith, in which he had been reared by a remarkably enthusiastic mother. When Charles was in the West Highlands, a warrant was issued for the seizure of the duke; and two Highland officers, Sir Patrick Murray of Auchtertyre, and Mr Campbell of Inverary, undertook to execute it, under circumstances extremely discreditable to them. Having asked themselves to his house to dinner, he invited them to come in the kindest terms, as friends and neighbours, and entertained them hospitably. Meanwhile they had ordered a military party to surround the house, and when all was prepared, they announced their warrant. The duke with difficulty restrained his temper, and told them he would step into a closet off the dining-room, to prepare himself to go with them. They, trusting that he could not escape, assented. He instantly went down a back stair, through his gardens, and into the adjoining wood, crawling on hands and knees to avoid being seen by the sentinels. Fortunately, he found a horse, though without a saddle, and only haltered, on which he rode to the house of his friend Moray of Abercairney.[1] Having thus escaped the fangs of the government, by which he should otherwise have been held in restraint till after the insurrection was over, he was now by no means less eager than

[1] *Jacobite Memoirs*, 16.

before to promote the cause of the house of Stuart, by personal service, and the aid of his numerous dependants, who of themselves nearly formed a regiment.

Charles received considerable reinforcements at Perth. Viscount Strathallan, a cadet of the Drummond family, Lord Ogilvie, son of the Earl of Airlie, and John Roy Stuart, a gentleman of Speyside, and the *beau idéal* of a clever Highland officer,[1] were amongst the most conspicuous persons of note who here joined him : the last-mentioned gentleman brought with him from abroad some very agreeable letters from persons of importance, promising assistance.[2] He had already been joined by the tenants of Lord Nairn, and the Lairds of Gask and Aldie. The Robertsons of Struan, Blairfitty, and Cushievale, the Stuarts who inhabited the uplands of Perthshire, and many of the tenants of the Duke of Athole, raised by the Marquis of Tullibardine, now poured themselves into the tide of insurrection. In raising the men of lower Perthshire, considerable difficulties were experienced by the chiefs and landlords. The Duke of Perth, having ordered his tenants to contribute a man for every plough, is said, though with extremely little probability, to have shot one refractory person, in order to enforce his orders among the rest. Tullibardine, from the equivocal nature of his title, found still greater difficulty in raising the tenants upon those estates which he conceived to be his own. But perhaps no one experienced so much difficulty in his levies as the good Laird of Gask, though he was at the same time perhaps the person of all others the most anxious to provide men for the service of his beloved Prince. This enthusiastic Jacobite was, it seems, so extremely incensed at

---

[1] John Roy was the son of the Baron of Kincardine on the Spey, and lineally descended from Robert II., the first of the Stuart kings. He was in the prime of life, an excellent soldier, and also a writer of verses, both English and Gaelic, many of which are still traditionally preserved in the Highlands. An old Highland woman, a few years ago (1827), describing John Roy's person, which she had seen, said that his eye in particular was very fine—her expression was, *like the eye of a horse*—of course an exaggeration, yet marking a feature of no common size and brilliancy.

[2] A Mr Johnstone, who afterwards wrote a memoir of the insurrection, also joined the Prince at Perth.

the resistance he received from some of his tenants, that he laid an arrestment or inhibition upon their corn-fields, by way of trying if their interest would not oblige them to comply with his request. The case was still at issue, when Charles, in marching from Perth, observed the corn hanging dead ripe, and inquired the reason. He was informed that Gask had not only prohibited his tenants from cutting their grain, but would not permit their cattle to be fed upon it, so that these creatures were absolutely starving. He instantly leaped from the saddle, exclaiming: 'This will never do,' and began to gather a quantity of the corn. Giving this to his horse, he said to those that were by that he had thus broken Gask's inhibition, and the farmers might now, upon his authority, proceed to put the produce of their fields to its proper use.[1]

When Charles entered Perth, he had only a single guinea in his pocket.[2] During his march hitherto, he had freely given his chiefs what sums they thought necessary for the subsistence of the men; and his purse was now exhausted, but fortunately at a moment when it was in his power to replenish it. By sending detachments of his men to various towns at no great distance, he raised some of the public money; and several of his Edinburgh friends now came in with smaller, but less reluctant subsidies. From the city of Perth he exacted £500.

Perhaps the most important accession to his force which Charles received at Perth was that of Lord George Murray, whom his brother, the Marquis of Tullibardine, brought down from Athole the day after the army entered the city. This gentleman was advanced to middle age, and had been in arms for the Stuarts at the affair of Glenshiel in 1719. Having served abroad since, in the Sardinian service, he possessed considerable military experience; but his talents and enterprising character were such as to render knowledge of his profession comparatively a matter of secondary moment. Charles had so much confidence in his abilities, as immediately to make him

---

[1] Tradition. [2] Home's Works, iii. 43.

lieutenant-general of his army—a trust for which he soon proved himself admirably qualified.

Charles was compelled to linger eight days at Perth, by the double necessity of providing himself with money, and gathering the Perthshire clans together. He did not, however, spend his time in vain. He seized this opportunity of reducing the ill-assorted elements of his army to some kind of order, and exerted himself to get the men instructed in the various evolutions of military discipline. The sturdy mountaineers were, as may be easily imagined, somewhat intractable, displaying great inaptitude in the conventional rules by which a whole body is to be governed, though, at the same time, every individual evinced a readiness and dexterity in the use of his own arms far beyond what is seen in ordinary soldiers. At a review held on the North Inch, a common near the town (September 7), Charles was observed to smile occasionally at the awkwardness of their general motions; at the same time he complimented their agility and wild elegance by calling them 'his *stags*.'[1] Lord George Murray now took some pains to furnish the men with many things which, though they make but a poor appearance in a romantic narrative, are yet eminently useful during the actual progress of a campaign. Amongst these were provisions, and the means of carrying them. He caused each man to be provided with a sacken knapsack, large enough to carry a peck of oatmeal—the food chiefly depended upon by these hardy soldiers. He also took measures for supplying meal and knapsacks to the clans who were on their march to join the Prince. By no other means could this little army have long been kept together.

It would almost appear that Charles occupied himself so closely in business while at Perth, as to have little time for amusement. Not only did he make a point of rising early every morning to drill his troops, but it is told of him that, being one night invited to a ball by the gentlewomen of Perth, he had no

[1] Henderson's *History of the Rebellion*, 37.

sooner danced one measure, than he made his bow, and hastily withdrew, alleging the necessity of visiting his sentry-posts. From a newspaper of the time,[1] it appears that he attended divine service on Sunday the 8th of September, when a Mr Armstrong, probably a clergyman of the Scottish Episcopal Church, preached from the text (Isaiah, xiv. 1, 2): 'For the Lord will have mercy on Jacob, and will yet choose Israel, and set them in their own land: and the strangers shall be joined with them, and they shall cleave to the house of Jacob. And the people shall take them, and bring them to their place: and the house of Israel shall possess them in the land of the Lord for servants and handmaids: and they shall take them captives, whose captives they were; and they shall rule over their oppressors.' The nature of the discourse may be easily conjectured from the text. It is said that this was the first time the Prince had ever attended a Protestant place of worship.

Many of the strangers whom Charles found at Perth attending the fair procured passports from him, to protect their persons and goods in passing through the country. To all these persons he displayed great courteousness of manner. One of them, a linendraper from London, had some conversation with the youthful adventurer, who desired him to inform his fellow-citizens that he expected to see them at St James's in the course of two months.[2]

[1] The *Caledonian Mercury*.   [2] *Edinburgh Evening Courant*.

CHAPTER VI.

ALARM OF EDINBURGH.

'Can you think to front your enemies' revenges with the easy groans of old women, the virginal palms of your daughters, or with the palsied intercession of such a weak dotard as you seem to be? Can you think to blow out the intended fire of your city with such weak breath as this?'—*Coriolanus.*

FOR upwards of a week after Cope's march into the Highlands, the people of Edinburgh had felt all the anxiety which civilians usually entertain regarding an impending action; but as yet they expressed little alarm about their own particular safety. The common talk of the day amongst the Whigs was, that Cope would soon 'cock up the Pretender's beaver'—that he would speedily 'give a good account of the Highland host'—and other vauntings, indicating great confidence. To speak in another strain was considered treason. Prudence joined with inclination, on the part of the Jacobites, to keep this tone of the public mind undisturbed. They knew it to be Charles's wish that the low countries, and also the government, should be as little alarmed as possible by his proceedings. They therefore conspired with the zealous Whigs to spread a general impression of his weakness.

The better to lull the town, and consequently the whole nation, into security, Charles, or some of his officers, thought proper to despatch a person of gentlemanly rank from their camp in Lochaber, with a report calculated to increase this dangerous confidence. They selected for this purpose James Macgregor, or Drummond, son to the celebrated Rob Roy; a man of not the purest character, but who seemed eligible on account of his address, and because he enjoyed some confidence amongst the Whig party. By way of making himself as useful as possible, Macgregor volunteered at the same time to carry with him to Edinburgh copies of the Prince's proclamations and manifestos, which he thought he should easily be able to get printed there, and disseminated amongst the friends of the cause. He reached Edinburgh on the 26th, and, being immediately admitted into the presence of the civil and civic officers, reported that the Highlanders, when he left them a day or two ago, were not above 1500 strong at most. As far as he could judge of them, they would run at the first onset of the royal army, being chiefly old men and boys, and very ill armed. When he had performed this part of his duty, he lost no time in setting about the other. His papers were printed by one Drummond, a zealous Jacobite;[1] and so speedily were they diffused throughout the town, that the magistrates were obliged, within three or four days after the arrival of this faithful messenger, to issue a proclamation offering a high reward for the discovery of the printer.

Macgregor's report, though partially successful in assuring the citizens, who immediately learned it through the newspapers, was not so completely effective with the public authorities as to prevent them from taking a measure next day which they had for some time contemplated—that of applying to the king for permission to raise a regiment, to be paid by voluntary subscription of the inhabitants, with which they might at once defend their property and advance his majesty's interests, in case of the town being attacked. Their previous security, however, was about this time slightly disturbed by a piece of intelligence brought to town by a Highland street-porter, who had been visiting his friends in the north. This man declared that when he saw the insurgents in Lochaber, their camp was as long as the space between Leith and the Calton Hill (at

---

[1] Drummond, some years afterwards, fell under the anger of the government for similar proceedings, and had his printing-office shut up; on which occasion the workmen being thrown idle, and public sympathy, at least with one party, being excited in their behalf, it was suggested to them to act the drama of the *Gentle Shepherd*, which had not before been represented on the stage, though many years published. Thus Drummond's men became the first performers of this celebrated pastoral.

least a mile) ;[1] a local illustration, which inspired a much more respectful idea of the Chevalier's forces than any they had yet entertained.

It was not till the 31st of August that the alarm of the city of Edinburgh became serious. On that day the inhabitants received intelligence of Cope's evasion of the Highland forces at Dalwhinnie, and of the consequent march of the Chevalier upon the low country. They had previously looked upon the insurrection as but a more formidable kind of riot, which would soon be quelled, and no more heard of; but when they saw that a regular army had found it necessary to decline fighting with the insurgents, who were consequently left at liberty to disturb the open country, it began to be looked upon in a much more serious light. Their alarm was, if possible, increased next day (Sunday, the 1st of September), by the Duke of Athole coming suddenly to town on his way from Blair, which, as already mentioned, he had left on the approach of the Highlanders. It was reported that his Grace had been compelled to take this step with greater precipitation than would have otherwise been necessary, by receiving a letter from his brother, the marquis, calling upon him to deliver up the house and estate which he had so long possessed unjustly. But the venerable Thomas Ruddiman, who gave currency to this rumour by means of his paper, the *Caledonian Mercury*, was obliged during the same week to acknowledge it false, beg the duke's pardon, and pay a fine of two guineas, besides being imprisoned for two days.

The friends of government now began to make preparations for the defence of the capital.

'' Piled deep and massive, close and high,'

and chiefly situated upon a steep and isolated hill, Edinburgh was then partly surrounded by a wall, and partly by a lake. The wall was of little use but to check smuggling, or evasion of the city customs ; it had no embrasures for cannon, and part of

---
[1] *Caledonian Mercury.* Henderson's *History of the Rebellion,* 37.

it was overlooked by lines of lofty houses, forming the suburbs; while the lake was fordable in many places. The friends of the Hanover succession were nevertheless of opinion that the city was capable of making a defence, provided that the inhabitants were determined upon it, and that arms were obtained from government. It was at least possible, they thought, to hold out until Cope's troops should come to their relief. On the other hand, a considerable section of the inhabitants, including the Lord Provost (Mr Archibald Stewart) and others of the magistracy, were Jacobites, though necessarily making no outward demonstration of such politics. Everything which they could safely or plausibly do to discourage the idea of defending the town was done; and doubtless their efforts were attended with some success. Burghal politics came in to add to the difficulties of the time. Opposed to the existing magistracy were the materials of a Whig one, which had been excluded from power for five years; at its head was Mr George Drummond, a man of virtuous and benevolent character, who had fought in behalf of government at Sheriffmuir. The time was approaching when, according to the custom of the burgh, a new election of magistrates should take place; and it was obviously the policy of the Whigs to profess an eagerness for the defence of the town. On the other hand, the existing magistracy, considering this as a mere mode of party warfare, or an appeal to mob feelings, were the more inclined to go upon the opposite side. 'Defend the town,' or 'not defend the town,' thus became party cries for the *ins* and *outs* of burghal office; and it would have been difficult for any cool onlooker to say whether the Whigs, in their profession of a wish to keep out Prince Charles, or the opposite party, in expressing their belief that the town was indefensible, were the least sincere.

The living force available for defence actually appears to have been of no great amount, although many more formidable enemies have been resisted with something much less. Now that Cope, with his infantry, was off the field, the whole of the regular forces in the south of Scotland, besides the invalids who garrisoned the fortresses, consisted of two regiments of dragoons —Hamilton's at Edinburgh, and Gardiner's at Stirling, both of them newly raised. In Edinburgh there was a body of military police, or *gendarmes*, called the Town-guard, generally amounting to 96 men, but now increased to 126 : these were for the most part elderly men, who had never been active soldiers, but they had the advantage of being pretty well disciplined. There was another body of militia connected with the city, called the Trained Bands, the members of which, exceeding 1000 in number, were ordinary citizens possessed of uniforms, in which they appeared once a year to fire off their pieces in honour of the king's birthday, but which none of them had adopted with the prospect of ever becoming active soldiers, or, indeed, with any other view than to enjoy the civic dinner which was given to them on that joyous anniversary. The Trained Bands had, at their first institution in the reign of King James VI., worn defensive armour, and carried the long Scottish spear; but in these degenerate days they only assumed a simple uniform, and were provided with firelocks so old as scarcely to be fit for service. To give the reader some idea of the military prowess of these citizen-soldiers, an extract may be made from a pamphlet of the day.[1] The author of this tract says that, when a boy, he used to see the Trained Bands drawn up on the High Street to honour the natal day of Britain's majesty, on which occasions, he affirms, it was common for any one who was bolder than the rest, or who wished to give himself airs before his wife or mistress, to fire off his piece in the street, without authority of his officers : and ' I. always observed,' says the pamphleteer, ' they took care to shut their eyes before venturing on that military exploit;' though he immediately afterwards remarks in a note, their fear was perhaps better grounded than he imagined, considering the danger there was of their firelocks bursting about their ears.

To increase this hopeful force, the state officers had instigated

---

[1] *Account of the Behaviour of Archibald Stewart.* London, 1748.

the magistrates, as already mentioned, to raise a regiment, which was to be paid by public subscription. The royal[1] permission was not procured for this purpose till the 9th of September, on which day a subscription-paper was laid before the citizens, and a drum sent through the town and its neighbourhood to enlist men. But it is unusual to yield to the solicitations of recruiting-sergeants for the direct purpose of fighting a severe action on the succeeding week. As may be easily imagined, more fortune than life was volunteered on the present occasion. The subscription-paper filled almost immediately; but, after a week, only about 200 men had been procured.

Besides this force, which was dignified with the name of the Edinburgh Regiment, a number of the loyal inhabitants associated themselves as volunteers into a separate band or regiment, for which 400 were ultimately collected. The discipline of all these men was wretched, or rather they had no discipline. The members of the Edinburgh Regiment were, in general, desperate persons, to whom the promised pay was a temptation, and who cared nothing for the cause in which they were engaged. The volunteers, on the other hand, were all decent tradesmen, or youths drawn from the counter and desk, inspired no doubt with a love of liberty and the Protestant religion, but little qualified to oppose the approaching Highlanders.

One circumstance may here be mentioned, which seems to have had a great effect in determining the subsequent events; namely, the ignorance which prevailed in the Lowlands regarding the real character of the insurgents. The people were indeed aware that, far in the north, there existed tribes of men living each under the rule of its own chief, wearing a peculiar dress, speaking an unknown language, and going armed even in their most ordinary and peaceful vocations. They occasionally saw specimens of these following the droves of black-cattle which were the sole exportable commodity of their country—

---

[1] The king arrived in great haste from Hanover on the 31st of August.

plaided, bonneted, belted, and brogued — and driving their bullocks, as Virgil is said to have spread his manure, with an air of great dignity and consequence.[1] To their immediate neighbours they were known by more fierce and frequent causes of acquaintance; by the forays which they made upon the inhabitants of the plains, and the tribute or protection-money which they exacted from those whose possessions they spared. Yet it might be generally said that little was known of them either in the Lowlands of Scotland or in England, and that the little which was known was only calculated to inspire sensations of fear and dislike. The idea, therefore, that a band of wild Highlanders, as they were called, were descending to work their will upon the peaceful inhabitants of the plains, occasioned a consternation on the present occasion such as it is now difficult to conceive, but which must have proved very fatal to the wish which the friends of government entertained of defending the country.

CHAPTER VII.

CHARLES'S MARCH UPON EDINBURGH.

French Herald. You men of Angiers, open wide your gates,
And let young Arthur, Duke of Bretagne, in.'
King John.

HAVING recruited both his purse and his muster-roll, and done something towards the organisation and discipline of his army, Charles left Perth on Wednesday the 11th of September. The direct road from Perth to Edinburgh was by the well-known passage across the Firth of Forth called the Queen's Ferry, and the cities were little more than forty miles distant from each other. But as all the boats upon that estuary had been

---

[1] Sir Walter Scott; *Quarterly Review.*

carefully brought to the south side, and as he could not have passed, at anyrate, without being exposed to the fire of a war-vessel lying in the Firth, as well as to whatever danger was to be apprehended from Gardiner's dragoons, who awaited his approach, he was obliged to take a more circuitous and safe route by a fordable part of the river above Stirling. Marching, therefore, to Dunblane, he was joined upon the way by sixty of the Macdonalds of Glencoe, in addition to as many more who had previously come to his standard; and by forty Macgregors, the retainers of Macgregor of Glencairnaig, who had deputed their command to James Mor Macgregor or Drummond, the same person who did the service at Edinburgh which has been before mentioned.[1]

The Prince remained a day at Dunblane, waiting till a portion of his army, which he had left at Perth, should come up to join the main body. On the evening of the 12th, the whole encamped about a mile to the south of Dunblane.

Charles proceeded on Friday, the 13th, towards the Ford of Frew. He passed by Doune, where an incident occurred which shewed that he was at least the elected sovereign of the ladies of Scotland. At the house of Mr Edmondstone of Cambus, in the neighbourhood of Doune, the gentlewomen of the district of Monteith had assembled to see him pass; and he was invited to stop and partake of some refreshment. He drew up before the house, and, without alighting from his horse, drank a glass of wine to the healths of all the fair ladies present. The Misses Edmondstone, daughters of the host, acted on this occasion as servitresses, glad to find an opportunity of approaching a person for whom they entertained so much reverence; and when Charles had drunk his wine, and restored his glass to the plate which they held for him, they begged, in respectful terms, the honour of kissing his royal highness's hand. This favour he granted with his usual grace; but Miss Clementina Edmondstone, cousin of the other young ladies, and then on a visit at Doune,

---

[1] Gartmore MS., quoted in Birt's *Letters* (2d ed.), ii. 351.

thought she might obtain a much more satisfactory taste of royalty, and made bold to ask permission 'to pree his royal highness's mou'.' Charles did not at first understand the homely Scottish phrase in which this last request was made; but it was no sooner explained to him than he took her in his arms and gave her a hearty kiss—to the no small vexation, it is added, of the other ladies, who had contented themselves with so much less liberal a share of princely grace.[1]

At this period of his career Charles lost an expected adherent in a mysterious manner. Stewart of Glenbuckie, the head of a small sept of that family in Balquhidder, and Macgregor of Glencairnaig, chief of his ancient and famous clan, were both passing Leny House (above Callander) with their respective 'followings,' to join the Prince, when Mr Buchanan of Arnprior, proprietor of the house, came out and invited the two gentlemen in to spend the night. Glencairnaig positively refused to stop, and marched on with his retainers; but Glenbuckie consented to accept of Arnprior's hospitality. He supped with his host, apparently in good spirits, and was in due time conducted to his bedroom. According to another account, Mr Buchanan went to meet Mr Stewart and his party in Strathyre, where they had a dispute about the majorship of the Duke of Perth's regiment.[2] In any case, Stewart lodged that night in Leny House, and was found next morning in his bed shot dead, with a discharged pistol in his hand. Mr Buchanan alleged that the unfortunate gentleman was the author of his own death; but was not generally believed. Glenbuckie's men took up the body of their master, carried it home to their own glen, and did not afterwards join the Prince.[3] Arnprior also abstained from joining in the enterprise, though well inclined to it. Notwithstanding practical neutrality, he was seized a short while before the battle of Culloden, and conducted to Carlisle, where an unsigned letter of his, which had been intercepted on its way

---

[1] Nimmo's *History of Stirlingshire*, edited by the Rev. Mr Macgregor Stirling, p. 564.
[2] Lyon in Mourning, MS.
[3] Information from a daughter of Glenbuckie, who was alive in 1827.

to the Highland army, proved sufficient, with the odium of Glenbuckie's suspected murder, to procure his condemnation. It is but justice to the memory of this gentleman to add, that, immediately before his death, he uttered, in presence of a clergyman, a solemn denial of all share in the death of Mr Stewart.[1]

The Ford of Frew, by which Charles had to cross the Forth, was a shallow part of the river, formed by the efflux of the

The Ford of Frew, from an original drawing.

Boquhan Water, about eight miles above Stirling. It was expected that Gardiner's dragoons would attempt to dispute the passage with the Highlanders; but those doughty heroes, who had hitherto talked of cutting the whole host in pieces as soon as it approached the Lowlands, now thought proper to retire

[1] The whole declaration is in the Lyon in Mourning, MS. in my possession.

upon Stirling. Charles, therefore, found no opposition to prevent him from taking this decisive and intrepid step, which was, everything considered, much the same to him as the passage of the Rubicon had been to a greater person. Hitherto he had been in a land where the Highlanders had a natural advantage over any troops which might be sent to oppose them; but he was now come to the frontier of a country where, if they fought at all, they must fight on equal, or perhaps inferior terms. The adventurer's heart was, however, screwed up to every hazard. Some of his officers had just questioned the propriety of venturing into a country so open and hostile; and various less decisive measures were proposed, and warmly advocated. But Charles was resolved to make promptitude and audacity his sole tactics and counsellors. Coming to the brink of the river, he drew his sword, flourished it in the air, and pointing to the other side, walked into the stream with an air of resolution. The river having been somewhat reduced by a course of dry weather, he found no difficulty in wading across. When he reached the opposite side, he paused upon the bank,[1] and congratulated every successive detachment as it reached the land.

Charles dined in the afternoon of this day at Leckie House, the seat of a Jacobite gentleman named Moir,[2] who had been seized on the preceding night in his bed, and hurried to Stirling Castle by the dragoons, on suspicion that he was preparing to entertain the Chevalier.[3] The remainder of the day's march was in a direction due south, to the Moor of Touch; and it was for a time uncertain whether Charles designed to attack Edinburgh or Glasgow. The latter presented great temptations, on account of its being unprotected, and quite as wealthy as Edinburgh; and Charles had sufficient reason to owe it a grudge, on account of its zeal against his family on all occasions

---

[1] Dougal Graham's *Metrical History*, 15.

[2] Mr Moir had married the heiress of Leckie: his own patrimonial estate was a very small one, at some distance. He would sometimes point out the latter to his friends at Leckie House, saying slily: 'Yon is my Hanover.'

[3] Lockhart Papers, ii. 487.

when such zeal could be displayed. But the *éclat* of seizing the seat of government, and the assurance of his Edinburgh friends that he would easily be able to do so, proved decisive in confirming his own original wishes to that effect. He, however, sent off a detachment to demand a subsidy of £15,000 from the commercial capital.[1]

The Highland army then moved eastwards, fetching a compass to the south of Stirling, in order to avoid the castle guns. Meanwhile, Colonel Gardiner, who had retreated from Stirling the preceding night, continued to retire before them, designing to fall back upon the other regiment, which was now lying near Edinburgh. In this day's march the Prince passed over the field of Bannockburn, where his illustrious ancestor, Bruce, gained the greatest victory that adorns the Scottish annals. He spent the night succeeding this brief day's march

---

[1] The conduct of the insurgent army on first entering the Lowlands is minutely portrayed by Dougal Graham, the metrical historian of the insurrection, who seems to have been present, and observed their proceedings. The reader will be surprised to find young Locheil, with all his amiable qualities, represented as shooting one of his clan for petty theft:

> 'Here for a space they took a rest,
> And had refreshment of the best
> The country round them could afford,
> Though many found but empty board.
> As sheep and cattle were drove away,
> Yet hungry men sought for their prey;
> Took milk and butter, kirn and cheese,
> On all kinds of eatables they seize:
> And he who could not get a share,
> Sprang to the hills like dogs for hare:
> There shot the sheep and made them fall,
> Whirled off the skin, and that was all;
> Struck up fires, and boiled the flesh;
> With salt and pepper did not fash.
> This did enrage the Camerons' chief,
> To see his men so play the thief;
> And finding one into the act,
> He fired, and shot him through the back;
> Then to the rest himself addressed:
> "This is your lot, I do protest,
> Whoe'er amongst you wrongs a man.
> Pay what you get, I tell you plain;
> For yet we know not friend or foe,
> Nor how all things may chance to go."'—P. 16.

in Bannockburn House, the seat of Sir Hugh Paterson, a gentleman attached in the most enthusiastic manner to his cause. Sir Hugh was descended from the last Archbishop of Glasgow, and was married to a sister of the Earl of Mar, who commanded the insurgent army in 1715. The army lay upon the neighbouring field of Sauchie, where King James III., in 1488, was defeated and slain by his rebellious subjects.[1] From this place Charles sent a message to the magistrates of Stirling, who submitted to him, and sent out provisions to be sold to the army.

On the 14th the Prince proceeded to Falkirk, where his army lay all night among some broom to the east of Callander House. He himself lodged in that mansion, where he was kindly entertained, and assured of faithful service, by the Earl of Kilmarnock. His lordship informing Charles that Gardiner's dragoons intended next day to dispute the passage of Linlithgow Bridge, Charles despatched a band of 900 well-armed Highlanders to attack him, who, without delay, marched during the night on this expedition. But the dragoons did not wait to come to blows. They retired precipitately to Kirkliston, eight miles nearer Edinburgh; and the Highlanders entered Linlithgow without disturbance before break of day.

Charles brought up the remainder of the army to Linlithgow about ten o'clock that forenoon, when he was only sixteen miles from Edinburgh. It was Sunday, and the people were about to attend worship in their ancient church; but the arrival of so distinguished a visitor suspended their pious duties for at least one day. Linlithgow, perhaps on account of its having been so long a seat of Scottish royalty, was possessed by a Jacobite spirit; and on the present occasion, it is said that even some of the magistrates could not restrain their loyal enthusiasm. Charles was conducted in triumph to the palace, where a handsome entertainment was prepared for him by Mrs Glen Gordon, the keeper of the house, who, in honour of the visit, set the palace well flowing with wine, of which she invited all the

[1] Lockhart Papers, ii. 444.

respectable inhabitants of the burgh to partake. The Prince mingled in their festivities with his usual grace.[1] The Highland army, at four o'clock in the afternoon, marched to a rising ground between three and four miles to the eastward (near the twelfth milestone from Edinburgh), where they bivouacked, while the Prince slept in a neighbouring house.[2] They proceeded next morning (Monday the 16th) towards Edinburgh, from which they were now distant only four hours' march.

On reaching Corstorphine, Charles thought proper, in order to avoid the guns of Edinburgh Castle, to strike off into a by-road leading in a southerly direction towards the little village of Slateford. His men there bivouacked for the night in a field called Gray's Park, which at that time bore a crop of pease nearly ripe. The tradition of Slateford relates, that the proprietor of the ground applied to Charles at his lodgings for some indemnification for the loss of his crop. He was asked if he would take the Prince Regent's bill for the sum, to be paid when the troubles of the country should be concluded. The man hesitated at the name of the Prince Regent, and said he would prefer a bill from some person whom he knew. Charles

---

[1] Mr Bucknay, provost of Linlithgow in 1745, was a keen Jacobite. On the 10th of June preceding the commencement of the insurrection, he had attended a sort of *fête* given in the palace by Mrs Glen Gordon, in honour of the old Chevalier's birthday, when a large bonfire was kindled in the inner court, the fountain in the centre adorned with flowers and green boughs, and King James's health drunk. When the Highland army drew near, the provost fled towards Edinburgh; but his wife and daughters remained, and waited upon the Prince, with tartan gowns and white cockades, and had the honour of kissing his hand at the cross.—See *Jacobitism Triumphant*; a pamphlet dated 1753, which appears to have been occasioned by the following ridiculous circumstance. Some of the Jacobite gentry around Linlithgow suspecting that the postmaster of the town (a notorious loyalist) was in the habit of opening their letters and exposing them to government, Mr James Dundas of Philipstoun wrote a letter to Provost Bucknay, of which the following are the *ipsissima verba:*

'Sir—Is it not very hard that you and I cannot keep up a correspondence for that damned villain of a postmaster? (Signed) Ja. Dundas.'
They expected that the object of their suspicions would open this epistle, and be overwhelmed with shame and rage. To their surprise, the letter passed inviolate. There remained, however, the joke, of which the postmaster became aware some years afterwards; and the pamphlet is a sort of memorial arising out of the process for defamation which he then instituted against Mr Dundas before the Court of Session.

[2] Lockhart Papers, ii. 445.

smiled at his caution, and asked if he would take the name of the Duke of Perth, who was his countryman, and at the same time a more credit-worthy man than he could pretend to be. The rustic accepted a promissory-note from the duke.

CHAPTER VIII.

CAPTURE OF EDINBURGH.

'*King Philip.* Now, citizens of Angiers, ope your gates;
Let in that amity which you have made.'

King John.

THE delay of the Highland army at Perth for a time subdued the alarm which had been excited in Edinburgh by the first intelligence of Charles's descent upon the Lowlands. But when he set out from that city, and was understood to be marching upon Edinburgh, all the terrors of the citizens were renewed, at least of that part of them who looked upon the Highland army as a public enemy, or who conceived their entrance into the city to be inconsistent with the safety of private property. On the other hand, the Jacobite part of the population could scarcely conceal their joy at the news of every successive day's march which Charles made towards the city.

The conflicting ferment into which the passions of all ranks of people were thrown by the course of public events, was now increased in a great degree by another agitating matter—the election of heads of incorporations, which began to take place on the 10th of September, as preparatory to the nomination of the magistrates. So engrossing a matter was this, that the magistrates were obliged to discontinue the repairs which they were making upon the city walls, because it was impossible to get workmen to attend to their respective occupations.

Sir John Cope had sent one of his captains from Inverness

early in the month, to order a number of transports to sail from Leith to Aberdeen, in which he might bring back his men to the shores of Lothian. These vessels sailed on the 10th, escorted by a ship of war; and as the weather was excellent, they were expected to return very soon with an army of relief. From that day the people of Edinburgh, according to Mr Home, were continually looking up with anxiety to the vanes and weathercocks, watching the direction of the wind.

As no certain dependence could be placed upon Cope's arrival, the Whigs did not, in the meantime, neglect in aught the training of their civic levies. Drills took place twice a day. Professor Maclaurin, the celebrated mathematician, exerted all his faculties in completing the works of defence which he had designed; and the walls began to bristle with old pieces of cannon, which had been hastily collected from the country around. The various gates or ports of the town were all strongly barricaded, and a guard appointed to each. If we are to believe this party, all their measures were thwarted and clogged by difficulties thrown in their way by the provost. To one proposal, he would object that he had no authority; to another, that it was treasonable—adding, with a sneer, that 'he knew no treason but what the law had made so:' some efforts of zeal he scoffed at; others he held as more productive of danger than safety. Personally, he afforded no active encouragement to any plan of a defensive nature: some were suspiciously blundered in the working: for example, in the digging of a ditch at the Wellhouse Tower, under the castle, the earth was thrown outwards, so as to be favourable to the assailing, rather than to the defending party. Now, also, he gave countenance and publicity to every rumour which magnified the insurgent forces. The Whigs accused him of having always had a set of Jacobites in his company, from whom he seemed to take counsel. Their own advices were, on the other hand, listened to with reluctance.

No incident of importance occurred in Edinburgh till Sunday the 15th, when, a false alarm reaching the city that the insurgents were advanced within eight miles, it was proposed that

Hamilton's and Gardiner's regiments of dragoons should make a stand at Corstorphine, supported by a body of infantry composed of the volunteers, Edinburgh Regiment, and Town-guard.

Public worship had commenced this day at the usual hour of ten, and the ministers were all preaching with swords by their sides, when the fire-bell was rung as a signal of approaching danger, and the churches were instantly deserted by their congregations. The people found the volunteers ranked up in the Lawnmarket, ready to march out of town; and immediately after, Hamilton's dragoons rode up the street, on their way from Leith to Corstorphine. These heroes clashed their swords against each other as they rode along, and displayed, in their language, the highest symptoms of courage. The volunteers, put into heart by the formidable appearance of these squadrons, uttered a hearty huzza, and the people threw up their hats in the air. But an end was soon put to this affectation of bravery. The mothers and sisters of the volunteers began to take alarm at seeing them about to march out to battle, and with tears, cries, and tender embraces, implored them not to hazard their precious lives. Even their male relations saw fit to advise them against so dangerous a measure, which, they said, staked their valuable persons against a worthless rabble. Many then began to demur, saying that they had engaged to defend the town, but not to march out of it. At this juncture Captain ex-provost Drummond, anxious to stop the spreading murmurs, led off his company down the West Bow towards the West Port, trusting that the rest would follow. His astonishment was great when, on reaching the Port, and looking round, he found that, so far from other companies having followed, his own had melted away in the course of its brief march, and he had only a few of his immediate friends behind him. Some had gone back to the Lawnmarket; others had slipped down *closes*, as lanes are called in Edinburgh, and thus vanished. A city wag afterwards compared their march to the course of the Rhine, which at one place is a majestic river flowing through fertile fields, but, being continually drawn off by little canals, at last becomes a small rivulet, and almost ceases to be distinguishable before reaching the ocean.¹

Drummond immediately sent back a lieutenant to know what had detained the regiment; and this gentleman, out of all who remained in the Lawnmarket, found one hundred and forty-one who still retained some sense of either shame or courage, and professed to be willing to march out of town. The lieutenant brought these down to the West Port, where, being added to the Town-guard and the half-fledged subscription-regiment, they made up a body of three hundred and sixty-three men, besides officers.

Even this insignificant band was destined to be further reduced before making a movement against the approaching danger. As they were standing within the West Port, before setting out, Dr Wishart, a clergyman of the city, and Principal of the College, came with several other clergymen, and conjured the volunteers to remain within the walls, and reserve themselves for the defence of the city. The words of the reverend man appealed directly to the sentiments of the persons addressed; only a few affected a courage which could listen to no proposals of peace. Happily, their manhood was saved the shame of a direct and point-blank retreat. Drummond having sent a message to the provost, bearing, that unless he gave his final permission for their march, they should not proceed, they were gratified with an answer, in which the provost congratulated them upon their resolution not to march; on which Drummond withdrew, with the air of a man who is balked by malice in a design for the public service; and all the rest of the volunteers dispersed, except a few, chiefly hot-headed college youths, who resolved to continue in arms till the end of the war.² Meanwhile the Town-guard and Edinburgh Regiment, in

---

[1] *True Account of the Conduct and Behaviour of Provost Archibald Stewart*, p. 18.

[2] A story is told of one John Maclure, a writing-master, who, knowing the irresolution of his fellow-volunteers, and that they would never fight, assumed what the reviewer of Mr Home's Works (*Quar. Rev.* No. 71) calls 'a professional cuirass:' namely, a quire of writing-paper, upon which he wrote: 'This is the body of John Maclure—pray, give it a Christian burial.' The same humorist, finding himself jostled in the ranks at the West Port, called out: 'Stand about! *we're all alike burgesses here.*'

number one hundred and eighty men, marched out, by order of the provost, to support the dragoons at Corstorphine; being the whole force which the capital of Scotland found it possible on this occasion to present against the descendant of its ancient kings.

It was generally expected that an attack would be made during the succeeding night. The walls were guarded by six or seven hundred men, consisting of trained bands, volunteers, armed seceders, and a few of the Duke of Buccleuch's tenants; but no pains were taken by the magistrates to encourage, refresh, or duly relieve these men. If a Whig reporter is to be believed, it was even found that, at eleven at night, one of the gates—one presented towards the position of the enemy—was standing wide open, without a sentry![1] In the course of the night, the two regiments of dragoons retired to a field betwixt Leith and Edinburgh, and the infantry entered the city. Brigadier-general Fowkes arrived on the same night from London, in order to take the command of this little army of protection. He did so next morning; and by an order from General Guest, governor of the castle, marched out to Colt-bridge, a place two miles to the west of the city, where he was joined in the course of the forenoon by the civic troops.

A person who saw these soldiers at their post,[2] describes them as having been drawn up in the open field to the east of the bridge, in the form of a crescent, with Colonel Gardiner at their head, who, on account of his age and infirm health, was muffled in a wide blue surcoat, with a handkerchief drawn round his hat, and tied under his chin. The Edinburgh Regiment and Town-guard he describes as looking extremely dismal; but certainly their hearts could not be fainter than those of the dragoons. The event shewed that few had escaped the panic of this momentous day.

[1] This important fact is stated, *from personal knowledge*, by a volunteer, in a paper (now in my possession) which appears to have been drawn up for the information of the Solicitor-general. The gate was that called Bristo Port, which might be considered, on this occasion, as the second in point of importance.
[2] Henderson's *History of the Rebellion*, 43.

On retreating the preceding night to their quarters between Edinburgh and Leith, the dragoons had left a small reconnoitring party at Corstorphine, which is about two miles in advance of Coltbridge. It was with this party that the panic commenced. The insurgents, observing them on their approach to Corstorphine, sent forward one or two of their number on horseback to take a view of them, and bring a report of their number. These gentlemen, riding up pretty near, thought proper to fire their pistols *towards* the party; and the poor dragoons immediately, in the greatest alarm, wheeled about, without returning a shot, and retired upon the main body at Coltbridge, to whom they communicated all their fears. The whole party immediately broke up, and commenced a retreat, not to Edinburgh, with the design of still defending it within the walls, but to the open country beyond it. In this movement, afterwards styled the *Canter of Coltbrigg*, the men rode over the ground now occupied by the New Town, where they were exposed to the view of the citizens. The Jacobites beheld the spectacle with ill-concealed pleasure, while the Whigs were proportionately discouraged.

A clamour immediately rose in the streets, which, till this period, had been crowded with anxious faces; and hundreds ran about, crying that it was madness to think of defending the town after the dragoons had fled, and that if this measure was persisted in, 'they should all be murdered!' A message from the young Chevalier[1] had previously been delivered to them, importing that, if they admitted him peaceably into the town, they should be civilly dealt with, but that resistance would subject them to all the pains of military usage; and the general cry now was, that the town should be surrendered. The provost, in returning from the West Port, where he had been giving orders, in consequence of the retreat of his militia, was assailed

[1] Delivered between ten and eleven in the forenoon by Mr Alves, a gentleman of Edinburgh, who had passed the Highland army on the road, and been intrusted with it by the Duke of Perth. Mr Alves was put into prison that afternoon by the provost, for having been so imprudent as to communicate the message to the people on the streets, instead of confining it to his lordship's own ear.

upon the street by multitudes of the alarmed inhabitants, and implored to call a meeting of the citizens, to determine what should be done. He consented with some reluctance to do so, or rather the people pressed so close around him and his council in their chamber, that a meeting was constituted without his consent. He then sent for the officers of the crown, whose advice he wished to ask; but it was found, to the still greater consternation of the people, that all these gentlemen had deserted the city. The meeting was then adjourned to a larger place, the New Church Aisle, where the question of 'Defend, or not defend, the town' being put, by far the greater part of those present exclaimed in favour of the latter alternative, and all who attempted to urge the contrary measure were borne down by clamour. Whig reporters of the time call this a packed assembly; but it appears to have fairly enough represented the general feeling of the moment. While the ferment was at its height, a letter was handed in from the door, addressed to the Lord Provost, Magistrates, and Town-council of Edinburgh. Deacon Orrock, a shoemaker, got this document into his hands, and announced that it was subscribed 'Charles, P. R.' On this the provost rose, and saying he could not be present at the reading of such a letter, left the assembly. He was, however, prevailed upon, after some time, to return, and permit the letter to be read, when it was found to run as follows:

'*From our Camp*, 16*th September* 1745.

'Being now in a condition to make our way into the capital of his majesty's ancient kingdom of Scotland, we hereby summon you to receive us, as you are in duty bound to do; and in order to it, we hereby require you, on receipt of this, to summon the Town-council, and to take proper measures for securing the peace of the city, which we are very desirous to protect. But if you suffer any of the usurper's troops to enter the town, or any of the cannon, arms, or ammunition now in it (whether belonging to the public or to private persons) to be carried off, we shall take it as a breach of your duty, and a heinous offence against the king and us, and shall resent it accordingly.

We promise to preserve all the rights and liberties of the city, and the particular property of every one of his majesty's subjects. But if any opposition be made to us, we cannot answer for the consequences, being firmly resolved, at anyrate, to enter the city; and in that case, if any of the inhabitants are found in arms against us, they must not expect to be treated as prisoners of war.   CHARLES, P. R.'

The tenor of this letter decided the meeting in their proposal for a capitulation, and a deputation, headed by Bailie Gavin Hamilton (father of the late ingenious inquirer into the national debt), was despatched to Slateford, where they understood Charles to have taken up his quarters for the night, with power to entreat time for deliberation.

In the course of the afternoon, when the inhabitants were violently debating in the New Church Aisle, a gentleman, whose person was not recognised by any one, rode up the West Bow upon a gray horse, and rushing rapidly along the lines of the volunteers, where they were standing in the Lawnmarket, cried with a loud voice that he had seen the Highlanders, and they were 16,000 strong! Without stopping to be questioned, he was out of sight in a moment; but the impression he made upon the faint-hearted volunteers was decisive. Four companies immediately marched up to the Castle-hill, and surrendered their arms to General Guest, from whom they had received them; and their example was speedily followed by all the different bodies of militia that had been supplied with arms from the castle magazine. When this transaction was completed, Edinburgh might be said to have virtually resigned all hope of defence, though the Trained Bands still continued upon the walls, with their rusty firelocks in their hands, and the gates were still barricaded.

Throughout these scenes of civic pusillanimity, there were not wanting instances of vigorous resolution and consistent loyalty. Mr Joseph Williamson, an advocate (son to the celebrated *Mass David Williamson*, minister of the West Church of

Edinburgh during the reigns of the last Charles and James), who had been intrusted with the keys of the gates, on account of his office of town-clerk, on being asked by the provost to deliver up his charge, absolutely refused to do so; and when commanded peremptorily by his lordship, implored that he might be permitted at least to escape over the walls, so as not to share in what he considered the general disgrace of the city.[1] A similar enthusiast, by name Dr Stevenson, though he had long been bed-rid through age and disease, sat for some days, as one of the guards, at the Netherbow Port, *in his arm-chair!*[2]

The deputies, who had gone out in a carriage to Slateford at eight o'clock, returned at ten, with a letter from Charles, reiterating his demand to be peaceably admitted into the town, and pointing out that his manifesto and his father's declaration were a sufficient guarantee for the protection of the city.[3] By this time the magistrates had been informed, though it afterwards appeared prematurely, that General Cope's transports were arrived off Dunbar (twenty-seven miles east from the city), and felt disposed to hold out, in the hope of speedy relief from a government army. A second deputation of two persons (one of whom was father of the late Mr Coutts, banker) was therefore sent to Slateford about two o'clock in the morning, with a petition for a little longer time.

According to one account, the Prince simply refused to admit

---

[1] Williamson *did* go over the walls through the night, and was the first man to reach London with the intelligence of the surrender of Edinburgh.

[2] MS. Note to a copy of Lord Hailes's pamphlet against the extension of the city of Edinburgh, 1753.

[3] The letter was as follows:

'His Royal Highness the Prince Regent thinks his manifesto, and the king his father's declaration, already published, are a sufficient capitulation for all his Majesty's subjects to accept of with joy. His present demands are to be received into the city as the son and representative of the king his father, and obeyed as such when he is there.

'His Royal Highness supposes that since the receipt of his letter to the Provost and Magistrates, no arms or ammunition have been suffered to be carried off or concealed, and will expect a particular account of all things of that nature.

'Lastly, he expects a positive answer to this before two o'clock in the morning, otherwise he will find himself obliged to take measures conform.

By his Royal Highness's command,
JOHN MURRAY.

'*At Gray's Mill, 16th Sept. 1745.*'

them to his presence; but Mr Home says that they prevailed on Lord George Murray to second their application; and from another source[1] we have the actual words of a reply sent to them : ' His Royal Highness has already given all the assurances he can, that he intends to exact nothing of the city in general, nor of any in particular, but what his character of regent entitles him to. This he repeats, and renews his summons to the magistrates to receive him as such.' Dated at three in the morning. The deputies were then ordered ' to get them gone.'[2]

Charles, during this anxious night, slept only two hours, and that without taking off his clothes.[3] Finding that the inhabitants of Edinburgh were paltering with him, and afraid that the city would soon be relieved, he gave orders, at an early hour in the morning, for an attempt to take the city by surprise. The gentlemen whom he selected for this purpose were Locheil, Keppoch, Ardshiel, and Sullivan. They were commanded to take the best armed of their respective parties, to the amount of about nine hundred, together with a barrel of powder, to blow up one of the gates if necessary. Mr Murray of Broughton, who was well acquainted with the localities, acted as guide. This band mustered by moonlight upon the Borough Moor, where they could hear the watches calling the rounds within the castle. Strict silence and abstinence from intoxicating liquors were enjoined the men. Several plans for breaking into the city were agitated; but at length it was determined to attempt getting access by stratagem. A select party of twenty-four was planted close to the Netherbow Port; another party of sixty took station in St Mary's Wynd, close by; while the remainder hung a little way off, but ready to advance at a moment's notice. Locheil then sent forward one of his men, disguised in a riding-coat and hunting-cap, so as to appear as the servant of an officer of dragoons, in which character he was to knock at the wicket, and request admission, under pretence of being sent by his master to bring something which had been forgot in the city.

[1] Lyon in Mourning, MS. [2] Provost Stewart's Trial. [3] *Caledonian Mercury.*

The man did as he was bid; but without success, the guard ordering him to retire, under pain of being shot at. The chiefs were now at a loss how to proceed, for morn was breaking, and Locheil was anxious to avoid using violence. Mr Murray of Broughton recommended that they should retire to St Leonard's Crags, and wait for further orders; and they were about to follow this advice, when an accident enabled them to accomplish their object. The hackney-coach which took out the last party of deputies to Slateford, and afterwards brought them back to the city, was now returning to its master's quarters in the Canongate. The port was opened, contrary to orders, to allow it egress; and no sooner had that been done, than the Highlanders, who had not yet retired, rushed in and took possession of the gate.[1] The guard was so slender, that this feat was much more easily performed than they expected; but not knowing what resistance they might meet, they rushed into the High Street, sword in hand, with one of those outcries with which they were accustomed to make an onset in the field of battle.[2] The neighbouring people, roused from their beds, looked over their windows, and beheld in the dusk of the morning their street filled with a thickening troop of those enemies whom they had been so anxious to exclude, while the pipes screamed out a stormy pibroch, such as might have suited a day of fight.[3] A first object of the intruding party was to seize the guard-house in the High Street, and disarm the men posted there. They then went to the different ports of the city, and also to all the posts upon the walls, and relieved the guards, as quietly, says Mr Home, as one guard relieves another in the

---

[1] The first man who entered the city was Captain Evan Macgregor, a younger son of Macgregor of Glencairnaig, and grandfather to Sir Evan Murray Macgregor, Bart., chief of this ancient clan. In consideration of his gallantry, he was that night raised to a majority by the Prince at Holyrood House.—*MS. Account of the Campaign by Duncan Macpharig.*

[2] Lockhart Papers, ii. 488.

[3] The tune was called *We'll awa to Sherramuir to haud the Whigs in order*, according to the report of an aged female, whose mother, servant at the time to Commissioner Cochrane (father of the mechanical Earl of Dundonald), saw from her master's windows in the Netherbow the scene above described.

routine of duty on ordinary occasions.[1] They fixed a strong guard at the head of the West Bow, to cut off all communication between the city and the castle, using the Weigh-house as their court of guard; and the remainder of the body drew themselves up in two lines upon the street, to await the arrival of the army. When the inhabitants began to stir at their usual hour of rising, they found the government of the city transferred from the magistrates in the name of King George, to the Highlanders in the name of King James.[2]

[1] Mr Home perhaps adopted this idea from a saying to the same effect which tradition puts into the mouth of a Highlander. A citizen of Edinburgh, taking a stroll round the walls on the morning of this momentous day, observed a mountaineer sitting astride upon a cannon, with an air of great vigilance and solemnity, as if deeply impressed with a sense of his duty as a sentinel. The citizen accosted him with a remark, that surely these were not the same troops which mounted guard yesterday. 'Och, no,' said the Highlander, 'she pe relieved.'

[2] At the period of these memorable transactions, there were two newspapers regularly published in Edinburgh—the *Evening Courant* and the *Caledonian Mercury*. The former continued throughout all the subsequent campaign to express such violent hostility to the insurgents, that the editor was burned in effigy at Rome on the 10th of June 1746, amongst the other festivities with which the birthday of the old Chevalier was there celebrated. The *Mercury*, on the contrary, was so enthusiastic a Jacobite, that it was afterwards very much discountenanced and even persecuted by government. There is something quite amusing in the conduct of the *Courant* on the occasion of Charles's entry into Edinburgh. So long as the Highlanders were at a distance, the editor talks of them with the most dignified contempt. Even when they had pushed their way to Perth, he describes them as 'a pitiful ignorant crew, good for nothing, and incapable of giving any reason for their proceedings, but talking only of *snishing, King Jamesh, ta rashant* [the regent], *plunter, and new progues*.' At every successive advance, however, which they made towards Edinburgh, and at every additional symptom of imbecility displayed by the protectors of the city, this tone is perceptibly decreased, till at last, in the number for Tuesday, September 17, it is altogether extinguished, and we only find a notice to the following effect: 'By order of Mr Murray of Broughton, Secretary. Since our last, the Prince, with his Highland army, has taken possession of this place; but we must refer you for particulars to our next.' Our *next*, however, did not come out for a week, instead of appearing, as it ought to have done, at the distance of two days; and during the whole stay of the Prince in Edinburgh, the editor seems fain to say as little on either side as possible. The *Mercury*, which, as already mentioned, was then under the charge of Ruddiman, the distinguished grammarian, both talks with more respect of the Highland army when at a distance, and afterwards becomes more readily its organ of intelligence, than the *Courant*. In the first publication after the capture of Edinburgh, 'affairs' are stated to have 'taken a surprising turn in this city since yesterday, Highlanders and bagpipes being now as common in our streets as formerly were dragoons and drums.' Then follows an account of the taking of the city, concluding with a statement that 'the Highlanders behave most civilly to the inhabitants, paying cheerfully for everything they get,' &c. Both papers are printed without the affix of a printer's or publisher's name—a circumstance which at once indicated their terror of government, and the compulsion under

CHAPTER IX.

PRINCE CHARLES'S ENTRY INTO EDINBURGH.

'To match this monarch, with strong Arcite came
Emetrius, king of Inde, a mighty name,
On a bay courser goodly to behold—
    *   *   *   *
His amber-coloured locks in ringlets run
With graceful negligence, and shone against the sun;
His nose was aquiline, his eyes were blue,
Ruddy his lips, and fresh and fair his hue:
Some sprinkled freckles on his face were seen,
Whose dusk set off the whiteness of his skin;
His awful presence did the crowd surprise,
Nor durst the rash spectator meet his eyes—
Eyes that confessed him born for kingly sway,
So fierce, they flashed intolerable day.'
Palamon and Arcite.

INTELLIGENCE of the capture of Edinburgh having been conveyed to the Prince, he prepared, at an early hour, to leave his lodgings in Slateford, and lead forward the remainder of his army. This march, though short, was not altogether free of

which the Highland army had laid them. They are also unstamped; because the Stamp-office, as well as the banks and other public offices, had been removed into the castle before the army approached.

It remains to be stated, that Provost Archibald Stewart was afterwards apprehended, and, being confined for fourteen months, and only liberated on finding bail to the enormous amount of £15,000, was tried by the High Court of Justiciary, upon an obsolete statute of the Scottish James II., 'for neglect of duty, and misbehaviour in the execution of his office.' The trial, which took place in March 1747, lasted for two or three days, and was considered the most solemn ever witnessed in this country. He was acquitted by a unanimous jury. My impression is, that Mr Stewart acted throughout exactly as might have been expected of a Jacobite who wished to keep a fair face towards the government. On the other hand, after the government troops had committed the blunder of leaving the Lowlands exposed, great daring for the repulse of the Highlanders was not to be reasonably expected in Edinburgh; and the citizens at large most unquestionably betrayed feelings which gave only too good a colour to the actual proceedings of their provost.

PRINCE CHARLES'S ENTRY INTO EDINBURGH.

danger; for he could see from his present position the flag of defiance flaunting on the battlements of the castle, and apparently daring him to venture within the scope of its guns. The eminent position of that fortress was such as to command nearly the whole country for miles around, and it was a matter of difficulty to discover a path which should conduct him to the city without being exposed to its fire. Some of his train, however, by their acquaintance with the localities, enabled him to obviate this petty danger.

By the direction of his guides, Charles made a circuit to the south of Edinburgh, so as not only to maintain a safe distance from the castle, but to keep some swelling grounds between, which screened him from its view. Debouching upon the open or turnpike road near Morningside, and turning towards the city, he reached a sequestered and almost obsolete crossroad, which turns off to the east by the house of Grange, and completely precludes the view of the city or castle. Charles conducted his army along this road, and soon entered the King's Park near Prestonfield, by a breach which had been made in the wall.[1]

It must have been with elated feelings that Charles traversed this venerable domain, whose recesses had so often sounded to the bugle-horn of his royal ancestors. Leaving his troops about noon in the Hunter's Bog, a deep and sheltered valley betwixt Arthur's Seat and Salisbury Crags, he rode forward, with the Duke of Perth on one hand, and Lord Elcho on the other,[2] some other gentlemen coming up behind. When he reached the eminence under St Anthony's Well, where he for the first time came within sight of the palace, he alighted from his horse,[3] and paused a few moments to survey the scene.

The park and gardens below, intervening betwixt the Prince and the palace, were now filled with the inhabitants of Edinburgh, who, on learning that he approached the city in this

---
[1] Lockhart Papers, ii. 446.
[2] This young nobleman, son of the Earl of Wemyss, had joined him the night before.
[3] *Hist. Reb., with an Account of the Genius and Temper of the Clans.*

quarter, had flocked in great numbers to see him. The crowd consisted of all ranks and persuasions of people, excepting only those who had taken a leading part in opposing his entrance into the city. The Jacobites of course abounded; and many of these now approached Charles, where he was standing beside his horse, and knelt to kiss his hand. He received their homage and congratulations with smiles, and bowed gracefully to the huzza which immediately after rose from the crowded plain below.[1]

Descending to the Duke's Walk, a footpath through the park, so called from having been the favourite promenade of his grandfather, he stood for a few minutes to shew himself to the people. As it was here that he might be said to have first presented himself to the people of Scotland, it may be necessary to describe his appearance.

The figure and presence of Charles are said by one of his historians, who saw him on this occasion,[2] to have been not ill suited to his lofty pretensions. He was in the prime of youth, tall and handsome, of a fair complexion; he wore a light-coloured peruke, the ringlets of which descended his back in graceful masses, and over the front of which his own pale hair was neatly combed. His complexion was ruddy, and, from its extreme delicacy, slightly marked with freckles. His visage was a perfect oval, and his brow had all the intellectual but melancholy loftiness so remarkable in the portraits of his ancestors. His neck, which was long, but not ungracefully so, had, according to the fashion of the time, no other covering or encumbrance than a slender stock buckled behind. His eyes were large and rolling, and of a light blue. The fair, but not ill-marked eyebrows which surmounted these features were beautifully arched. His nose was round and high, and his

---

[1] 'He came to the royal palace, at the abbey of Holyrood House, amidst a vast crowd of spectators, who, from town and country, flocked together to see this uncommon sight, expressing their joy and surprise together by long and loud huzzas. Indeed the whole scene, as I have been told by many, was rather like a dream, so quick and amazing seemed the change, though no doubt wise people saw well enough we had much to do still.'— *Journalist in Lockhart Papers*, ii. 489.

[2] Mr Home.

mouth small in proportion to the rest of his features. He was above five feet ten in stature, and his body was of that straight and round description which is said to indicate not only perfect

PRINCE CHARLES EDWARD STUART.
From Strange's contemporary engraving.

symmetry, but also the valuable requisites of agility and health. In the language of one of his adherents,[1] he was as 'straight

[1] *The Wanderer, or Surprising Escape, &c.* Glasgow, 1752; p. 17. It is added by that writer that he 'would fight, run, or leap with any man in the Highlands.'

as a lance, and as round as an egg.' By all ladies who ever saw him, his person was excessively admired; and the powers of fascination which he could exercise over the male sex have been sufficiently attested. On the present occasion he wore a blue velvet bonnet, bound with gold lace, and adorned at top with a white satin cockade, the well-known badge of his party. He had a short tartan coat, on the breast of which hung the star of the order of St Andrew. A blue sash, wrought with gold, came gracefully over his shoulder. He wore small-clothes of red velvet, a pair of military boots, and a silver-hilted broadsword.[1]

After he had stood for a few minutes in the midst of the people, he mounted a fine bay gelding, which had been presented to him by the Duke of Perth, and slowly rode towards the palace. Being an excellent horseman, a murmur of admiration ran at this moment through the crowd, which soon amounted to, and terminated in, a long and loud huzza. Around him, as he rode, there was a small guard of ancient Highlanders,[2] whose outlandish and sunburned faces, as they were occasionally turned up with reverence towards the Prince, and occasionally cast with an air of stupid wonder over the crowd, formed not the least striking feature in this singular scene.

The Jacobites, delighted beyond measure by the gallant aspect of their idol, were now indulging themselves in the most extravagant terms of admiration. With their usual propensity to revert to the more brilliant periods of the Scottish monarchy, they fondly compared Charles to King Robert Bruce, whom they said he resembled in his figure,[3] as they fondly anticipated he would also do in his fortunes. The Whigs, however, though compelled to be cautious in the expression of their sentiments, talked of him in a different style. They acknowledged he was a goodly person, but observed that, even in that triumphant

---

[1] *Hist. Reb., with an Account of the Genius and Temper of the Clans.*
[2] Most of them stooping with age, and imperfectly armed. See *Hist. of the Rise, Progress, and Extinction of the Reb. in Scot.* 8vo. London, sold by R. Thomson, &c., p. 30. (A violent party production.)
[3] Home's Works, iii. 71.

hour, when about to enter the palace of his fathers, the air of his countenance was languid and melancholy; that he looked like a gentleman and man of fashion, but not like a hero or a conqueror.[1]

Charles approached Holyrood House by the same path over which George IV., seventy-seven years after, was drawn thither in his daily progresses from Dalkeith. As he was parading along, the Duke of Perth stopped him a little, while he described the limits and peculiar local characteristics of the King's Park. It was observed on this occasion by an eye-witness, that during the whole five minutes the duke was expatiating, Charles kept his eye bent sideways upon Lord Elcho (who stood aside at a little distance), and seemed lost in a mental speculation about that new adherent. As the procession—for such it might be termed—moved along the Duke's Walk, the crowd greeted the principal personage with two distinct huzzas, which he acknowledged with bows and smiles. The general feeling of the crowd seemed to be a very joyful one, arising in some cases from the influence of political prepossessions, in many others from gratified curiosity, and perhaps in still more from the satisfaction with which they had observed the fate of the city so easily decided that morning. Many had previously conceived Charles to be only the leader of a band of predatory barbarians, at open warfare with property, and prepared to commit any outrage for the accomplishment of his purposes. They now regarded him in the interesting light of an injured prince, seeking, at the risk of life, one single noble object, which did not very obviously concern their personal interests. All, more or less, resigned themselves to the charm with which the presence of royalty is so apt to be attended. Youthful and handsome; gallant and daring; the leader of a brave and hardy band; the commander and object of a most extraordinary enterprise; unfortunate in his birth and prospects, but making apparently one manly effort to retrieve the sorrows of his fate;

---

[1] Home's Works, iii. 71.

the descendant of those time-honoured persons by whose sides the ancestors of those who saw him had fought at Bannockburn and Flodden; the representative of a family peculiarly Scottish, but which seemed to have been deprived of its birthright by the machinations of the hated English—Charles was a being calculated to excite the most fervent emotions amongst the people who surrounded him. The modern sovereign, as he went over the same ground in his splendid chariot, was beheld with respect, as the chief magistrate of the nation; but the boot of Charles was dimmed, as he passed along, with kisses and tears.

A remarkable instance of the effect of these feelings occurred as Charles was entering the palace. When he had proceeded along the piazza within the quadrangle, and was just about to enter the porch of what are called the Hamilton apartments, the door of which stood open to receive him, a gentleman of mature age stepped out of the crowd, drew his sword, and, raising it aloft, marshalled the way before him up-stairs. James Hepburn of Keith, in East Lothian, who adopted this conspicuous mode of enlisting himself, did not act altogether under the influence of a devoted attachment to the Stuart family, but was stimulated by a sense of the injustice of the Union, which he said had ruined his country, and reduced a Scottish gentleman from being a person of some estimation to being the same as nobody. Since the insurrection of 1715, in which he was engaged, he had for thirty years kept himself in constant readiness to strike another blow for what he considered the independence of his country. Learned and intelligent, advanced in life, and honoured by all parties of his countrymen, this man is said by Mr Home, who knew him, to have been a perfect model of ancient simplicity, manliness, and honour. That he was inspired with as pure and noble a sense of patriotism as any Whig that ever breathed, it is impossible to doubt. The Jacobites beheld with pride a person so accomplished set the first example in Edinburgh of joining the Prince; auguring that his 'silver hairs' would 'purchase them a good opinion.' The Whigs, on the other hand, by whom he was equally admired, looked with pity upon a brave and worthy gentleman thus offering himself up a sacrifice to the visionary idea of national independence.[1]

The Prince being thus established in his paternal palace, it was the next business of his adherents to proclaim his father at the Cross. The party which entered the city in the morning had taken care to secure the heralds and pursuivants whose business it was to perform such ceremonies. About one o'clock, therefore, an armed body was drawn up around the Cross; and that venerable pile, which, notwithstanding its association with so many romantic events, was soon after removed by the magistrates, had the honour of being covered with carpet for the occasion.[2] The officers were clothed in their fantastic but rich old dresses, in order to give all the usual *éclat* to this disloyal ceremony. David Beatt, a Jacobite teacher of Edinburgh,[3] then proclaimed King James, and read the commission of regency, with the declaration dated at Rome in 1743, and a manifesto in the name of Charles Prince Regent, dated at Paris, May 16, 1745. An immense multitude witnessed the solemnity, which they greeted with hearty but partial huzzas. The ladies, who viewed the scene from their lofty lattices in the High Street, strained their voices in acclamation, and waved white handkerchiefs in honour of the day.[4] The Highland guard looked round the crowd with faces expressing wild joy and triumph, and, with the license and extravagance appropriate to the occasion, fired off their pieces in the air. The bagpipe was not wanting to greet the name of James with a loyal pibroch; and during the ceremony, Mrs Murray of Broughton, whose enthusiasm was only surpassed by her beauty, sat on horseback beside the Cross, with a drawn sword in her hand, and her person profusely decorated with white ribbons, which signified devotion to the house of Stuart.[5]

---

[1] Home's Works, iii. 72.　　　　　[2] *Caledonian Mercury.*
[3] Boyse's *History of the Rebellion.*　　[4] Mr Home.　　[5] Boyse, 77.

CHAPTER X.

COPE'S PREPARATIONS.

'Cope sent a letter from Dunbar,
Saying : " Charlie, meet me if ye daur,
And I'll learn you the art of war,
 Right early in the morning." '
 Jacobite Song.

WHILST the Highlanders were proclaiming King James at the Cross of Edinburgh, Sir John Cope was landing his troops at Dunbar. The evasive movement of this general had been most unfortunate, as it completely deprived the Lowlands of such protection as his troops were able to afford. He shewed, however, all possible anxiety to repair the consequences of his error, marching his army without delay from Inverness to Aberdeen, where it was embarked with the design of landing in some Lowland port, and in the hope of still being in time to protect the principal parts of the kingdom.

Sir John's infantry was reinforced at Dunbar by the craven dragoons, who had fled thither as the safest place within their reach. Of their flight an amusing, though perhaps highly coloured account has been given in a pamphlet already quoted.[1] 'Before the rebels,' says the writer, 'came within sight of the king's forces [then posted at Coltbridge], before they came within three miles' distance of them, orders were issued to the dragoons to wheel, which they immediately did with the greatest order and regularity imaginable. As it is known that nothing is more beautiful than the evolutions and movements of cavalry, the spectators stood in expectation of what fine manœuvre they might terminate in, when new orders were immediately issued

---

[1] *A True Account of the Behaviour and Conduct of Archibald Stewart, Esq., late Lord Provost of Edinburgh, in a Letter to a Friend.* London, 1748.

to retreat; they instantly obeyed, and began to march in the usual pace of cavalry. Orders were repeated every furlong to quicken their pace; and, both precept and example concurring, they quickened it so well, that before they reached Edinburgh, they quickened it to a very smart gallop. They passed in inexpressible hurry and confusion through the narrow lanes at Barefoot's Parks, in the sight of all the north part of Edinburgh, to the infinite joy of the disaffected, and equal grief and consternation of all the other inhabitants. They rushed like a torrent down to Leith, where they endeavoured to draw breath; but some unlucky boy (I suppose a Jacobite in his heart) calling to them that the Highlanders were approaching, they immediately took to their heels again, and galloped to Prestonpans, about five [nine] miles farther. There, in a literal sense, *timor addidit alas*—there fear added wings, I mean to the rebels; for, otherwise, they could not possibly have imagined these formidable enemies to be within several miles of them. But at Prestonpans the same alarm was repeated. The Philistines be upon thee, Samson! They galloped to North Berwick; and being now about twenty miles to the other side of Edinburgh, they thought they might safely dismount from their horses, and look out for victuals. Accordingly, like the ancient Grecian heroes, each began to kill and dress his provisions—*egit amor dapis atque pugnæ*—they were actuated by the desire of supper and of battle. The sheep and turkeys of North Berwick paid for this warlike disposition. But behold the uncertainty of human happiness! When the mutton was just ready to be put upon the table, they heard, or thought they heard, the same cry of Highlanders. Their fear proved stronger than their hunger; they again got on horseback; but were informed of the falseness of the alarm time enough to prevent the spoiling of their meal. By such rudiments as these, the dragoons were so thoroughly initiated in the art of running, that at the battle of Preston they could practise it of themselves, though even there the same good example was not wanting. I have seen an Italian opera called *Cesare in Egitto*—Cæsar in Egypt—where, in the first scene, Cæsar is introduced in a great hurry, giving orders to his soldiers, *Fugge, fugge ; allo scampo*—Fly, fly ; to your heels! This is a proof that the commander at Coltbridge is not the first hero that gave such orders to his troops.'

The 'Canter of Coltbridge' is related by Mr Home with circumstances somewhat different, but not less ridiculous. After passing through Leith and Musselburgh, they encamped for the evening in a field near Colonel Gardiner's house at Preston. Between ten and eleven at night, one of their number, going in search of forage, fell into a disused coal-pit, which was full of water, and making an outcry for assistance, impressed his companions with a belief that their dreaded enemy was upon them. Not stopping to ascertain the real cause of the noise, or to relieve their unfortunate fellow-soldier, the whole mounted their horses, and with all imaginable speed galloped off to Dunbar. Colonel Gardiner, awaking in the morning, found a silent and deserted camp, and was obliged, with a heavy heart, to follow in the direction which he learned they had taken. There was little danger that he should have missed their track, for, as he passed along, he found the road strewed with swords, pistols, and firelocks, which they had thrown away in their panic. He caused these to be gathered, and conveyed in covered carts to Dunbar, where he arrived in time to greet General Cope as he landed.

The disembarkation of the troops, artillery, and stores was not completed till the 18th of September; when Mr Home, author of the History already quoted, presented himself at the camp, and gave the general all the information he could desire regarding the numbers and condition of the Highland army. The author of *Douglas* had gone to the different posts about the city, and counted the men there stationed; he had then ascended the hill which overlooked the bivouac of the main body, and reckoned them as they sat at food in lines upon the ground. The whole number, in his estimation, did not exceed two thousand; but he had been told that several bodies from the north were on their march to join them. The general asked his informant what sort of appearance they made, and, in particular, how they were armed; to which the young poet replied, that most of them seemed to be strong, active, hardy men, though many were of an ordinary size, and, if clothed like Lowlanders, would appear inferior to the king's troops. The Highland garb, he said, favoured them, as it shewed their naked limbs, which were strong and muscular; while their stern countenances, and bushy uncombed hair, gave them a fierce, barbarous, and imposing aspect. As to their arms, he continued, they had no artillery of any sort but one small unmounted cannon, which he had seen lying upon a cart, drawn by a little Highland pony. Fourteen or fifteen hundred of them were armed with firelocks and broadswords, and many others had only either the one or the other of these weapons. Their firelocks were of all sorts and sizes—muskets, fusees, and fowling-pieces; but they must soon provide themselves more generally with that weapon, as the arsenal of the Trained Bands had fallen into their hands. In the meantime, he had seen one or two companies, amounting altogether perhaps to a hundred men, each of whom had no other weapon than the blade of a scythe fastened end-long upon a pole.[1] General Cope dismissed Mr Home, with many compliments for bringing him so accurate an account of the enemy.

The king's army was joined at Dunbar by several judges and other civil officers, who, having fled from Edinburgh on the evening before the Prince had entered it, now resolved to remain with the royal troops, not as fighting men, but as anxious and interested spectators of the approaching action. There also came a few noblemen and gentlemen of the country, attended by their tenants in arms. Among these was the Earl of Home, who, being then an officer in the Guards, thought it his duty to offer his services when the king's troops were in the field. The retinue which this nobleman brought along with him was such as to surprise many persons. At the time when

[1] Home's Works, iii. 76.

the Lowlands of Scotland were equally warlike, and equally under the influence of the feudal system with the Highlands, his lordship's ancestors could have raised as many men upon their dominions in Berwickshire as would have themselves repelled the Chevalier's little army. In 1633, the Earl of Home had greeted Charles I., as he crossed the Border to visit Scotland, at the head of six hundred well-mounted gentlemen, his relations and retainers. The whole force that the present earl could bring, besides himself, to assist his sovereign in opposing a public enemy, consisted of *two body-servants!*[1]

It was not till the day succeeding the disembarkation, Thursday, the 19th of September, that the royal army left Dunbar to meet the insurgents. It is said to have made a great show upon its march; the infantry, cavalry, cannon, and baggage occupying several miles of road. The country-people, long unaccustomed to wars and arms, flocked from all quarters to see an army going to fight a battle in Lothian, and with infinite concern and anxiety beheld this uncommon spectacle.[2]

The army halted for the night in a field to the west of Haddington, sixteen miles east of Edinburgh. In the evening, it was proposed to employ some young people who followed the camp to ride betwixt Haddington and Edinburgh during the dark hours, lest the Highlanders, whose movements were rapid, should march in the night-time and surprise the army. Accordingly sixteen young men, most of whom had been volunteers at Edinburgh, and among whom the author of *Douglas* was one, offered their services. About nine at night eight of them set out, in four parties, by four different roads, for Duddingston, where they understood the Highlanders to be encamped. They returned safe at midnight, reporting that all was quiet; and the other eight then set out in the same manner.[3]

---

[1] Home's Works, iii. 77.   [2] Ibid. iii. 78.
[3] It was the duty of two of this little corps to pursue the coast road towards Musselburgh. Their names were Francis Garden and Robert Cunningham—the one afterwards better known by his judicial title of Lord Gardenstone, and the other by his official designation of General. On approaching Musselburgh, says Sir Walter Scott in a lively contribution to the *Quarterly Review*, 'they avoided the bridge, to escape observation, and crossed the

On the morning of the succeeding day, Friday the 20th of September, Cope continued his march towards Edinburgh by the ordinary post-road from Haddington. After marching a very few miles, it occurred to him that the defiles and enclosures near the road would, in case of an attack, prove unfavourable to the action of cavalry, and he resolved to adopt a less frequented and more open path. On coming to Huntington, therefore, he turned off to the right, and took what is called the *Low Road;* that is, the road which traverses the low country near the sea, passing by St Germains and Seton. At the same time he sent forward his adjutant-general, the Earl of Loudon, accompanied by the Earl of Home, to mark out a camp for the army near Musselburgh, intending to go no farther that day.

Esk, it being then low water, at a place nigh its junction with the sea. Unluckily, there was at the opposite side a snug thatched tavern kept by a cleanly old woman called Luckie F——, who was eminent for the excellence of her oysters and sherry. The patrol were both *bon vivants;* one of them, whom we remember in the situation of a senator, was unusually so, and a gay, witty, agreeable companion besides. Luckie's sign, and the heap of ʟoyster-shells deposited near her door, proved as great a temptation to this vigilant forlorn-hope as the wine-house to the abbess of Andouillet's muleteer. They had scarcely got settled at some right *pandores*, with a bottle of sherry as an accompaniment, when, as some Jacobite devil would have it, an unlucky north-country lad, a writer's (that is, attorney's) apprentice, who had given his indentures the slip, and taken the white cockade, chanced to pass by on his errand to join Prince Charlie. He saw the two volunteers through the window, knew them, and guessed their business: he saw the tide would make it impossible for them to return along the sands, as they had come. He therefore placed himself in ambush upon the steep, narrow, impracticable bridge, which was then, and for many years afterwards, the only place of crossing the Esk: and how he contrived it I could never learn, but the courage and assurance of his province are proverbial, and the Norland whipper-snapper surrounded and made prisoners of the two unfortunate volunteers before they could draw a trigger.'—*Quarterly Review*, vol. xxxvi. 177.

They were immediately conducted to the camp at Duddingston, and put into the hands of John Roy Stuart, commander of the Prince's bodyguard, who at once pronounced them spies, and proposed to hang them accordingly. Thrown into consternation by this sentence, they luckily recollected that a youthful acquaintance, by name Colquhoun Grant, bore a commission in the very body which John Roy commanded; and they entreated him to lead them before that person, who was able to attest their innocence. Colquhoun Grant, who lived many years afterwards as a respectable writer to the signet in Edinburgh, used to relate that he never was so much surprised in his life, and at the same time amused, as when his two young friends were brought up to him for his verdict. Stuart introduced them with the following words: 'Here are two fellows who have been caught prowling near the camp. I am certain they are spies, at least this oldest one [Mr Garden]; and I propose that, to make sure, we should hang them baith.' Mr Grant, of course, interfered in behalf of his friends, and afterwards getting them into his own custody, took it upon him to permit their escape.—Information by the late Henry Mackenzie, author of the *Man of Feeling.*

The soldiers are described as having been in high spirits during the march; the infantry feeling confident in the assistance of the cavalry, and the cavalry acquiring some portion of the same courage by a junction with the infantry.

The first files of the troops were entering the plain betwixt Seton and Preston, when Lord Loudon came back at a round pace with information that the Highlanders were in full march towards the royal army. The general, surprised, but not disconcerted by this intelligence, and thinking the plain which lay before him a very proper place to receive the enemy, called a halt there, and drew up his troops with a front to the west. His right was thus extended to the sea, and his left towards the village of Tranent. Soon after he had taken up his ground, the Chevalier's army came in sight.

CHAPTER XI.

THE PRINCE'S MARCH TO PRESTON.

> 'When Charlie looked this letter upon,
> He drew his sword the scabbard from,
> Crying : " Follow me, my merry, merry men,
> And we'll meet Johnnie Cope in the morning."'
> *Jacobite Song.*

THREE days of rest in Edinburgh, where they were supplied with plenty of food, and did not want opportunities of improving their appointments, had meanwhile increased in no inconsiderable degree the efficacy and confidence of the Highland army. Learning that Cope had landed at Dunbar, and was marching to give him battle, the Prince came on Thursday night to Duddingston, where, calling a council of war, he proposed to march next morning and meet the enemy half-way. The council agreed that this was the only thing they could do; and

Charles then asked the Highland chiefs how they thought their men would behave in meeting a general who had already avoided them. The chiefs desired Macdonald of Keppoch to speak for them, as he had served in the French army, and was thought to know best what the Highlanders could do against regular troops. Keppoch's speech was brief, but emphatic. He said that the country having been long at peace, and few or none of the private men having ever seen a battle, it was difficult to foretell how they would behave; but he would venture to assure his royal highness that the gentlemen would be in the midst of the enemy, and that the clansmen, devoted to their chiefs, and loving the cause, would certainly not be far behind them. Charles, catching the spirit of the moment, exclaimed he would be the first man to charge the foe! But the chiefs discountenanced this imprudent proposal, declaring that in his life lay the strength of their cause, and that, should he be slain, they would be undone beyond redemption, whether victorious or defeated. They even went so far as to declare that they would go home, and endeavour to make the best terms they could for themselves, if he persisted in so rash a resolution. This remonstrance with difficulty repressed the ardour of their young commander, whose great passion at this moment seems to have been to strike a decisive blow, and share personally in its glory.[1]

On the morning of Friday the 20th of September, when the king's army was commencing its march from Haddington, the Highlanders roused themselves from their bivouac near Duddingston, and prepared to set forward. They had been reinforced since daybreak by a party of Grants from Glenmorriston,[2] as they had been the day before by some

[1] Home's Works, iii. 81.
[2] Grant of Glenmorriston arrived with his little party in great haste, anxious not to be too late for the first battle. He had travelled all night, and was of course travel-soiled and unshaven. When he rushed into the Prince's presence at Holyrood House, his appearance drew an ill-timed, but probably half-jocular remark from Charles as to his beard. The chief turned away with kindling wrath, saying: 'Sir, it is not beardless boys who are to do your business.'—*Information from the late Mr W. Grant, W.S.*

Maclachlans and Athole men. The Prince, putting himself at the head of his army, thus increased by 250, presented his sword, and said aloud: 'My friends, I have thrown away the scabbard!'[1] He was answered by a cheerful huzza; and the band then set forward in three files, Charles marching on horseback by their side, along with some of his principal officers.

The army proceeded from Duddingston Park, where they had what was called their camp, by the road which passes Easter Duddingston, and enters the main or post road near Magdalen Bridge. A lady, who in early youth had seen them pass the last-mentioned village,[2] was able, in 1827, to describe the memorable pageant. The Highlanders strode on with their squalid clothes and various arms, their rough limbs and uncombed hair, looking around them with an air of fierce resolution. The Prince rode amidst his officers at a little distance from the flank of the column, preferring to amble over the dry stubble-fields beside the road. My informant remembered, as yesterday, his graceful carriage and comely looks, his long light hair straggling below his neck, and the flap of his tartan coat thrown back by the wind, so as to make the jewelled St Andrew dangle for a moment clear in the air by its silken ribbon. He was viewed with admiration by the simple villagers; and even those who were ignorant of his claims, or who rejected them, could not help wishing him good fortune, and at least no calamity.

Soon after falling into the post-road, the insurgents continued their march till they entered the Market-gate of Fisherrow—an old narrow street leading to the bridge across the Esk. One there went up to a new house upon which the tilers were engaged, and took a long slip of wood, technically called a *tile-lath;* from another house he abstracted an ordinary broom, which he tied upon the end of the pole. This he bore aloft over his head, emblematising what seemed to be the general sentiment of the army, that they would sweep their enemies off the face of the earth. The shouts with which the symbol was

---

[1] *Caledonian Mercury.*   [2] The late Mrs Handasyde of Fisherrow.

hailed on the present occasion testified the high courage and resolution of the troops, and but too truly presaged the issue of the approaching conflict. Charles, in passing along the Marketgate, bowed gracefully to the ladies who surveyed him from their windows.[1]

The army now passed along the ancient bridge of Musselburgh—a structure supposed to be of Roman origin, and over which the Scottish army had passed, two centuries before, to the field of Pinkie. Proceeding directly onward, the column traversed, not the town of Musselburgh, but the old post-road which winds to the south, behind the gardens of Pinkie House. When passing these gardens, Lord George Murray, who led the van, received intelligence that Cope was at or near Preston, and was likely to seek the high grounds to the south, so as to obtain an advantage over the Highland army. Being convinced that the Highlanders could do nothing unless they got above the enemy, he immediately struck off through the fields to the right, with which he was well acquainted, ordering the army to follow him. By half an hour of quick marching, he reached the height near Falside, and then marched slow, that the rear might close up. He now became aware that Cope had remained content with his position at Preston, and therefore commenced a slanting march down-hill towards Tranent. On coming within half a mile of that village, the army halted. During the last two miles of their march, they had had the enemy within sight.[2]

At this early stage of the campaign, the mode of *forming* the Highland army was extremely simple, on account of the want of horse and artillery. The column in which it always moved was merely halted at the proper place, and then facing about, became at once a line. Such was the evolution by which, on the present occasion, Charles brought his men to their first *tête-à-tête* with the devoted host of his antagonist.

When the royal troops first perceived the Highlanders they raised a spirited shout, to which the others readily replied.

[1] Tradition in Fisherrow.
[2] Lord George Murray's Narrative *Jacobite Memoirs*, 36.

The two armies were about a mile distant from each other, with a gentle slope and a long strip of marshy ground between. It was a little after noon, and the weather was favourable for immediate combat. Both armies had marched the equal distance of eight miles, and were alike fresh and ardent. It was Charles's wish, as it had been his expectation, to engage the enemy before nightfall; and the ground appeared perfectly favourable for the purpose. The descent towards Cope's position, though gentle, was sufficient to increase the natural speed and impetuosity of the Highlanders, whose ancestors had been always successful in conflicts fought in that manner. But Cope had not the same eager desire of battle; and various considerations, arising from the nature of the ground, interposed to prevent an immediate attack on the part of the Highlanders.

The English general had at first arranged his troops with their front to the west, expecting the enemy to come directly from Musselburgh; but when he saw them appear on the southern heights, he altered his position accordingly, and now lay upon a plain swelling gently up from the coast, with Cockenzie and the sea behind him, the intricate little village of Preston, with its numerous parks and garden-walls, on his right, Seton House at a distance on his left, and a deep ditch or drain traversing the morass before him. On all sides but the east he was inaccessible, except, perhaps, by a column which no enemy could ever have thought of directing against him.

By examining the country-people, who, as usual, flocked about him in great numbers, the Prince soon learned that to attack General Cope across the morass was impracticable, except at a great risk. In order to ascertain the point still more satisfactorily, Lord George Murray despatched Colonel Ker of Graden, an officer of experience, to survey and report upon the ground. Mounted upon a little white pony, Mr Ker descended alone from Tranent, and with great deliberation approached the post of the enemy. When very near it, he rode slowly along the edge of the morass, carefully inspecting the ground on all sides, and scanning the breadth and depth of the ditch. Some of the king's troops moved along the ditches, and shot at him; but he was not in the least discomposed. Coming to a stone fence which he required to cross, he dismounted, pulled down a piece of the dike, and then led his horse through the breach. When he had completely satisfied himself, he returned to the army, and reported his observations to the lieutenant-general. The morass, he said, could not be passed without the troops being exposed to several unreturned fires, and was therefore not to be thought of.[1] When Charles learned this, he moved a considerable part of his army back to Dolphingston, and affected to meditate an attack upon Cope's west or right flank. The English general observing this, resumed his first position, in order to meet the insurgents with the front of his army.

Charles, probably deterred from making an attack in this quarter by the park-dikes, which so effectually screened the enemy's front, now once more shifted his ground, and returned to his first station near Tranent. The king's army faced round at the same time. The whole afternoon was occupied by these evolutions. When evening approached, General Cope found himself still in possession of the advantageous ground he had originally chosen; but it was feared by some unconcerned spectators that he had been perhaps over-cautious in his evolutions; that he had cooped himself up in a narrow place, while the Highlanders were at liberty to move about as they pleased; and that he had disheartened his men by keeping them so carefully on the defensive, while the Highlanders were proportionably animated by feeling themselves in the predicament of an attacking party.[2]

Cope had not acted altogether on the defensive. Sullivan had posted fifty of Locheil's men at the parish church at the bottom of the village, 'for what reason,' says Lord George Murray, 'I could not understand.' The enemy brought their cannon to bear on this post, and fired off a few shots, which

---

[1] Home's Works, iii. 84. 'Without risking the loss of the whole army,' is the expression put into Mr Ker's mouth by the author of an account of the young Chevalier's operations, printed in the Lockhart Papers.
[2] Home's Works, iii. 85.

they accompanied with huzzas, being under the impression that the Highlanders were very liable to be frightened by cannon. They soon wounded one or two men, when Lord George Murray sent an order for the party to join the main body. Charles, however, posted 500 men under Lord Nairn at Preston, to the west of Cope's position, to prevent him from stealing a march in that direction.

Since the insurgents had first risen in Lochaber, the weather had been generally fine. The nights, however, though calm, were chill, as generally happens in the finest autumn weather under our northern climate. The night of Friday, the 20th of September 1745, set in with a cold mist, which, without doing any particular injury to the hardy children of the north, was annoying to their opponents, less accustomed to bivouacking, and obliged to be more upon the alert, in apprehension of a night attack. General Cope lighted great fires all round his position, to warm and inspirit his men,[1] and threw off a few cohorns during the night, to let the enemy know he was on his guard. At an early period of the evening he had planted pickets, with great care, in every direction around him, especially towards the east; he had also sent his military chest and baggage down to Cockenzie under a strong guard.

The royal army was arranged along the front of the morass in a manner displaying sufficient military skill. The centre consisted of eight companies of Lascelles's regiment, and two of Guise's. On the right were five companies of Lees's; on the left the whole of Sir John Murray's. Besides these, there were a number of recruits for different regiments at present abroad, and a few small parties of volunteers, comprising the gentlemen with their tenants already mentioned, and some persons who had been induced to join by religious considerations. The infantry was protected on the right flank by Gardiner's, on the left by Hamilton's dragoons, who stood each with two troops to the front, and one in the rear, for a reserve. Some

---

[1] Lockhart Papers, ii. 489, 490.

Highland companies composed a second line in the rear. The cannon, six pieces in all, guarded by a company of Lees's regiment, commanded by Captain Cochrane, and under the orders of Lieutenant-colonel Whiteford, were placed on the right of the army, near the wagon-road or railway from Tranent to Cockenzie.

The army of Cope altogether consisted of 2100 men; but a number of these did not fight in the subsequent engagement, being engaged elsewhere as videttes and guards. The artillery corps was by far the most hopeless part of the army. At the time when General Cope marched to the north, there were no gunners or matrosses to be had in Scotland but one old man, who had belonged to the Scots train of artillery before the Union. This person, with three old invalid soldiers, the general carried with him to Inverness; and the hopeful band was afterwards reinforced by a few sailors from the ship of war which escorted the troops to Dunbar. A more miserable troop could hardly have been intrusted with so important a charge.

As soon as it became dark, the Highland army moved from the west to the east side of Tranent, where the morass seemed to be more practicable; and a council of war being called, it was resolved to attack the enemy in that quarter at break of day. The Highlanders, wrapping themselves in their plaids, then laid themselves down to sleep upon the stubble-fields. Charles, whose pleasure it had all along been to share in the fatigues and privations of his men, rejecting the opportunity of an easier couch in the village, also made his lodging upon the ground. During the night not a light was to be seen and not a word to be heard in his bivouac, in obedience to an order which had been issued, for the purpose of concealing their position from Sir John Cope.[1]

[1] Home's Works, iii. 92.

CHAPTER XII.

THE BATTLE OF PRESTON.

'Brutus. Slaying is the word ;
It is a deed in fashion.'
Julius Cæsar.

A YOUNG gentleman named Robert Anderson (son of Anderson of Whitburgh, in East Lothian), who joined the insurgents at Edinburgh, had been present at the council which determined the place and mode of attack, but did not take the liberty to speak or give his opinion. After the dismissal of the council, Anderson told his friend, Mr Hepburn of Keith, that he knew the ground well,[1] and thought there was a better way to come at the king's army than that which the council had resolved to follow. 'I could undertake,' he added, 'to shew them a place where they might easily pass the morass without being seen by the enemy, and form without being exposed to their fire.' Hepburn listened attentively to this information, and expressed his opinion of it in such terms, that Anderson desired he would carry him to Lord George Murray. Mr Hepburn advised him to go alone to the lieutenant-general, with whom he was already perfectly well acquainted, and who would like best to receive any information of this kind without the presence of a third party. Anderson immediately sought Lord George, whom he found asleep in a field of cut pease, with the Prince and several of the chiefs lying near him. The young gentleman immediately awoke his lordship, and proceeded to inform him of his project. To Lord George it appeared so eligible that he

---

[1] Mr Anderson, while residing occasionally with his relatives, the Andersons of St Germains, had often shot snipes on this ground. Such, I have been informed by his family, was the accident by which he gained this valuable piece of knowledge.

hesitated not a moment to use the same freedom with the Prince which Mr Anderson had used with him. Charles sat up on his bed of pease-straw, and listened to the scheme with great attention. He then caused Locheil and the other leaders to be called and taken into counsel. They all approved of the plan, and a resolution was instantly passed to take advantage of Mr Anderson's offers of service.[1]

Lord Nairn's party being recalled from Preston, the Highland army began to move about three o'clock in the morning (Saturday, 21st September), when the sun was as yet three hours below the horizon. It was thought necessary, on this occasion, to reverse the order of march, by shifting the rear of the column to the van. Colonel Ker managed this evolution with his characteristic skill and prudence. Passing slowly from the head to the other end of the column, desiring the men, as he went along, to observe the strictest silence, he turned the rear forwards, making the men wheel round his own person till they were all on the march.[2] Mr Anderson led the way. Next to him was Macdonald of Glenaladale, major of the Clanranald regiment, with a chosen body of sixty men, appointed to secure Cope's baggage whenever they saw the armies engaged.[3] Close behind came the army, marching, as usual, in a column of three men abreast. They came down by a sort of valley, or hollow, that winds through the farm of Rigganhead. Not a whisper was heard amongst them. At first their march was concealed by darkness, and, when daylight began to appear, by the mist. When they were near the morass, some dragoons, who stood upon the other side as an advanced guard, called out: 'Who's there?' The Highlanders made no answer, but marched on. The dragoons, soon perceiving who they were, fired their pieces, and rode off to give the alarm.[4]

The ditch so often mentioned as traversing the morass became a mill-course at this easterly point, for the service of Seton Mill with water. The Highlanders had therefore not

[1] Home's Works, iii. 88.
[2] Lockhart Papers, ii. 449.
[3] Lockhart Papers, ii. 491.
[4] Home's Works, iii. 89.

only the difficulty of wading through the bog knee-deep in mud, but also that of crossing a broad deep stream by a narrow wooden bridge. Charles himself jumped across the dam, but fell on the other side, and got his legs and hands beslimed. The column, as it gradually cleared this impediment, moved directly onwards to the sea, till it was thought by those at the head that all would be over the morass; a line was then formed, in the usual manner, upon the firm and level ground.

The arrangement of the Highland army for the battle about to take place was ruled by some fanciful considerations. The great clan Colla, or Macdonalds, formed the right wing, in consequence of a tradition that Robert Bruce had assigned it that station at the battle of Bannockburn, in gratitude for the treatment he had received from its chief when in hiding in the Hebrides, and because it had assumed that station in every battle since, except that of Harlaw, on which occasion the post of honour was voluntarily resigned in favour of the Macleods.[1] The Camerons and Appin Stuarts composed the left wing, perhaps for some similar reason; while the Duke of Perth's regiment and the Macgregors stood in the centre. The Duke of Perth, as oldest lieutenant-general, commanded the right wing, Lord George Murray the left.

Behind the first line a second was arranged, at the distance of fifty yards, consisting of the Athole men, the Robertsons, the Macdonalds of Glencoe, and the Maclachlans, under the command of Lord Nairn. Charles took his place between the two lines. The whole army was rather superior in numbers to that of General Cope, being probably about 2400; but as the second line never came into action, the real number of combatants, as stated by the Prince's authority after the battle, was only 1456.

Surprise being no part of the Prince's plan, no regret was expressed at the alarm which the videttes had carried to the king's army; but it was thought necessary to form the lines as quickly as possible. When this was effected, Charles addressed

---

[1] Lockhart Papers, ii. 510.

his men in these words: 'Follow me, gentlemen, and by the blessing of God I will this day make you a free and happy people!'[1] The Duke of Perth then sent Mr Anderson to inform Lord George Murray that he was ready to march. Anderson met an aide-de-camp sent by Lord George to inform the duke that the left wing was moving. Some time of course elapsing before the right wing was aware of this motion, it was a little behind the left, and the charge was thus made in an oblique manner.[2]

It was just dawn, and the mist was fast retiring before the sun when the Highlanders set out upon their attack. A long uninterrupted series of fields, from which the grain had recently been reaped, lay between them and General Cope's position. Morn was already on the waters of the Forth to their right, and the mist was rolling in large masses over the marsh and the crofts to their left; but it was not yet clear enough to admit of either army seeing the other. An impervious darkness lay between, which was soon, however, to disclose to both the exciting spectacle of an armed enemy. On the part of the Highlanders there was perfect silence, except the rushing sound occasioned by their feet going through the stubble: on that of General Cope, only an occasional drum was to be heard, as it hoarsely pronounced some military signal.

At setting out upon the charge, the Highlanders pulled off their bonnets, and looking upwards, uttered a short prayer.[3] The front-rank men, most of whom were gentlemen, and all of whom had targets, stooped as much as they could in going forward, keeping their shields in front of their heads, so as to protect almost every part of their bodies, except the limbs, from the fire which they expected.[4] The inferior and worse-armed men behind endeavoured to supply the want of defensive weapons by going close in rear of their companions. Every chief charged in the centre of his regiment, supported immediately on both sides by his nearest relations and principal

[1] The Prince's authorised account of the battle, *Caledonian Mercury*.
[2] Home's Works, iii. 91.   [3] *Caledonian Mercury*.   [4] Ibid.

officers ;[1] any one of whom, as of the whole clan, would have willingly substituted his person to the blow aimed at that honoured individual.

A little in advance of the second line, Charles himself went on, in the midst of a small guard. His situation was not so dangerous as it would have been if he had persisted in his wish of going foremost into the enemy's lines, but yet such as a gallant man might have been glad to have. As his courage has been most absurdly challenged, it is the more necessary to be particular as to his conduct on this occasion. A Highland gentleman, who wrote a journal of the campaign, relates that, just before the moment of the onset at Preston, he saw the Prince leave his guard, and go forward to the front line to give his last orders to the Duke of Perth and Clanranald. Passing the reporter of the circumstance on his return, and recognising him, he said, with a smile: '*Gres-ort, gres-ort!*'—that is, 'Make haste, make haste!'[2]

Not only was the front line, as already mentioned, oblique, but it was soon further weakened from another cause. After commencing the charge, it was found that the marsh retired southwards a little, and left some firm ground unoccupied by that extremity of the army, so that it would have been possible for Cope to turn their flank with a troop of dragoons. In order to obviate this disadvantage, the Camerons were desired by Lord George Murray to incline that way, and fill the open ground. When they had done so, there was an interval in the centre of the line, which was ordered to be filled up from the second line; but it could not be done in time.[3] Some of the Prince's officers afterwards acknowledged that, when they first saw the regular lines of the royal army, and the level rays of the new-risen sun reflected at a thousand points from the long extended series of muskets, they could not help expecting that the wavering, unsteady clusters into which their own line was broken would be defeated in a moment, and

---

[1] Highland tradition. [2] Lockhart Papers, ii. 491. [3] Ibid. ii. 449.

swept from the field.[1] The issue was destined to be far otherwise.

Sir John Cope, who had spent the night at the little village of Cockenzie, where his baggage was disposed under a guard, hastened to join his troops on first receiving intelligence that the Highlanders were moving towards the east. His first impression regarding their movements seems to have been, that, after finding it impossible to attack him either across the morass or through the defiles of Preston, they were now about to take up a position on the open fields to the east, in order to fight a fair battle when daylight should appear. It does not seem to have occurred to him that they would make the attack immediately; and, accordingly, although he thought proper to form his lines, and turn them in the direction of the enemy, he was at last somewhat disconcerted, and his men were not a little surprised, when it was given out by the sentries that the Highlanders were upon them.[2]

The mode of fighting practised at this period by the Highlanders, though as simple as can well be conceived, was well calculated to set at nought and defeat the tactics of a regular soldiery. It has been thus described by the Chevalier Johnstone, who was engaged in all the actions fought during this campaign: They advanced with the utmost rapidity towards the enemy, gave fire when within a musket-length of the object, and then throwing down their pieces, drew their swords, and holding a dirk in their left hand along with the target, darted with fury on the enemy through the smoke of their fire. When within reach of the enemy's bayonets, bending their left knee, they contrived to receive the thrust of that weapon on their

---

[1] Home's Works, iii. 92.
[2] The circumstances which lead to this conclusion were the following. According to the journal-writer already quoted, the advancing mountaineers, on first coming within sight of Cope's army, heard them call out: 'Who is there? Who is there? Cannons! cannons! Get ready the cannons, cannoniers!' Andrew Henderson, a Whig historian, has also mentioned, in his account of the engagement, that the sentries, on first perceiving the Highland line through the mist, thought it a hedge which was gradually becoming apparent as the light increased. The event, however, was perhaps the best proof that the royal army was somewhat taken by surprise.

targets; then raising their arm, and with it the enemy's point, they rushed in upon the soldier, now defenceless, killed him at one blow, and were in a moment within the lines, pushing right

A full-armed Highland Gentleman.—From a unique drawing in possession of W. F. Watson, Esq.

and left with sword and dagger, often bringing down two men at once. The battle was thus decided in a moment, and all that followed was mere carnage.

Cope, informed by his retreating sentries that the enemy was

THE BATTLE OF PRESTON.

advancing, had only time to ride once along the front of his lines to encourage the men, and was just returned to his place on the right of the infantry, when he perceived, through the thin sunny mist, the dark clumps of the clans rushing swiftly and silently on towards his troops; those which were directly opposite to him being most visible, while on the left they faded away in an interminable line amongst the darkness from which they seemed gradually emerging. The numerous clusters in which they successively burst upon his sight—the rapidity with which they advanced—the deceptive and indefinite extent given to their appearance by the mist—all conspired to appal the royal troops. Five of the six cannon were discharged against the left of the advancing host, with such effect as to make that part of the army hover for a moment upon the advance; and one volley of musketry went along the royal lines from right to left as the clans successively came up. But all was unavailing against the ferocious resolution of the Highlanders.

The victory began, as the battle had done, among the Camerons. That spirited clan, notwithstanding their exposure to the cannon, and although received with a discharge of musketry by the artillery guard, ran on with undaunted speed, and were first up to the front of the enemy. Having swept over the cannon, they found themselves opposed to a squadron of dragoons under Lieutenant-colonel Whitney, which was advancing to attack them. They had only to fire a few shots, when these dastards, not yet recovered from their former fright, wheeled about, and fled over the artillery guard, which was accordingly dispersed. The posterior squadron of dragoons, under Colonel Gardiner himself, was then ordered to advance to the attack. Their gallant old commander led them forward, encouraging them as well as he could by the way; but they had not proceeded many steps, when, receiving a few shots from the Highlanders, they reeled, turned, and followed their companions. Locheil had ordered his men to strike at the noses of the horses, as the best means of getting the better of their masters; but they never found a single opportunity of practising this *ruse*, the men having chosen to retreat while they were yet some yards distant.

Hamilton's dragoons, at the other extremity of the army, no sooner saw their fellows flying before the Camerons, than they also turned about and fled, without having fired a carabine, and while the Macdonalds were still at a little distance.

The infantry, when deserted by those from whom they were taught to expect support, gave way on all hands, without having reloaded their pieces, or stained a single bayonet with blood. The whole at once threw down their arms, either to lighten them in their flight, or to signify that they surrendered; and many fell upon their knees before the impetuous Highlanders, to beg the quarter which, in the hurry of the moment, could scarcely be given them. One small party alone, out of the army, had the resolution to make any resistance. They fought for a brief space under the command of Colonel Gardiner, who, deserted by his own troop, and observing their gallant behaviour, had put himself at their head. They only fled when they had suffered considerably, and when their brave leader was cut down by numerous wounds. Such was the rapidity with which the Highlanders in general bore the royal soldiers off the field, that their second line, though only fifty yards behind, and though it ran fully as fast as the first, on coming up to the place, found nothing upon the ground but the killed and wounded.[1] The whole battle, indeed, is said to have lasted only four minutes.

In the panic flight which immediately ensued, the Highlanders used their weapons with unsparing vigour, and performed many feats, such as might rather adorn the pages of some ancient romance than the authentic narrative of a modern battle. A small party of Macgregors, in particular, bearing for their only arms the blades of scythes, fastened end-long upon poles, clove heads to the chin, and cut off the legs of horses. With even the broadsword, strength and skill enabled them to do prodigious execution. Men's feet and hands, and also

---

[1] Chevalier Johnstone's *Memoirs*, 37.

the feet of horses, were severed from the limbs by that powerful weapon; and it is a well-authenticated fact, that 'a Highland gentleman, after breaking through Murray's regiment, gave a grenadier a blow which not only severed the arm raised to ward it off, but cut the skull an inch deep, so that the man immediately died.'[1]

While the clans on the right and left behaved with distinguished bravery, a portion of the centre, including some of the Lowland tenantry of the Duke of Perth, acted in a manner resembling the conduct of the royal troops. They are said, on approaching the enemy's lines, to have 'stood stock-still like oxen.'[2] It was to this regiment that the scythe-armed company of Macgregors belonged. These at least evinced all the ardour and bravery which were so generally displayed that day by their countrymen. Disregarding the example of their immediate fellows, they continued to rush forward, under the command of their captain, Malcolm Macgregor. A space being left betwixt them and their clan-regiment, which went on beside the Camerons, under command of Glencairnaig, their chief, they edged obliquely athwart the field in that direction, in order to rank themselves beside their proper banner—an evolution which exposed them in a peculiar manner to the fire coming at that moment from the British regiments. Their captain fell before this fire, pierced with no fewer than five bullets, two of which went quite through his body. Stretched on the field, but unsubdued in spirit, he raised himself upon his elbow, and cried out, as loud as he could: 'Look ye, my lads, I'm not dead; by G—, I shall see if any of you does not do his duty!' This speech, half-whimsical as it was, is said to have communicated an impulse to his men, and perhaps contributed, with other acts of individual heroism, to decide the fate of the day.[3]

The general result of the battle of Preston may be stated as

---

[1] *Caledonian Mercury*, September 25, 1745.
[2] Manuscript by Duncan Macpharig, temporarily in the possession of the late Rev. Mr Macgregor Stirling.
[3] Chevalier Johnstone's *Memoirs*.

having been the total overthrow and almost entire destruction of the royal army. Most of the infantry falling back upon the park-walls of Preston, were there huddled together, without the power of resistance, into a confused drove, and had either to surrender or be cut in pieces. Many, in vainly attempting to climb over the walls, fell an easy prey to the ruthless claymore. Nearly 400, it is said, were thus slain, 700 taken, while only about 170 in all succeeded in effecting their escape.

The dragoons, with worse conduct, were much more fortunate. In falling back, they had the good luck to find outlets from their respective positions by the roads which run along the various extremities of the park-wall, and they thus got clear through the village with little slaughter; after which, as the Highlanders had no horse to pursue them, they were safe. Several officers, among whom were Fowkes and Lascelles, escaped to Cockenzie and along Seton Sands, in a direction contrary to the general flight.

The unfortunate Cope had attempted, at the first break of Gardiner's dragoons, to stop and rally them, but was borne headlong, with the confused bands, through the narrow road to the south of the enclosures, notwithstanding all his efforts to the contrary. On getting beyond the village, where he was joined by the retreating bands of the other regiment, he made one anxious effort, with the Earls of Loudon and Home, to form and bring them back to charge the enemy, now disordered by the pursuit; but in vain. They fled on, ducking their heads along their horses' necks to escape the bullets which the pursuers occasionally sent after them.[1] By using great exertions, and holding pistols to the heads of the troopers, Sir John and a few of his officers induced a small number of them to halt in a field near St Clement's Wells, about two miles from the battle-ground. But, after a momentary delay, the accidental firing of a pistol renewed the panic, and they rode off once more in great disorder. Sir John Cope, with a portion of them, reached

---

[1] Report of Cope's Examination.

Channelkirk at an early hour in the forenoon, and there halted to breakfast, and to write a brief note to one of the state officers, relating the fate of the day. He then resumed his flight, and reached Coldstream that night. He next morning proceeded to Berwick, whose fortifications seemed competent to give the security he required. He everywhere brought the first tidings of his own defeat.

The number of dragoons who accompanied the general was about 400; besides which, there were perhaps half as many who dispersed themselves in different directions. A small party which made for the castle of Edinburgh permitted themselves to be pursued and galled the whole way by a single cavalier, without ever once having the courage to turn about and face him. Colquhoun Grant, who had the hardihood to perform this feat, was a man of great bodily strength, and was animated by a most heroic zeal for the interests of the Chevalier. After performing some valorous deeds on the field of Preston, he mounted the horse of a British officer, whom he had brought down with his broadsword, and rode after the fugitive dragoons with all possible speed. Within an hour after the battle, the inhabitants of Edinburgh were informed of the result, by seeing these dispirited men galloping up their principal street, followed by a single enemy! The troopers got into the castle in safety, and Grant, when he arrived there, finding the gate closed behind them, stuck into it his bloody poniard, which he left in token of defiance. He then rode back, and was allowed to pass from the town without interruption.[1] Another single pursuer was less fortunate. This was Mr David Threipland, eldest son of Sir David Threipland of Fingask, in Perthshire. He was in delicate health, but animated by great courage and zeal. On his own horse he pursued a party of dragoons till they came to the place where Cope was endeavouring to rally his troopers near St Clement's Wells. Here, pausing a moment,

---

[1] Information by a surviving friend of Mr Grant. Sir Walter Scott gives a somewhat different version of apparently the same story, in which it is stated that the dragoons were refused admission.—See *Tales of a Grandfather*.

they became aware that they were pursued by only a single gentleman, with two servants. They turned, and cut him down with their swords. He was buried on the spot. 'I remember, when a child,' says Sir Walter Scott, 'sitting on his grave, where the grass long grew rank and green, distinguishing it from the rest of the field. A female of the family then residing at St Clement's Wells used to tell me the tragedy, of which she had been an eye-witness, and shewed me, in evidence, one of the silver clasps of the unfortunate gentleman's waistcoat.' It is not unworthy of notice, that so lately as 1824, in the course of some legal proceedings, a lady, who was cousin-german to Mr Threipland, gave evidence of the fact of his death, stating that she remembered being put into mourning on his account.[1]

'The cowardice of the English,' says the Chevalier Johnstone, in allusion to their conduct at Preston, 'surpassed all imagination. They threw down their arms, that they might run with more speed, thus depriving themselves of the only means they had of arresting the vengeance of the Highlanders. Of so many men, in a condition, from their numbers, to preserve order in their retreat, not one thought of defending himself. Terror had taken complete possession of their minds. I saw,' he continues, 'a young Highlander, scarcely formed, who was presented to the Prince as a prodigy, having killed, it was said, fourteen of the enemy. The Prince asked him if this were true. "I do not know," replied he, "if I killed them, but I brought fourteen soldiers to the ground with my broadsword!" Another Highlander brought ten soldiers to the Prince, whom he had made prisoners of war, driving them before him like a flock of sheep. This Highlander, from a rashness without example, having pursued a party to some distance from the field of battle, along the road between the two enclosures, struck down the

---

[1] The horse on which Mr Threipland rode was observed next year in a fair at Perth, by the *grieve* or land-steward of Fingask, having found its way thither in the possession of a horse-dealer, who had probably obtained it from some marauding Highlander. The animal was purchased with a melancholy pleasure by the family, and kept sacred from work till the end of its days.

THE BATTLE OF PRESTON.

hindermost with a blow of his sword, calling at the same time: "Down with your arms!" The soldiers, terror-struck, threw down their arms without looking behind them; and the Highlander, with a pistol in one hand and his sword in the other, made them do just as he pleased.'

From the eagerness of the Highlanders to secure as much plunder as possible, they did not improve their victory by a very eager or long-continued pursuit. A great proportion remained upon the field, investing themselves with the spoils of the slain and wounded, while others busied themselves in ransacking the house of Colonel Gardiner, which happened to be immediately adjacent to the field. A small party, among whom were the brave Macgregors, continued the chase for a mile and a half, when, in the words of Duncan Macpharig, 'the Prince came up, and successively took Glencairnaig and Major Evan in his arms, congratulating them upon the result of the fight. He then commanded the whole of the clan Gregor to be collected in the middle of the field; and a table being covered, he sat down with Glencairnaig and Major Evan to refresh himself, all the rest standing round as a guard, and each receiving a glass of wine and a little bread.' In regard to Charles's conduct after the battle, the report of another eye-witness, Andrew Henderson, author of a historical account of the campaign, is as follows: 'I saw the Chevalier, after the battle, standing by his horse, dressed like an ordinary captain, in a coarse plaid and large blue bonnet, with a narrow plain gold lace about it, his boots and knees much dirtied, the effects of his having fallen in a ditch. He was exceedingly merry, and twice cried out, with a hearty laugh: "My Highlanders have lost their plaids." But his jollity seemed somewhat damped when he looked upon the seven standards which had been taken from the dragoons; at this sight he could not help observing, with a sigh: "We have missed some of them!" After this he refreshed himself upon the field, and with the greatest composure ate a slice of cold beef and drank a glass of wine.' Mr Henderson ought to have mentioned that Charles had, before thus attending to his own personal wants, spent several hours in providing for the relief of the wounded of both armies; preserving (to use the language of Mr Home), from temper or from judgment, every appearance of moderation and humanity. It remains to be stated that, after giving orders for the disposal of the prisoners and for securing the spoils, which comprised the baggage, tents, cannon, and a military chest containing £4000, he left the field, and rode towards Pinkie House, the seat of the Marquis of Tweeddale, where he lodged for the night.

Though the general behaviour of the king's army on this memorable morning was the reverse of soldierly, there were not wanting in it instances of respectable conduct. The venerable Gardiner, whose name has been rendered familiar by the affectionate biography of his friend Doddridge, afforded a noble example of fidelity to duty. On the previous afternoon, though so weak that he had to be carried forward from Haddington in a postchaise, he urged the propriety of instantly attacking the Highlanders, and even, it is said, offered Cope his neighbouring mansion of Bankton as a present, provided he would consent to that measure, which he felt convinced was the only one that could insure victory. When he found this counsel decidedly rejected, he gave all up for lost, and began to prepare his mind by pious exercises for the fate which he expected to meet in the morning. In the battle, notwithstanding his gloomy anticipations, he behaved with the greatest fortitude, making more than one of the insurgents fall around him. Deserted by his dragoons, and severely wounded, he put himself at the head of a small body of foot which still refused to yield; and he only ceased to fight when brought to the ground by severe and repeated wounds. He expired in the manse of Tranent, after having rather breathed than lived a few hours.[1]

[1] Doddridge's *Life of Colonel Gardiner.* A large thorn-tree, in the centre of the battleground, marks the spot where Gardiner fell. He was buried in the north-west corner of the church of Tranent, where eight of his children had been previously interred. Some years ago, on the ground being incidentally disturbed, his head was found marked by the stroke of the weapon which despatched him, and still adhered to by his military *club*, which, bound firmly with silk, and dressed with powder and pomatum, seemed as fresh as it could have been on the day he died.

Another redeeming instance of self-devotion was presented by Captain Brymer of Lees's regiment, the only officer in the army who had ever before seen the Highlanders attack regular troops. He had witnessed the wild onset of the Macdonalds at Sheriffmuir, which impressed him with a respect for the instinctive valour of the race. At Haddington, two nights before, when all the rest of the officers were talking lightly of the enemy, and anticipating an easy victory, Brymer retired to solitary meditation, assured that the danger which approached was by no means inconsiderable. When the dread moment of fight arrived, he disdained to fly like the rest, but fell at his station, 'with his face to the foe.'

The wounded of the royal army were treated by their conquerors with a degree of humanity which might have been well imitated by the regular troops on a subsequent occasion. The conduct of the Prince has been spoken of: that of his lieutenant-general, Lord George Murray, was not less kind, if we are to believe his own statement. A party, whose wounds were not very severe, was conducted by Lord George to Musselburgh, he walking by their side, and allowing some of them to use his horses. At Musselburgh he obtained accommodation for them in an empty house, and slept beside them that night, to protect them from any violence on the part of his troops.[1] This precaution seems scarcely to have been necessary. The Clanranald journalist says:[2] 'Whatever notion our Low-country people may entertain of the Highlanders, I can attest they gave many proofs this day of their humanity and mercy. Not only did I often hear our common clansmen ask the soldiers if they wanted quarter, and not only did we, the officers, exert our utmost pains to save those who were stubborn, or who could not make themselves understood, but I saw some of our private men, after the battle, run to Port Seton for ale and other liquors to support the wounded. As one proof for all, of my own particular observation, I saw a Highlander carefully, and with patient

[1] *Jacobite Memoirs*, 42.   [2] Lockhart Papers.

kindness, carry a poor wounded soldier on his back into a house, where he left him, with a sixpence to pay his charges. In all this,' adds the journalist, 'we followed not only the dictates of humanity, but also the orders of our Prince, who acted in everything as the true father of his country.'

Of the Highlanders themselves, only thirty were killed, including three officers, and about seventy or eighty wounded. The greater part of the wounded of both armies were taken into Colonel Gardiner's house, where it was thought possible, a few years ago, to see upon the oaken floors the dark outlines or prints of the tartaned warriors, formed by their bloody garments, where they lay.[1]

Whatever humanity may have been displayed by the common Highlanders towards the wounded, they exhibited quite as much activity in despoiling the slain. Every article they conceived to be of the least value they eagerly appropriated; often, in their ignorance of civilised life, making the most ludicrous mistakes. One who had got a watch, sold it soon afterwards to some person for a trifle, and remarked, when the bargain was concluded, with an air of great self-congratulation, that he was glad to be quit of it, for it had died last night; the machine having in reality stopped for want of winding up. Another exchanged a horse for a horse-pistol. Rough old Highlanders were seen going with the fine shirts of the English officers over the rest of their clothes, while little boys went strutting about with large gold-laced cocked-hats on their heads, and bandoleers dangling down to their heels. One of the Highlanders was seen soon after passing through Stirling, on his way to the north, carrying

---

[1] The greater part of the slain were interred at the north-east corner of the park-wall so often alluded to, where the ground is still perceptibly elevated in consequence. A considerable number were also buried round the thorn-tree already mentioned, which is said to have marked the centre of Cope's first line. The country-people, of whom it might truly be said that

'With more dismay
They saw the fight, than those that made the fray,'

were drawn forth and employed in this disagreeable duty; which they performed by carting quantities of earth, and emptying it upon the bloody heaps.

a military saddle on his back: he probably thought he had secured a competency for life.[1]

When the search for spoil had ceased, the Highlanders began to collect provisions. They fixed their mess-room in one of the houses of Tranent, and, sending abroad through the neighbouring parks, seized such sheep as they could conveniently catch. The

[1] Information by a bishop of the Scottish Episcopal Church.—A quantity of chocolate, found in General Cope's carriage, was afterwards sold publicly in the streets of Perth, under the denomination of *Johnnie Cope's saw*—that is, salve. The carriage itself was employed to carry home old Robertson of Struan, who had come down from the Highlands with his clan, but was unable, from age, to accompany the expedition any farther. At that time there was no coach-road to Struan's residence; but when he had driven as far as he could, the vehicle was carried forward over the remaining tract by the clansmen. After lying in the courtyard at Mount Alexander till almost rotten, it was broken up for firewood.

In the blind eagerness of the Highlanders for spoil, it is said that they plundered many of the inhabitants of Edinburgh and other neighbouring towns who came, during the course of the day, to see the battle-ground. The whimsical Skirving, in his ballad of *Tranent Muir*, says:

> ' That afternoon, when a' was done,
> I gaed to see the fray, man ;
> But had I wist what after past,
> I 'd better stayed away, man.
> On Seton sands, wi' nimble hands,
> They picked my pockets bare, man ;
> But I wish ne'er to dree sic fear,
> For a' the sum and mair, man.'

In this rude but clever composition, the honest farmer embodies almost the whole talk of the times regarding the actors on both sides. He animadverts in severe terms upon the conduct of the British officers, one of whom betrayed an especial degree of cowardice, and that under circumstances which also disgraced his humanity. This was a Lieutenant Smith, of Hamilton's regiment, and of Hibernian extraction :

> ' When Major Bowle, that worthy soul,
> Was brought down to the ground, man,
> His horse being shot, it was his lot
> For to get many a wound, man.
> Lieutenant Smith, of Irish birth,
> Frae whom he called for aid, man,
> Being full of dread, lap owre his head,
> And wadna be gainsaid, man.
>
> He made sic haste, sae spurred his beast,
> 'Twas little there he saw, man ;
> To Berwick rade, and falsely said
> The Scots were rebels a', man.
> But let that end, for weel it 's kenned
> His use and wont 's to lie, man ;
> The Teague is naught—he never faught
> When he had room to fly, man.'

So famous did this scandal become in a little time, that an advertisement was inserted in

people of the village have a tradition of their coming straggling in every now and then during the day, each with a sheep upon his back, which he threw down at the general dépôt with the exclamation : 'Tare 's mhair o' Cope's paagage !' When men's minds are agitated by any mirthful or triumphant emotion, they are pleased with wonderfully small jokes.

the *Edinburgh Courant* of the 6th of January 1746, to the following effect: 'Whereas there has been a scandalous report spread, to the prejudice of Lieutenant Peter Smith of General Hamilton's dragoons, that he refused to assist Major Bowles, when dismounted at Preston: I, the said Major Bowles, do affirm it to be an infamous falsehood, Lieutenant Smith not being in the same squadron with me; nor did any officer of the corps refuse me his assistance on that occasion. Witness my hand, at Prestonpans, this 1st of January 1746. (Signed) RICHARD BOWLES.' It is needless to say that the lame and limited circulation of this exculpatory evidence went but little way to recover the unfortunate lieutenant's fame. Smith seems, therefore, to have at last aimed at another mode of redress. He is said to have come to Haddington, with the intention of challenging Mr Skirving, and to have sent a friend to the house of that gentleman, in order to settle the preliminaries of a personal combat. Here, however, poor Smith was quite as much at fault as ever. The farmer was busy forking his dunghill when the *friend* approached, whose hostile intentions he no sooner learned, than he proceeded to put that safe barrier between his own person and that of the challenger; after which, he patiently waited till the gentleman disclosed his errand. When he had heard all, and paused a little to consider it, he at last replied with great coolness: 'Gang awa back to Mr Smith; tell him that I hae nae time to come to Haddington to gie him satisfaction; but say, if he likes to come here, I 'll tak a look o' him; and if I think I 'm fit to fecht him, I 'll fecht him; and if no, I 'll just do as he did—I 'll rin awa!' This Mr Skirving was the father of a very clever artist in the department of crayon portraits, long well known in Edinburgh.

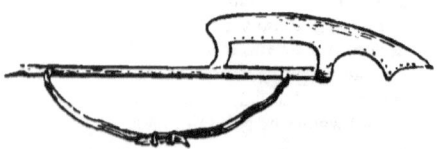

The weapon which slew Colonel Gardiner.

CHAPTER XIII.

PRINCE CHARLES AT HOLYROOD.

'What says King Bolingbroke?'
Richard II.

THE Camerons entered Edinburgh scarcely three hours after the battle, playing their pipes with might and main, and exhibiting, with many marks of triumph, the colours they had taken from Cope's dragoons.[1] But the return of the main body of the army was reserved for the succeeding day (Sunday), when an attempt was made to impress the citizens with as high an idea as possible of the victory they had achieved. The clans marched in one long extended line into the lower gate of the city, with bagpipes exultingly playing the cavalier air, *The king shall enjoy his own again.*[2] They bore, besides their own standards, those which had been taken from the royal army; and they displayed, with equally ostentatious pride, the vast accession of dress and personal ornament which they had derived from the vanquished. In the rear of their own body came the prisoners,[3] at least half as numerous as themselves, and then followed the wounded in carts.[4] At the end of all, were the baggage and cannon under a strong guard. They paraded through the principal streets of the city, as if anxious to leave no one unimpressed with the sight of their good fortune. Charles himself did not accompany the procession, but came in the evening to Holyrood House,

---

[1] *The Wanderer, or Surprising Escape* (Glasgow, 1752), p. 43.
[2] Boyse's *History*, 82.
[3] The prisoners were confined, the officers in Queensberry House, and the privates in the jail and church of the Canongate. The wounded were committed to the Royal Infirmary, where the utmost possible pains was taken to heal them. In the course of a few days after the battle, the officers were liberated on parole, and permitted to lodge in the town. Afterwards, on one person breaking his word by going into the castle, the whole were sent to Cupar-Angus; and the private men were put into custody at Logierait in Athole.
[4] Boyse's *History*.

where, according to the *Caledonian Mercury*, he was 'welcomed with the loudest acclamations of the people.'

It is difficult to describe the extravagant rejoicings with which the Jacobites hailed the news of Preston. They received the messengers and homeward-bound Highlanders, who everywhere dispersed the intelligence, with unbounded hospitality; and they no longer made any scruple to disclose those sentiments in public which they had hitherto been obliged to conceal as treasonable. The gentlemen drank fathom-deep healths to the Prince, who, in their own language, 'could eat a dry crust, sleep on pease-straw, take his dinner in four minutes, and win a battle in five;'[1] whilst the ladies busied themselves in procuring locks of his hair, miniature portraits of his person, and ribbons on which he was represented as 'the Highland laddie.' But perhaps the most extraordinary instance of individual zeal in his behalf was one afforded by an old nonjurant clergyman of the Scottish Episcopal communion, who had attended his camp before Preston, as some of the violent Presbyterians, on the other hand, followed that of Cope. This zealous partisan, immediately after the battle, set out on foot for his place of residence beyond Doune in Perthshire; and, having travelled considerably more than fifty miles, next morning gave out the news of the victory from his own pulpit, at the ordinary hour of worship, invoking a thousand blessings on the arms and person of the Chevalier.[2]

The conduct of the Prince himself was marked by a becoming moderation. On Monday the 23d, he issued several proclamations, in one of which he expressed his anxiety that no interruption should be experienced by persons passing to and from Edinburgh on business, and formally granted protection to the inhabitants and the country-people around 'from all insults, seizures, injuries, and abuses of our army against them respectively.' In another, he alluded to a wish which had been expressed by many, that his victory should be marked by public

---

[1] *Caledonian Mercury*. [2] Information by a bishop of the Scottish Episcopal Church.

rejoicings, and added: 'We, reflecting that, however glorious it may have been to us, and however beneficial to the nation in general, as the principal means, under God, for the recovery of their liberty; yet, in so far as it has been obtained by the effusion of the blood of his majesty's subjects, and has involved many unfortunate people in great calamity, we hereby forbid any outward demonstrations of public joy; admonishing all true friends to their king and country to return thanks to God for His goodness towards them, as we hereby do for ourselves.'

An addition to this proclamation was elicited by a circumstance which came into notice on the preceding day. On the Saturday evening Charles sent messengers to the clergy of the city, requesting them to hold public worship as usual, and apprehend no disturbance from him. To his surprise, not one of the regular clergy appeared in his pulpit on the Sunday: it was found that they had all deserted the town. He therefore added to the above proclamation: 'And we hereby repeat, what we have so often declared, that no interruption shall be given to public worship, but, on the contrary, all protection to those concerned in it; and if, notwithstanding hereof, any shall be found neglecting their duty in that particular, let the blame lie entirely at their own door, as we are resolved to inflict no penalty that may possibly look like persecution.' The clergy, as a body, continued absent during the remainder of his stay in Edinburgh. It has been stated [1] 'that they sent a deputation of their number to know whether they would be permitted, in the course of divine service, to pray for King George, when it was answered, on the part of Charles, that to grant the request would be in so far to give the lie to those family pretensions for the assertion of which he was in arms, but that, notwithstanding, he would give them his royal assurance that they should not be called to

[1] *Tales of a Grandfather*, third series, iii. 38. During Charles's stay at Holyrood House, a sermon was preached before him from Joshua xxii. 22: 'The Lord God of gods, the Lord God of gods, he knoweth, and Israel he shall know; if it be in rebellion, or if in transgression against the Lord, save us not this day.'—*Information by the late Mr George Robertson, author of 'Ayrshire Families,'* &c.

account for any imprudent language they might use in the pulpit.' This assurance, if it was ever made, did not induce any of the ministers to return to duty. There was, however, a suburban clergyman, by name Macvicar, who, having some countenance from the guns of the castle, continued to preach as usual, and offer up the ordinary prayers for the king. He also added, though several of the Highland army were present: 'As to this young person who has come among us seeking an earthly crown, do Thou, in thy merciful favour, grant him a heavenly one!'[1]

Amongst other traits of real or affected liberality, the Prince proclaimed immunity to all who might have distinguished themselves by acting against himself, his father, or grandfather, provided they should, within twenty days, formally engage to live inoffensively for the future.

He was at the same time obliged to publish an edict less creditable to his little army. It appears that, in searching for arms, the Highlanders used some license in regard to other matters of property; though it is also allowed that many persons unconnected with the army assumed the appearance of clansmen, and were the chief perpetrators of the felonies complained of. Whole bands, indeed, went about the country, shewing forged commissions, and affecting to sell protections in Charles's name, for which they exacted considerable sums of money.[2] The Highland army were partly blamable for these misdemeanours, because they had opened the public jails wherever they came, and let loose the culprits; and because, since their

---

[1] The *ipsissima verba* of this singular prayer, as given in Ray's *History of the Rebellion*, were these: 'Bless the king; Thou knows what king I mean—may the crown sit long easy upon his head, &c. And for the man that is come among us to seek an earthly crown, we beseech Thee in mercy to take him to thyself, and give him a crown of glory!'

[2] Among the rest, a certain malefactor named Ratcliff, who has been made well known to the public by means of a popular novel, seems to have been by no means the least active. It is mentioned in the *Caledonian Mercury* for October 11, that 'the *very villain* James Ratcliff, who has spent his whole life in pilfering and robbing, and who has escaped twenty several times from jail, particularly twice when under sentence of death in this city, was yesternight apprehended in the Grassmarket, and committed to the Thief's Hold. He had gone about the country since he last got out of jail, at the head of a gang of villains in Highland and Lowland dress, imposing upon and robbing honest people.'

arrival in Edinburgh, the sword of justice had been suspended. Charles, however, who was not personally blamable, made every exertion to suppress practices which tended so much to bring his cause into bad repute; and his exertions seem to have been not altogether ineffectual.[1] It unfortunately happened that, while he did all he could to prevent small or individual robberies, the necessities of his own exchequer compelled him to authorise others of considerable magnitude upon the public bodies of the kingdom. From the city of Edinburgh he exacted a thousand tents, six thousand pair of shoes, and a vast quantity of smaller articles, for the use of his troops; the expense of which was so great as to call for an assessment of half-a-crown a pound on the rental of the city. He seized all the goods in the custom-houses of Leith and Borrowstounness, and immediately converted them into money, by selling them back to the smugglers from whom they had been taken. From the city of Glasgow he raised £5500.

Though with 2000 men he had now obtained possession of

[1] It is the confident assertion of all who witnessed and have described the transactions of this time, that many persons really belonging to the Highland army *did commit acts of depredation*. It was common, for instance, for well-dressed persons to be stopped in the streets by men who presented their pieces with a threatening aspect, and who, on being asked what they wanted, usually answered: 'A *paapee*,' that is, a halfpenny. Sometimes these persons were contented with a still humbler tribute—a pinch of snuff. When we consider the extreme moderation of these demands, we can scarcely visit the practice with anything but a smile. Even this was only practised by the *canaille* of the clans, or rather perhaps by those loose persons who hang upon the skirts of all armies, and whose only motive for carrying arms is, that they may take advantage, for their own proper profit, of the license which more or less accompanies the presence of all military bodies whatever. The general tradition of the Lowlands is, that the Highlanders behaved with great civility as they were advancing in their expedition, and that it was only when retreating, and when their pride of spirit had been in a great measure destroyed, that their conduct in this respect was to be complained of.

A worthy Quaker in Edinburgh, by name Erskine, and by trade a brewer, called upon Charles at Holyrood House, to complain of a robbery which had been committed upon him by a troop wearing the Highland dress and cognizance, and concluded his remonstrance with these words: 'Verily, friend Charles, thou art harder to deal with than our present ruler: George only takes a part of our substance, but thou takest it all.' It is said that the Prince told this strange expostulator that what he had lost was little enough to compensate for the long arrears of tax and duty which he was owing to the king *de jure*. But he appears, on the contrary, to have taken measures for bringing the perpetrators of the robbery to deserved punishment. There is an advertisement in the *Courant* of the time, proceeding from him, in which he offers a reward for the robbers, and requires all to whom the stolen goods might be offered for sale to restore them to the owner.

Scotland, excepting the fortresses, it was impossible with that small force to take any immediate step for the advancement of his cause. It was necessary to wait for some time, that his forces might be augmented, either by accessions of his Scottish partisans, or by aid from abroad. He therefore encamped his troops at Duddingston, and, taking up his own residence in Holyrood House, enjoyed for a short period the privileges of undisputed sovereignty. Even at this most brilliant part of his career his deportment was generally thought pensive. He nevertheless gave a few balls to the ladies [1] who favoured his cause, and generally dined in public with his officers. On these occasions, if not uniformly cheerful, he at least endeavoured to appear pleased with what he saw of Scotland, its people, and whatever was peculiar to it. He was heard to say at dinner, that, should his enterprise be successful, he would make Scotland his *Hanover*, and Holyrood his *Herrenhausen*—thus conveying at once a compliment to the Scotch, and a sarcasm at the partiality of King George for his native dominions and palace. At his balls, which were held in the picture-gallery, he took care to dress very elegantly, wearing on some occasions ' a habit of fine silk tartan (with crimson-velvet breeches), and at other times an English court dress, with the ribbon, star, and order of the Garter.' Here his affability and great personal grace wrought him high favour with the ladies, who, as we learn from the letters of President Forbes, became generally so zealous in his cause as to have some serious effect in inducing their admirers to declare for the Prince. There was, we know for certain, a Miss Lumsden, who plainly told her lover, a young artist named Robert Strange, that he might think no more of her unless he should immediately join Prince Charles; and thus actually prevailed upon him to take up arms. It may be added that he survived the enterprise, escaped with great difficulty, and married the lady. He was afterwards the best line-engraver of his time, and received the honour of knighthood from George

---

[1] A tune to which he danced with Lady Betty Wemyss on one or more of these occasions has been preserved and published.

III.[1] White ribbons and breast-knots became at this time conspicuous articles of female attire in private assemblies. The ladies also shewed considerable zeal in contributing plate and other articles for the use of the Chevalier at the palace, and in raising pecuniary subsidies for him. Many a posset-dish and snuff-box, many a treasured necklace and repeater, many a jewel which had adorned its successive generations of family beauties, was at this time sold or laid in pledge, to raise a little money for the service of Prince Charlie.[2]

The external graces and accomplishments of the Prince have never been denied; but much doubt has been expressed

---

[1] Miss Lumsden, who was a most accomplished and high-minded person, was sister of Mr Andrew Lumsden, an adherent of the Prince. Mr Strange had no predilection for the Stuart cause, but solely obeyed the dictates of his lady-love.

[2] One of his officers has given the following account of the Prince's daily life at Holyrood House: 'In the morning, before the council met, the Prince Regent had a levee of his officers, and other people who favoured his cause. Upon the rising of the council, which often sat very long—for his counsellors frequently differed in opinion with one another, and sometimes with him—he dined in public with his principal officers. After dinner, he rode out to Duddingston (where the army lay encamped after their return to Edinburgh). In the evening he returned to Holyrood House, and received the ladies who came to his drawing-room. He then supped in public, and generally there was music at supper, and a ball afterwards.'—*Home's History.*

The following description of Charles was drawn during his stay at Holyrood House by an Englishman, who was sent from York in the middle of October as a spy, to report upon the appearance of himself and his forces: 'I was introduced to him on the 17th, when he asked me several questions as to the number of the troops, and the affections of the people of England. The audience lasted for a quarter of an hour, and took place in the presence of other two persons. The young Chevalier is about five feet eleven inches high, very proportionably made; wears his own hair, has a full forehead, a small but lively eye, a round brown-complexioned face; nose and mouth pretty small; full under the chin; not a long neck; under his jaw a pretty many pimples. He is always in a Highland habit, as are all about him. When I saw him, he had a short Highland plaid [*tartan*] waistcoat; breeches of the same; a blue garter on, and a St Andrew's cross, hanging by a green ribbon, at his button-hole, but no star. He had his boots on, *as he always has.* He dines every day in public. All sorts of people are admitted to see him then. He constantly practises all the arts of condescension and popularity—talks familiarly to the meanest Highlanders, and makes them very fair promises.'—Excerpt from a MS. in the possession of the late George Chalmers, Esq., given in his *Caledonia,* vol. ii. p. 717. That learned antiquary adds, that the description corresponds with a bust by Le Moine, executed after his return to Paris.

The description which the spy gives of the Highlanders is also worthy of quotation, though not flattering. 'They consist,' he says, 'of an odd medley of gray-beards and no-beards—old men fit to drop into the grave, and young boys whose swords are near equal to their weight, and I really believe more than their length. Four or five thousand may be very good determined men; but the rest are mean, dirty, villainous-looking rascals, who seem more anxious about plunder than their Prince, and would be better pleased with four shillings than a crown.'

whether he possessed the genuine qualities of head and heart which would have given him true esteem, had he been established on the throne. Without here entering upon the whole question, it may at least be asserted with confidence, that, throughout the affair of 1745-6, he gave eminent proofs of a merciful and forgiving disposition, insomuch as to offend many adherents, and shewed himself to be superior to all low and cruel arts for advancing his cause. Mr Maxwell of Kirkconnel, who joined him at Edinburgh, and has left a memoir of the campaign,[1] presents the following illustrations of this point: 'Everybody,' says he, 'was mightily taken with the Prince's figure and personal behaviour. There was but one voice about them. Those whom interest or prejudice made a runaway to his cause, could not help acknowledging that they wished him well in all other respects, and could hardly blame him for his present undertaking. Sundry things had concurred to raise his character to the highest pitch, besides the greatness of the enterprise, and the conduct that had hitherto appeared in the execution of it. There were several instances of good nature and humanity that had made a great impression on people's minds. I shall confine myself to two or three. Immediately after the battle, as the Prince was riding along the ground that Cope's army had occupied a few minutes before, one of the officers came up to congratulate him, and said, pointing to the killed: "Sir, there are your enemies at your feet." The Prince, far from exulting, expressed a great deal of compassion for his father's deluded subjects, whom he declared he was heartily sorry to see in that posture. Next day, when the Prince was at Pinkie House, a citizen of Edinburgh came to make some representation to Secretary Murray about the tents that city was ordered to furnish against a certain day. Murray happened to be out of the way, which the Prince hearing of, called to have the gentleman brought to him, saying he would rather despatch the business, whatever it was, himself, than have the gentleman

---

[1] Printed at Edinburgh, 1841. 4to.

wait, which he did by granting everything that was asked. So much affability in a young prince flushed with victory, drew encomiums even from his enemies. But what gave the people the highest idea of him, was the negative he gave to a thing that very nearly concerned his interest, and upon which the success of his enterprise perhaps depended. It was proposed to send one of the prisoners to London, to demand of that court a cartel for the exchange of prisoners taken, and to be taken, during the war, and to intimate that a refusal would be looked upon as a resolution on their part to give no quarter. It was visible a cartel would be of great advantage to the Prince's affairs; his friends would be more ready to declare for him if they had nothing to fear but the chances of war in the field; and if the court of London refused to settle a cartel, the Prince was authorised to treat his prisoners in the same manner as the Elector of Hanover was determined to treat such of the Prince's friends as fell into his hands. It was urged that a few examples would induce the court of London to comply. It was to be presumed that the officers of the English army would make a point of it. . . . . Though this scheme was plausible, and represented as very important, the Prince could never be brought into it; it was below him, he said, to make empty threats, and he would never put such as those into execution; he would never in cold blood take away lives which he had saved in the heat of action at the peril of his own. These were not the only proofs of good nature the Prince gave about this time. Every day produced something new of this kind.[1] These things

---

[1] Perhaps we are to consider in this light a ceremony which he consented to perform under the following circumstances: When at Perth, he had been petitioned by a poor woman to *touch* her daughter, a child of seven years, who had been afflicted with the king's evil ever since her infancy. He excused himself by pleading want of time, but directed that the girl should be brought to him at Edinburgh; to which she was accordingly despatched, under the care of a sick-nurse, and a day was appointed when she should be introduced to his presence in the palace. When the child was brought in, he was found in the picture-gallery, which served as his ordinary audience-chamber, surrounded by his principal officers and by many ladies. He caused a circle to be cleared, within which the child was admitted, together with her attendant, and a priest in his canonicals. The patient was then stripped, and placed upon her knees in the centre of the circle. The clergyman having pronounced an appropriate prayer, Charles approached the kneeling

softened the rigour of a military government, which was only imputed to the necessity of his affairs, and which he endeavoured to make as gentle and easy as possible.'

As yet, excepting a letter he had addressed to Lord Barrymore from Perth, Charles had had no correspondence with the friends of his family in England. On the day after the battle of Preston, he despatched an agent, named Hickson, with instructions drawn up, probably by himself, in the following brief but forcible terms: 'You are hereby authorised and directed to repair forthwith to England, and there notify to my friends, and particularly to those in the north and north-west, the wonderful success with which it has hitherto pleased God to favour my endeavours for their deliverance. You are to let them know that it is my full intention, in a few days, to move towards them; and that they will be *inexcusable before God and man, if they do not all in their power to assist and support me in such an undertaking.* What I demand and expect is, that as many of them as can, should be ready to join me; and that they should take care to provide provisions and money, that the country may suffer as little as possible by the march of my troops. Let them know that there is no more time for deliberation; *now or never is the word.* I AM RESOLVED TO CONQUER, OR PERISH. If this last should happen, let them judge what they and their posterity have to expect. C. P. R.' Hickson was apprehended on the 27th at Newcastle, with this document in his cloak-bag. He was put into prison, where he next morning attempted to take away his life by cutting his throat, but without immediately succeeding in his object.[1] What afterwards became of him does not appear.

On the 10th of October, Charles issued a proclamation 'unto

girl, and with great solemnity touched the sores, pronouncing at every different application the words: 'I touch, but God heal!' The ceremony was concluded by another prayer from the priest; and the patient, being again dressed, was carried round the circle, and presented with little sums of money by all present. The story goes on to say that, precisely twenty-one days from the date of her being submitted to Charles's touch, the ulcers closed and healed, and nothing remained to shew that she had been afflicted except the scars or marks left upon the skin! These marks my informant had himself touched.

[1] Culloden Papers, 226.

all his majesty's subjects, of what degree soever,' in which he made an earnest appeal to their affections, and took occasion to explain his views on some important points in the political state of the country.[1] He declared that his father's sole intention was 'to reinstate all his subjects in the full enjoyment of their religion, laws, and liberties.' 'Our present attempt,' said he, 'is not undertaken in order to enslave a free people, but to redress and remove the encroachments made upon them; not to impose upon any a religion which they dislike, but to secure them all in the enjoyment of those which are respectively at present established amongst them either in England, Scotland, or Ireland.' He promised to respect the national debt, but said he could upon no account be induced to ratify the Union. He alluded to the endeavours which were made by ill-designing men to prejudice the people against himself and his undertaking. 'Do not,' says he, 'the pulpits and congregations of the clergy, as well as your weekly papers, ring with the dreadful threats of popery, slavery, tyranny, and arbitrary power, which are now ready to be imposed upon you by the formidable powers of France and Spain? Is not my royal father represented as a blood-thirsty tyrant, breathing out nothing but destruction to all who will not immediately embrace an odious religion? Or have I myself been better used? But listen only to the naked truth.

'I with my own money, hired a small vessel, ill supplied with money, arms, or friends; I arrived in Scotland, attended by seven persons; I publish the king my father's declaration, and proclaim his title, with pardon in one hand, and in the other liberty of conscience, and the most solemn promises to grant whatever a free parliament shall propose for the happiness of a people. I have, I confess, the greatest reason to adore the goodness of Almighty God, who has in so remarkable a manner protected me and my small army through the many dangers to

---

[1] Lord Mahon expresses his opinion that this document was of his own composition, notwithstanding that Mr Murray of Broughton, in his examination, states it to have been drawn up by Sir Thomas Sheridan and Sir James Steuart.

which we were at first exposed, and who has led me in the way to victory, and to the capital of this ancient kingdom, amidst the acclamations of the king my father's subjects. Why, then, is so much pains taken to spirit up the minds of the people against this my undertaking?

'The reason is obvious; it is, lest the real sense of the nation's present sufferings should blot out the remembrance of past misfortunes, and of the outcries formerly raised against the royal family. Whatever miscarriages might have given occasion to them, they have been more than atoned for since; and the nation has now an opportunity of being secured against the like for the future.

'That our family has suffered exile during these fifty-seven years, everybody knows. Has the nation, during that period of time, been the more happy and flourishing for it? Have you found reason to love and cherish your governors, as the fathers of the people of Great Britain and Ireland? Has a family, upon whom a faction unlawfully bestowed the diadem of a rightful prince, retained a due sense of so great a trust and favour? Have you found more humanity and condescension in those who were not born to a crown, than in my royal forefathers? Have their ears been open to the cries of the people? Have they, or do they consider only the interest of these nations? Have you reaped any other benefit from them than an immense load of debts? If I am answered in the affirmative, why has their government been so often railed at in all your public assemblies? Why has the nation been so long crying out in vain for redress against the abuse of parliaments, upon account of their long duration, the multitude of placemen which occasions their venality, the introduction of penal laws, and, in general, against the miserable situation of the kingdom at home and abroad? All these and many more inconveniences must now be removed, unless the people of Great Britain be already so far corrupted that they will not accept of freedom when offered to them, seeing the king, on his restoration, will refuse nothing that a free parliament can ask for the security of the religion, laws, and liberty of his people. ....

'It is now time to conclude, and I shall do it with this reflection. Civil wars are ever attended with rancour and ill-will, which party rage never fails to produce in the minds of those whom different interests, principles, or views set in opposition to one another. I therefore earnestly require it of my friends to give as little loose as possible to such passions; this will prove the most effectual means to prevent the same in the enemies of our royal cause. And this my declaration will vindicate to all posterity the nobleness of my undertaking, and the generosity of my intentions.'[1]

[1] This document was burlesqued on the spur of the occasion by Mrs Cockburn, author of the beautiful song, *The Flowers of the Forest*, and whose wit, as here exemplified, may for the future check in some degree the too confident assertion that the Muses were exclusively Jacobite. The verses form a kind of parody of a song called *Clout the Cauldron*:

> 'Have you any laws to mend?
>   Or have you any grievance?
> I am a hero to my trade,
>   And truly a most leal prince.
> Would you have war, would you have peace,
>   Would you be free of taxes,
> Come chapping to my father's door,
>   You need not doubt of access.
>
> Religion, laws, and liberty,
>   Ye ken are bonnie words, sirs;
> They shall be a' made sure to you,
>   If you'll fecht wi' your swords, sirs.
> The nation's debt we soon shall pay,
>   If ye'll support our right, boys;
> No sooner we are brought in play,
>   Than all things shall be tight, boys.
>
> Ye ken that by a Union base,
>   Your ancient kingdom's undone,
> That a' your ladies, lords, and lairds,
>   Gang up and live at London.
> Nae langer that we will allow,
>   For, crack—it goes asunder—
> What took sic time and pains to do;
>   And let the warld wonder.
>
> I'm sure, for seven years and mair,
>   Ye've heard o' sad oppression;
> And this is all the good ye got
>   By the Hanover succession.

CHAPTER XIV.

GATHERING AT EDINBURGH.

'To wanton me, to wanton me,
Ken ye what maist wad wanton me?
To see King James at Edinburgh Cross,
Wi' fifty thousand foot and horse,
And the usurper forced to flee;
Oh, this is what maist wad wanton me!'
Jacobite Song.

THE court of St James's, thoroughly alarmed at Charles's progress and success, were now taking measures to present a large force against him. About the end of September, the king ordered a strong body of troops, consisting of several battalions of foot and some squadrons of horse, to march directly to Scotland, under the command of Marshal Wade. They were

'For absolute power and popery,
Ye ken it's a' but nonsense:
I here swear to secure to you
Your liberty of conscience.

And, for your mair encouragement,
Ye shall be pardoned byganes;
Nae mair fight on the continent,
And leave behind your dry banes.
Then come away, and dinna stay;
What gars ye look sae landart?
I'd have ye run, and not delay,
To join my father's standard.'

Sir Walter Scott, in a manuscript note which he communicated to the author of this history, says: 'I remember having heard repeated a parody on Prince Charles's proclamation, in burlesque verse, to the tune of *Clout the Cauldron*. In the midst of the siege or blockade of the castle of Edinburgh, the carriage in which Mrs Cockburn was returning from a visit to Ravelston was stopped by the Highland guard at the West Port; and as she had a copy of the parody about her person, she was not a little alarmed for the consequences, especially as the officer talked of searching for letters and correspondence with the Whigs in the city. Fortunately the arms on the coach were recognised as belonging to a gentleman favourable to the cause of the adventurer, so that Mrs Cockburn escaped, with the caution not to carry political squibs about her person in future.'

appointed to assemble at Doncaster, and Wade set out from London on the 6th of October to assume the command. It was not till the 29th of October that this army reached Newcastle, on their way to meet the Highland army, by which time Charles was on the point of marching into England.[1]

This force being still considered too small, the king, besides using every endeavour to enlist new men, ordered home a considerable portion of his veteran army from Flanders, along with its youthful commander, William, Duke of Cumberland, his second son, who had already distinguished himself at the well-fought though unsuccessful battle of Fontenoy. Thirteen regiments of infantry and two of cavalry were also in the course of being raised by the nobility and gentry of England to oppose the insurgents; and the king, the better to carry on the war, was favoured with a loan of £700,000, by the proprietors of two privateer vessels, which had recently taken upwards of that sum in specie from the French. The royal assent was also given, October 21, to a bill for suspending the Habeas Corpus Act; and many persons of importance were arrested on suspicion.

To oppose forces thus leisurely collected, and in such quantities, Charles exerted himself, for six weeks after his victory, to raise the clans which had not at first declared themselves, and to organise his little army as well as time and circumstances would allow. This was the more necessary, as, in addition to the regular forces mustered by the government, President Forbes was exerting himself to raise a loyal force in the Highlands out of the *followings* of the Laird of Grant, the Earl of Sutherland, Monro of Foulis, and a few other well-affected landlords, and for this purpose had obtained from court twenty commissions for an equal number of *independent companies*, as they were called, of 100 men each. On the 24th of September,

---

[1] Wade, on the 30th of October, issued a proclamation, addressed to such as had been forced by their superiors into rebellion, offering them his majesty's free pardon, on condition of their returning to their homes before the 12th of November.

Charles despatched Mr Alexander Macleod of Muiravonside, a cousin of young Clanranald, as a messenger to the Isle of Skye, to assure Sir Alexander Macdonald and the Laird of Macleod, that, not imputing their inactivity to disaffection, he was ready to receive them and their powerful clans as the most favoured of his father's loyal subjects. From Skye, this messenger was commissioned to go to Castle Downie, the residence of Lord Lovat, and to deliver to him the same message. He met with no success in Skye, where Duncan Forbes had been exerting himself to confirm the two recusant chiefs in their loyalty. At Castle Downie he found Lovat still undecided as to which course he should take. This aged chief had been greatly rejoiced by the tidings of Preston. It is said that, momentarily hurried from his prudent course, he pronounced it a victory of unparalleled brilliancy, and descending to his courtyard, and casting his hat upon the ground, drank, in a bumper of wine, 'Success to the White Rose, and confusion to the White Horse and all its adherents!'—the white rose being a badge of the house of Stuart, and the white horse a conspicuous object on the armorial shield of the house of Hanover. Still he was too much in fear of the government, and too closely watched by his neighbour, President Forbes, to commit himself in the character of a declared partisan of the Chevalier. It occurred to Lovat's subtle, but at the same time superficial mind, that he might give the Prince the use of his clan, as a portion of his army, while he himself might keep up a fair face towards the government, and thereby save his person and estates from risk. He therefore caused the clan to be mustered by his subalterns, the chief of whom was Fraser of Gortuleg; and summoning his son, a youth of eighteen, from college at St Andrews, forced him to assume the appearance of a rebellious young chief, determined to muster and lead away the clan for the service of the Chevalier, against the will of an aged father, unable by personal infirmity to prevent him.

The letters addressed by Lovat to President Forbes during the time when these transactions were going on have been preserved and published,[1] and perhaps we have nowhere more faithful illustrations of that mean cunning, the natural language of which Hogarth has so well expressed in his lordship's portrait. On the 7th of October, he speaks with indignation of the 'villainous, malicious, and ridiculous reports' that had been circulated respecting his conduct, and to which Forbes had alluded, assuring the President that 'there was nothing ever out of hell more false.' Forbes replied on the same day, in terms expressing full confidence in his continued prudence and loyalty. On the 11th, Lovat writes again, representing (this was an important part of his system) his health as extremely bad; he could not move without the assistance of three or four men. He is full of intelligence favourable to the Chevalier's object—a French army landed in the south of England—the Duke of Beaufort, Sir Watkins William Wynne, and Morgan of Tredegar, at the head of a native English army of six thousand men—all the gentry of Banff, Aberdeen, Perth, and Stirling, and many of the clans, flocking to the standard at Edinburgh. The contagion of disloyalty has reached his men, and he finds it morally impossible to prevent them from arming in behalf of the 'mad young gentleman.' He really does not know how to act: he wishes he had been in any part out of Britain for these twelve months past. Finally, he craves the Lord President's advice. On the night of the 16th, a large party of Lovat's clan, under some of his subalterns, made an unsuccessful attack on Culloden House, in order to seize the person of the President, for which, it will be recollected, he had obtained a warrant from Prince Charles, not dictated in such unscrupulous terms as he had wished. Apparently, on hearing of this attack, he wrote to the Lord President in condoling terms; but the letter has not been preserved. Of course, he would disclaim all connection with the attempt, though there is no doubt that it was of his own scheming. In the same letter, as we can judge from the President's answer, he must have stated that his son had put

[1] Culloden Papers, 4to.

himself at the head of the clan, and was about to conduct it to the standard of the Chevalier. On the 20th, he renews this subject, with many affected complaints as to the distresses of his situation. 'This Prince's landing,' says he, 'was as great a surprise to me as it was to any man in Scotland; but who can prevent accidents, or the designs of Providence? It is certain that what he has done since he landed seems rather to be a miracle, than the effects of men's heads or hands; and how far that favourable providence may follow him, or conduct him, God alone knows; for *he seems at present in a fair and probable way of succeeding.*' For this, which probably was his genuine opinion, he adduces facts; particularly the great number of his adherents in Scotland, and the succours expected from abroad. Nevertheless, 'I do solemnly declare to your lordship that nothing ever vexed my soul so much as the resolution of my son to go and join the Prince. . . . . This mad resolution struck him in the head as soon as he heard of the Prince's landing; and after what Macleod said to him, and what Gortuleg said to him, and what myself said to him, I know by his answers to Macleod, Gortuleg, and me, that all the creation will not keep him from going to live and die with that Prince. I refer it to your lordship, who has a true sense of the danger of my family from his going out, what a load and weight of grief must be upon my soul to see my son, myself, and my family in such danger and jeopardy. But I cannot help it. I must submit to the will of God, and there must leave it.'

In this letter he whiningly complains that his son, when he ventures to remonstrate with him, only 'smiles and laughs :' in another of the 27th, we have the young man described as flying in his face 'like a wild-cat' whenever he but speaks of his folly. The President having, in a reply dated the 29th, plainly intimated that, in an age of such suspicion, the Master of Lovat's conduct might be the ruin of his father and family, the old chief, on the 30th, exclaims loudly against the very idea of such a thing, than which, he says, there never could have been greater injustice among the Turks or Persians. 'Am I, my lord, the first man that has had ane undutiful son? Or am I the first man that has made a good estate, and saw it destroyed in his own time by the foolish actings of ane unnatural son, who prefers his own extravagant fancies to the solid advice of ane affectionate old father? I have seen instances of this in my own time; but I never heard till now that the foolishness of a son would take away the liberty and life of a father, that lived peaceably, that was ane honest man, and well inclined to the rest of mankind. But I find the longer a man lives, the more wonders and extraordinary things he sees.' On the 6th of November, he entreats the Lord President to continue his friendship, and to represent his case in the most favourable light in important quarters—adding, with that view, a recital of how his clan had been infected by the general enthusiasm, how they had gone off to the Prince, leaving me 'a contemptible old infirm fellow in my house, and no more notice taken of me than if I was a child'—and finally, how he was, after all, exerting himself to make up a regiment for the government, 'most of them pretty fellows, though some of them are between sixty and seventy years of age' (many of them, he elsewhere says, 'about my own age,' that is, on the borders of eighty!), and at whose head he was to put a set of 'pretty gentlemen.' He was determined to live at home in peace, and, if he should suffer on his son's account, it would be a greater severity than was ever practised to any subject. 'My house and green,' he adds, 'has been like a market-place for some time past; and my son was such a fool, that he entertained, and does entertain, every man he thinks favours his part, and he is ten times [more] master of this house than I am; but I have resolved from the beginning, and still continue firm in my resolution, let them do or say what they will, I will never black paper with them; and as soon as I am able to travel out of this house, I'll stay no longer in it, for I am downright killed with vexation of heart and spirit, to see my health much hurt, my family in danger, and any money and rent I have foolishly spent and squandered away. There is no help for it; I must submit to Divine Providence.' Then, after a few matters of no importance, he tells how the Earl of Cromarty and Lord Macleod had come to Beaufort, on their way to join the Prince. ' So your lordship sees that the *wise and worldly* people of the Mackenzies are infected; so that it's no wonder that the Frasers, *who never were thought worldly or wise*, should be infected with a contagion, though never so foolish or dangerous.'

It is very remarkable, amidst all these proofs of refined cunning, to observe the want of the simplest wisdom in Lovat. From the magnificent accounts he gives of the Prince's circumstances and prospects, he appears to have been among the most credulous and easily deceived men of his day.

The Master of Lovat—afterwards the well-known General Fraser of the British army—led out the Frasers, it has always been said, with great reluctance, but not in time to join the army before its march into England.

Although the President was generally successful in his negotiations, he could not prevent a considerable number of the clans from marching to join the Prince's standard. As he himself declares in one of his letters, rebels stalked out from families for whose loyalty he could have previously staked his life; and even his own nephew, to his great astonishment and mortification, one day assumed the white cockade, and joined the insurgents. It would indeed appear that he was in some cases, besides that of Lovat, egregiously deceived; and that, by a policy not less fine-spun than his own, many whom he considered his friends had only assured him of their loyalty in order to lull him into security, and that they might be able to circumvent him in their turn. Under these circumstances, it is not surprising that the Independent Companies did not at first muster very quickly. The Earl of Loudoun came to Inverness to take the command on the 11th of October; but only two companies had been gathered at the end of that month, and only four more during the first half of the next.

Edinburgh was in the meantime experiencing some of the miseries of civil war. For a few days after the battle of Preston, the communication between the city and castle continued open.

The Highlanders kept guard at the Weigh-house, an old building situated in the centre of the street leading to the castle, about four hundred yards from the fortress itself; and they at first allowed all kinds of provisions to pass, particularly for the use of the officers. But, the garrison soon beginning to annoy them with cohorns and cannon, orders were issued, on the 29th of September, that no person should be permitted to pass. General Guest then sent a letter to the city, threatening to use his cannon against the stations of the Highland guards, unless they permitted a free communication. As that involved the safety of the town to a great extent, the inhabitants—for there were no magistrates—implored a respite for a single night, which was granted. They then waited upon Prince Charles, and shewed him General Guest's letter. He immediately gave them an answer in writing, that they might shew it to the governor, expressing his surprise at the barbarity of the officer who threatened to bring distress upon the citizens for not doing what was out of their power, and at the extravagance which demanded his renunciation of all the advantages he possessed by the fortune of war. He concluded by threatening to retaliate upon the garrison, in reprisals upon their estates, and also upon those of 'all known abetters of the German government.' Upon presenting this letter to General Guest, and making earnest entreaty for a further respite, the citizens obtained a promise that no shots should be fired till his majesty's pleasure should be known upon the subject, providing that the besiegers should, during that time, offer no annoyance to the garrison.

This condition was broken next day by the levity of the Highlanders, who fired off their pieces, to frighten some people who were carrying provisions up the Castle-hill. The governor then considered himself justified in firing upon the guard. Charles, on learning what had taken place, published a proclamation, prohibiting all intercourse with the castle, upon pain of death, and gave orders to strengthen the blockade, by posting additional guards at several places. The garrison retaliated for this measure, by firing at all the Highlanders they could see. On the 4th of October, they commenced a bombardment of the city. When it grew dark, the cannonading ceased, and a party sallying out, threw up a trench across the Castle-hill, where they planted cannon, and fired balls and small-shot down the street. They also set fire to one or two deserted houses at the head of the street, and on the people running to extinguish the flames, destroyed some innocent lives. The people, then greatly alarmed, began to busy themselves in transporting their aged and infirm friends to the country, along with their most valuable effects; and the streets, on which the bullets were every moment descending, were soon as completely deserted by day as they usually were by night. In running down to Leith for shelter, a great party met the inhabitants of that town hurrying for the same purpose towards Edinburgh, because a British ship of war, lying off in the roads, and whose intercourse with the shore had been cut off by the Highlanders, was firing into their streets with the same fatal effect. All was perplexity and dismay; and the unhappy citizens stood still, wringing their hands, and execrating the cruel necessities of war.

The distress which the blockade of the castle had brought upon the city was now found to be so unfavourable to Charles's cause, that he was obliged, for the sake of that cause, to take it off. He did so by proclamation on the evening of the day succeeding its commencement. The cannonade then ceased on the part of the castle, into which provisions were thenceforth conveyed without molestation.

The prisoners taken at Gladsmuir had meanwhile been sent to distant parts of the country—the officers to Perth, and the private men to Logierait in Athole. Some sergeants, corporals, and private men were prevailed upon to enlist in the victorious army; but most of them afterwards deserted. It will be found that most of the officers, who, besides their parole, had also taken an oath not to serve against the house of Stuart for a twelvemonth, held as little faith with their captors. The Prince not only freed those private soldiers who had been severely wounded (about seventy in number), but, with his usual humanity, gave them money to bear them to their homes. Many travelled into England as beggars, shewing their dreadful gashes wherever they went; by which means the curiosity of the English populace was at once gratified, and their minds impressed with no small terror for the claymore.

The accessions of force which Prince Charles received at Edinburgh were not inconsiderable. The first that joined him was Lord Ogilvie, eldest son of the Earl of Airlie, who arrived in town on the 3d of October with a regiment of 600 men, most of whom were of his own name, and from the county of Forfar. Next day came Gordon of Glenbucket, with 400 men from the head of Aberdeenshire, forming a regiment, of which he and his kinsmen were the officers. Lord Pitsligo arrived on the 9th, with a great body of gentlemen from the counties of Aberdeen and Banff, attended by their servants, all well armed and mounted; as also a small body of infantry. On the 16th, Lord Lewis Gordon, brother of the Duke of Gordon, arrived, and kissed the Chevalier's hand. It was understood that he on this occasion represented his brother, who was not inclined to appear in person.[1] These valuable recruits were from the northern part of the Lowlands of Scotland, where non-jurancy might be said to have its principal citadel, and where the Episcopal and Roman Catholic forms of worship still flourish. Various other gentlemen from the north, along with some inferior septs of Highland families, joined the army before the end of October, when the whole amount was somewhat less than 6000.

[1] Amongst many who declared for the Chevalier a cautious policy was adopted. In cases where the head of a family and proprietor of an estate went out, he would previously make over his property to his eldest son, who remained at home in possession. When the father, on the contrary, was averse to active partisanship, a son went out, along with all the forces, both in the way of men and money, which the house could contribute, assured that, although the youth should fall or be attainted, he had still brothers to inherit the patrimonial property for the behoof of the family. Some of the Highland gentlemen themselves saw fit to adopt this policy. The Macdonalds of Clanranald, and also those of Glengarry, were led out by the sons of their respective chiefs. At a subsequent period of the campaign, the *wife* of the chief of the Mackintoshes raised the clan in behalf of Charles, while Mackintosh himself served as an officer in the militia raised for the defence of government.

K

The Chevalier, notwithstanding the success of Preston, found few adherents in Edinburgh, or in any part of the country south of the Forth. Even when he was in complete possession of the city, only about three hundred of the inhabitants, and those not the most respectable, did him the honour of assuming the white cockade.[1] In fact, his enterprise was a thing quite foreign to the feelings and ordinary pursuits of the Lowland population. It was also opposed by the stern Presbyterian principle of dislike to his family, originating in the religious persecutions to which his ancestors had subjected a portion of the people of Scotland. It is true that the most rigid sect of Presbyterians had, since the revolution, expressed a strong desire to coalesce with the Jacobites, with the hope, in case the house of Stuart were restored, to obtain what they called a covenanted king; and that 1000 of this sect had assembled in Dumfriesshire, at the first intelligence of the insurrection, bearing arms and colours, and supposed to contemplate a junction with the Chevalier. But these religionists were now almost as violently distinct from the Established Church of Scotland as ever they had been from those of England and Rome, and had long ceased to play a prominent part in the national disputes. The established clergy, and the greater part of their congregations, were averse to Charles upon considerations perfectly moderate, but at the same time not easy to be shaken.

Some instances have been reported which shew the efficacy of these sentiments against Charles's cause, and at the same time prove the disinclination to war which an age of domestic peace and increasing commerce had produced in the Lowlands. When the Earl of Kilmarnock exerted himself in 1715 for the defence of government, he found no difficulty in raising a large regiment among his tenants and dependants, all of whom were at once willing to attend their baronial master, and hearty in the cause for which he desired their services; but on the son of that earl coming to Kilmarnock in 1745, and requesting the

---

[1] *Edinburgh Packet Opened*, 1745. 8vo. P. 12.

inhabitants to arm themselves in behalf of the house of Stuart, there was a very different result. The people were acquiring wealth by the manufacture of carpets and nightcaps, and had got different lights regarding feudal servitude, which, added to their prejudices against the pope and the Pretender, caused them fairly to rebel against their baronial superior. His lordship assembled them in the town-hall, and tried them first with entreaties, and then with threats; but not one man would consent to join his standard. He then confined his demands to their arms; for, weavers as they were, they still retained the old muskets and rusty swords of their covenanting ancestors, and occasionally displayed them at bloodless wapenshaws. But this requisition they were equally prepared to resist; and one of them even told his lordship, that 'if they presented him with their guns, it would be *with the muzzle till him!*'[1] The Earl of Kilmarnock, therefore, brought none but himself and his body-servants to the Prince's army.

The Earl of Kellie was equally unsuccessful in his attempt to raise his dependants. This eccentric nobleman is described in the *Mercury* as going over to Fife, in order to raise a regiment for the Prince's service upon his estates in that well-affected district. He never got above three men—himself as colonel, an old Fife laird for lieutenant-colonel, and a serving-man, who had to represent all the rest of the troop by his own single person!

Several other Lowland gentlemen joined the Prince at this time—amongst the rest William Hamilton of Bangour, an amiable man and pleasing poet, who became the laureate of the enterprise, and seems at one time to have designed being its historian. Another of some note was the Honourable Arthur Elphingstone of Balmerino, who had been an officer in Queen Anne's army, and who, in the ensuing January, while engaged in the enterprise, succeeded to his family title of Lord Balmerino. 'I might easily,' said this brave veteran in his *last*

---

[1] Tradition at Kilmarnock.

speech, 'have excused myself taking arms on account of my age; but *I never could have had peace of conscience* if I had stayed at home, when that brave Prince was exposing himself to all manner of dangers and fatigue both night and day.' An adherent of still greater importance, and one whose becoming so occasioned more surprise, was Sir James Steuart of Goodtrees and Coltness, afterwards distinguished as the author of the first British work of importance on political economy, and unquestionably a man of considerable talents. Descended of a Whig family, Sir James had, nevertheless, allowed himself, in the course of his travels, to form an intimacy with the Stuart princes and some of their principal adherents. He had more lately been piqued at the treatment he had received at an election from one of the officers of the government. He was disposed to join the enterprise of the Prince, but wished that, in doing so, he should not appear quite a free agent. His sister's husband, the Earl of Buchan, a good man, of moderate understanding,[1] was brought by him to the same views, and they agreed with Lady Steuart's brother, Lord Elcho, that they should be seized in a public place, and carried to Holyrood House, as if against their will. Walking next day at the Cross of Edinburgh, Sir James and the earl were seized accordingly, and conducted to the palace. There a message was sent from an anteroom to the Chevalier, mentioning their presence. The Prince, who in the meanwhile had heard of the manner of their visit, returned for answer, that if the Earl of Buchan and Sir James Steuart came as willing partisans to befriend his cause, he should be proud and happy to see them, but not otherwise. This bluntness, though honourable to the Prince's candour, displeased Buchan, whose resolution, perhaps, had already begun to give way. He therefore made a low bow to the officer, and said: 'Please inform his royal highness that I have the honour to be his most obedient humble servant;' after which he instantly left the palace. Sir James, too much offended with the government to

---

[1] Though the father of two uncommonly clever men—the Honourable Henry Erskine, and Lord Erskine, Chancellor of England.

retrace his steps, remained to see the Prince upon the terms prescribed.[1]

When the old Chevalier was first informed of Charles's departure for Scotland, he, though disapproving of the enterprise, did all he could to favour its success. Besides remitting 200,000 francs to O'Brien, his chief agent at Paris, to pay off the debts contracted by the Prince, he deposited another sum of 50,000 francs in the hands of Waters, junior, his banker there, to be at O'Brien's disposal for the service of the enterprise, and soon after sent 80,000 Roman crowns for the same purpose, promising soon to follow the same up with a still further remittance of 28,000 crowns, which he said would exhaust his treasury.[2] He likewise wrote a letter (August 5, new style—July 24, old style) to the king of France, pressingly urging him to second the Prince's attempt by an efficient force.[3] He at the same time addressed the Cardinal Tencin, the Maréchal de Noailles, and indeed the whole of the French ministers, to the same effect. Immediately after his taking possession of Edinburgh, the Prince despatched Mr Kelly to France, to give an account of his marvellous success, and urge it as a reason for the government sending him the much-desired aid.[4] He now sent Sir James Steuart, in the more formal character of an ambassador, to enforce the arguments of Kelly. Meanwhile the young Duc de Bouillon, with whom Charles had formed a romantic friendship, was exerting all his eloquence with the king and ministers to the same effect. The various means taken to obtain French aid were in some degree successful. Early in October several ships from France arrived at Montrose, Stonehaven, and other ports in the north with arms and ammunition. The first of these brought £5000 in money, and 2500 stand of arms, besides a Monsieur de Boyer, styled Marquis d'Eguilles, who, on the 10th, was received with

---

[1] The family tradition, communicated by the late Sir Henry Steuart of Allanton.
[2] Stuart Papers, appendix to Browne's *History*.
[3] Stuart Papers, Browne's *History*.
[4] Kelly went by Campvere, in Holland, where he was near being arrested by the Conservator of Scots Privileges, an agent kept by the Scottish merchants at that port.

studious parade at Holyrood House as the French ambassador. It was given out that this gentleman brought letters from Louis XV., promising that an armament should be immediately despatched to the Prince's assistance, under the conduct of his brother, the Duke of York. Another vessel, besides some money and arms, brought a few French-Irish officers. A third landed part of a company of artillerymen, with six field-pieces. A difficulty was experienced in getting these stores transported to Edinburgh, as the bridge of Stirling was under command of the castle, and the Firth of Forth was swept by British cruisers. The expedient adopted was to erect a battery of four or five guns at Higgins' Nook, near Airth, and a similar one on the other side of the Forth, to guard that narrow passage from the boats of the cruisers. The stores were brought over by this way in a hundred and eighty-five carts, under the conduct of a guard, and arrived at Dalkeith just in time to accompany the army on its southward march.

The account given by Maxwell of Kirkconnel presents a favourable view of the character and conduct of the Prince, as both appeared during his residence in Edinburgh. One less flattering has been given by Lord Elcho, who likewise left a memoir respecting the insurrection. Lord Elcho's account of the Chevalier's council is peculiarly valuable, because we nowhere else obtain the same light; but some allowance must be made for the bitter personal feeling under which he evidently writes. 'The Prince,' says he, 'formed a council, which met regularly every morning in his drawing-room. The gentlemen whom he called to it were the Duke of Perth, Lord Lewis Gordon, Lord George Murray, Lord Elcho, Lord Ogilvie, Lord Pitsligo, Lord Nairn, Locheil, Keppoch, Clanranald, Glencoe, Lochgarry, Ardshiel, Sir Thomas Sheridan, Colonel O'Sullivan, Glenbucket, and Secretary Murray. The Prince, in this council, used always first to declare what he himself was for, and then he asked everybody's opinion in his turn. There was one-third of the council whose principles were, that kings and princes can never either act or think wrong; so, in consequence, they always confirmed what the Prince said. The other two-thirds, who thought that kings and princes thought something like other men, and were not altogether infallible, and that this Prince was no more so than others, begged leave to differ from him, when they could give sufficient reasons for their difference of opinion. This very often was no difficult matter to do; for as the Prince and his old governor, Sir Thomas Sheridan, were altogether ignorant of the ways and customs of Great Britain, and both much for the doctrine of absolute monarchy, they would very often, had they not been prevented, have fallen into blunders which might have hurt the cause. The Prince could not bear to hear anybody differ in sentiment from him, and took a dislike to everybody that did; for he had a notion of commanding the army as any general does a body of mercenaries, and so let them know only what he pleased, and expected them to obey without inquiring further about the matter. This might have done better had his favourites been people of the country; but as they were Irish, and had nothing to risk, the people of fashion, that had their all at stake, and consequently ought to be supposed likely to give the best advice of which they were capable, thought they had a title to know and be consulted in what was good for the cause; and if it had not been for their insisting strongly upon it, the Prince, when he found that his sentiments were not always approved of, would have abolished this council long ere he did.

'There was a very good paper sent one day by a gentleman in Edinburgh, to be perused by his council. The Prince, when he heard it read, said that it was below his dignity to enter into such a reasoning with subjects, and ordered the paper to be laid aside. The paper was afterwards printed, under the title of "The Prince's Declaration to the People of England," and is esteemed the best manifesto published in those times, for those that were printed at Rome and Paris were reckoned not well calculated for the present age.

'The Prince created a committee for providing the army with forage. It was composed of Lord Elcho, president;

Graham of Duntroon, whom they called Lord Dundee; Sir William Gordon of Park; Hunter of Burnside; Haldane of Lanark, and his son; Mr Smith; and Mr Hamilton. They issued out orders, in the Prince's name, to all the gentlemen's houses who had employments under the government, to send in certain quantities of hay, straw, and corn upon such a day, under pain of military execution if not complied with; but their orders were very punctually obeyed.

'There were courts-martial sat every day for the discipline of the army, and some delinquents were punished with death.'

During the stay of the Chevalier in Edinburgh, the newspapers served as organs of intelligence in his favour, and were the chief vehicles of his proclamations. While the *Courant* submitted to this necessity with the reluctance which might have been expected from its principles, the *Mercury* not only complied with promptitude, but rejoiced in the opportunity thus afforded of indulging its natural propensities without constraint. Ruddiman himself had retired to the country, after having only once, as he himself informs us (in the preface to his *Dissertation concerning the Competition between Bruce and Baliol*), seen his Prince *for two minutes*. At the age of seventy-one, he could not promote by any active measures the cause of his heart. During his absence, however, the paper was conducted with sufficient vigour by his partner, James Grant, a young man of more violent political prejudices than himself, and who eventually took arms in behalf of the Chevalier. Grant did all that the command of such a tool put into his power to further the views of the Highland army. Making allowance for the partiality displayed in his paragraphs, many of them contain curious memorabilia of the time.

Friday, September 27.—' Several sergeants and corporals, with a vast many private men, have entered into the Prince's service; so that, with the volunteers who come in, the clerks of the office have not leisure to eat, drink, or sleep, by enlisting. These sergeants and volunteers are now beating for volunteers to serve Prince Charles.

' The poor soldiers who were wounded at the late battle daily die of their wounds, both in town and country; and such of them as have been able to crawl to town, are cheerfully succoured by the inhabitants.

' His Royal Highness, whose robust and hardy constitution supports his natural inclination to fatigue and hardships, lay last night in a soldier's tent at the camp, preferring that tent to the royal palace of Holyrood House.'

Monday, September 30.—' There is now forming, and pretty well advanced, a body of horse life-guards for his Royal Highness the Prince, commanded by the Right Honourable the Lord Elcho. Their uniform is blue, trimmed with red, and laced waistcoats; they are to consist of four squadrons of gentlemen of character.

'The Prince's tent has been erected in the camp near Duddingston, where his Royal Highness lies every night wrapped up in his Highland plaid. He takes the utmost pleasure in reviewing his people, and is highly beloved by them. There was yesterday a general review.

' Several persons of distinction, and a vast number of private gentlemen, have joined the Prince's army since our last.

' A gentleman, a citizen of London, arrived yesterday in the Prince's camp, and offered himself a volunteer.

GATHERING AT EDINBURGH.

'Ever since the castle has been blocked up somewhat strictly on the *side of this city*, the friends of the garrison have the night-long conveyed up by ropes to them whatever necessaries they want, by the corner of the West Port side.'

Wednesday, October 2.—' Among the observables of this time, one is, that there is not in the city jail one single prisoner for crime, debt, or otherwise. The like, perhaps, never could have been said before.'

Some of the subsequent publications overflow with flattering accounts of the rising in the north, and intimate the highest hopes regarding the issue of the expedition. The clans are described as descending in thousands from their fastnesses, and every party which really came to the camp is greatly exaggerated. Cheerful accounts are also given of the readiness with which the contributions of the towns and rents of the forfeited estates are paid to the Prince. Altogether, from the magnificence of the reports which the *Mercury* puts into circulation, it is scarcely to be wondered at that so many sober men saw fit to embark in the expedition. I should suppose that Lord Lovat must have been a constant reader of the *Mercury*.

Wednesday, October 16.—' On Monday last, Monseigneur de Boyer, a French person of quality, arrived at the palace of Holyrood House with dispatches from the court of Versailles. He has brought with him a great quantity of arms, ammunition, money, &c.

' Yesternight, the Right Honourable Lord Lewis Gordon, third son of the deceased Alexander, Duke of Gordon, came and kissed the Prince's hand, and joined his Royal Highness's standard. His lordship was some time an officer in the navy. The court, which was very numerous and splendid, seemed in great joy on this occasion, as several gentlemen, not only of the name of Gordon, but many others in the shires of Aberdeen, Banff, and Murray, who had declined joining the Prince's standard, unless some one or other of the sons of the illustrious house of Gordon was to head them, will now readily come up and join the army.'

Monday, October 21.—' Friday last, at one afternoon, a woman was observed by the sentinels on duty at the park of artillery near Holyrood House, carrying, as they believed, dinner to some of the guard; under which colour she actually got past the outer sentinels, and even made an attempt to get by the inner sentinels; but, being pushed back, she stept to the south-east wall of the park, and actually got upon it, though the sentinels called out and fired upon her. She was immediately apprehended, and there were found upon her several combustible affairs. The people asking what business she had within the artillery ground, where so much powder was, with her straw, fagots, &c., she only answered that she believed it was a churchyard, and pretended to be delirious. It is assured that two suspicious-looking fellows were at the same time seen stepping over the easter wall of the park, but that they unhappily escaped by the surprise everybody was in.'

Monday, October 28.—' Saturday last, his Royal Highness the Prince reviewed the Macdonells of Glengarry at Musselburgh; they made a most noble appearance.'

Besides innumerable paragraphs of local news, calculated more or less to favour the Chevalier's enterprise, Grant inserted in his paper a detailed account, compiled from the records of parliament, of the Massacre of Glencoe; also a life of Viscount Dundee, and some letters by the Duke of Berwick, lauding the conduct of Prince Charles at the siege of Gaeta —the whole tending to throw infamy upon the Whigs, and lustre on the Cavaliers. It is worthy of remark, that, after the accession of several Lowland gentlemen, the position of the insurgent army is always termed the *Scots* Camp, probably to give it a more national and respectable appearance in print.

CHAPTER XV.

INVASION OF ENGLAND.

> 'Cock up your beaver, and cock it fu' sprush,
> We 'll over the Border and gie them a brush ;
> There 's somebody there we 'll teach better behaviour—
> Hey, brave Johnnie lad, cock up your beaver.'
> *Old Song.*

THE closing days of October saw Charles in possession of an army of between 5000 and 6000 men, with a small park of artillery, and abundance of arms and ammunition, while still further reinforcements were preparing for him in the north, though not likely to join immediately. At the same time large bodies of troops were collecting against him in England, and even in the north of Scotland. In such circumstances, it would have been difficult for the most prudent head to say what step ought to be taken. Charles, who had had no maxim in the business but that the nearer he could advance to the seat of government the better, determined for the most vigorous course, and surprised his council one day by the announcement that he designed to march for Newcastle, and give battle to Marshal Wade, who, he was convinced, would fly before him. The proposal was combated by the more cautious of his friends, but ultimately agreed to.

Orders were now therefore given to call in all the various parties which had been posted in different parts of the country, and the Chevalier held a final review of his whole force upon the beach betwixt Leith and Musselburgh,[1] now known by the name of Portobello Sands.

During the latter half of October the army had not lain at

---

[1] Boyse's *History*, 95.

Duddingston, but in more comfortable lodgings within and around the city. On the 26th, the main body left Edinburgh, and pitched a camp a little to the west of Inveresk church, where they had a battery pointing to the south-west. At a still later period of the month they removed to a strong situation above Dalkeith, having that town on their left, the South Esk in front, the North Esk in rear, and an opening on the right towards Polton.[1]

At six o'clock on the evening of Thursday the 31st of October, Prince Charles finally left the palace and capital of his paternal kingdom, and, accompanied by his life-guards, rode to Pinkie House. Having slept there that night, he rode next day at noon to Dalkeith, where he gave orders for the march of his army. In order to deceive Marshal Wade as to the point in which he designed to invade England, he had previously sent orders for quarters to all the towns upon the road to Berwick, and despatched little detachments of his men in various other directions. His actual resolution was to enter England by the western border, at once with the view of eluding the army at Newcastle, and that he might gather the troops which he expected to come to his standard in Lancashire and Wales, which were unusually well affected. He now also appointed his principal officers—the Duke of Perth and Lord George Murray to be lieutenant-generals, Lord Elcho colonel of the life-guards, the Earl of Kilmarnock colonel of the hussars, and Lord Pitsligo colonel of the Angus horse.

The army was at this time in the best possible condition, and provided with all the conveniences which could attend a deliberate campaign. The men were fresh, by their long rest at Edinburgh, well clothed and well appointed; they carried with them provisions for four days: and their baggage was promptly transported, by about 150 wains, and as many sumpter-horses,[2] carrying large baskets across their backs.

At the commencement of this singular march, the insurgents

[1] Merchant's *Hist. Reb.*, p. 127.
[2] They had pressed 800 horses into their service out of the county of Mid-Lothian alone.

amounted in gross numbers to 6000, 500 of whom were cavalry; and 3000 Highlanders. Thirteen regiments, many of them very small, were composed of the Highland clans; five regiments, generally more numerous, of Lowlanders; and besides the two troops of horse-guards, who wore a uniform, and were commanded by Lords Elcho and Balmerino, there were bodies of horse under the orders of Kilmarnock and Pitsligo, the first coarsely dressed and indifferently armed, and the last clothed in the ordinary fashion of country-gentlemen, each armed with such weapons as he pleased to carry, or could most readily command. A small body of the lighter horse was selected to scour the country for intelligence.[1]

The Highland regiments were commanded by their chiefs, and generally officered by the kinsmen of that dignitary, according as they were near of kin. Each regiment had two captains,

[1] The following list will convey a more distinct view of the Highland army, as constituted at this interesting period. It is from the *Life of the Duke of Cumberland*. 8vo. London, 1767.

CLAN REGIMENTS, AND THEIR COMMANDERS.

Locheil—Cameron of Locheil.................................700
Appin—Stuart of Ardshiel..................................200
Clanranald—Macdonald [younger] of Clanranald..............300
Keppoch—Macdonald of Keppoch..............................200
Kinlochmoidart—Macdonald of Kinlochmoidart................100
Glencoe—Macdonald of Glencoe..............................120
Mackinnon—Mackinnon of Mackinnon..........................120
Macpherson—Macpherson of Cluny............................120
Glengarry—Macdonell of Glengarry..........................300
Glenbucket—Gordon of Glenbucket...........................300
Maclachlan—Maclachlan of that ilk.........................260
Struan—Robertson of Struan................................200
Glenmorriston—Grant of Glenmorriston......................100

                                                        2960

LOWLAND REGIMENTS.

Athole—Lord George Murray.................................600
Ogilvie—Lord Ogilvie, Angus men...........................900
Perth—Duke of Perth.......................................700
Nairn—Lord Nairn..200
Edinburgh—Roy Stuart......................................450

HORSE.

Lord Elcho and Lord Balmerino.............................120
Lord Pitsligo.. 80
Earl of Kilmarnock... 60

two lieutenants, and two ensigns. The front rank of the regiments was filled by men of good birth, who in the Highlands, however poor in fortune, are styled gentlemen, and who had for pay one shilling a day, while that of the ordinary men was only sixpence. The pay of the captains was half-a-crown, of the lieutenants two shillings, of the ensigns one shilling and sixpence. Each of the gentlemen of the front rank was completely armed, in the fashion of the Highlanders, with a musket, a broadsword, a pair of pistols, a dirk at the belt, to which were also attached a knife and fork; the left arm sustained a round target, made of wood and leather, and studded with nails; and some who chose to be armed with extraordinary care, besides the dagger at the belt, carried a smaller one stuck into the garter of the right leg, which they could use in certain situations, when the other was beyond their reach. The undistinguished warriors of the rear ranks were in general armed in a much inferior manner, many of them wanting targets.

On the evening of Friday the 1st of November, a considerable portion of the army, under the command of Lord George Murray, took the road for Peebles, intending to proceed to Carlisle by Moffat. The remainder left Dalkeith on the 3d, the Prince walking at their head, with his target over his shoulder. He had previously lodged two nights in the palace of the Duke of Buccleuch. This party took a route more directly south, affecting a design of meeting and fighting Marshal Wade at Newcastle. On passing this morning by Prestonhall gate, the Prince found breakfast prepared for him there by order of the Duchess of Gordon, the lady of the neighbouring mansion; for which act of hospitality her Grace lost a pension of £1000, which the government had bestowed upon her in consideration of her bringing up her family in the Protestant religion.[1] In like manner, as he passed Fala Dams, the ladies of Whitburgh, sisters of his valuable adherent Robert Anderson, gave him and his immediate attendants a refection in the open air; after

[1] Tradition.

which, in compliance with their request for a keepsake, he cut for them a piece of velvet from the hilt of his sword. Passing over Soutra Hill, he concluded the first day's march at Lauder, where he took up his quarters in Thirlstane Castle, the seat of the Earl of Lauderdale. Next day, on account of a false report that there was a strong body of dragoons advancing in this direction to meet him, he fell back upon Channelkirk, in order to bring up the rear of his troops, who had lingered there during the night. He marched that day (the 4th) to Kelso, walking all the way on foot, in order to encourage the men. A third party assumed a middle course, by Galashiels, Selkirk, Hawick, and Mosspaul.

The western division, which had charge of the cannon and most of the baggage, arrived at Peebles on the evening of Saturday the 2d of November. The sun was setting as the first lines devolved from the hills which environ the place on every side, and, throwing back a thousand threatening glances from the arms of the moving band, caused alarm among the peaceful townsmen, who had only heard enough about the insurrection and its agents to make them fear the worst from such a visit. Contrary to expectation, the mountaineers neither attempted to cut the throats nor to violate the property of the inhabitants. They let it be known, wherever they went, that they required certain acts of obedience on the part of the people; and that, if these were not willingly rendered, they had the will, as they possessed the power, of using force. The leader demanded payment of the cess, on pain of military execution; and little parties, calling upon various householders within and without the town, requested such supplies of provisions as could be properly spared, with the alternative of having their houses given up to plunder. But scarcely any incivility was ever shewn in the outset.[1]

This division of the insurgents, after spending a day or two at Peebles, went up Tweedsmuir to Moffat, and then, directing their route down Annandale, entered England near Longtown.

[1] Tradition at Peebles.

Charles remained at Kelso from the Monday when he arrived till Wednesday, preserving the further direction of his march a secret. In order the better to perplex the army which awaited him at Newcastle, he sent orders to Wooler, a town upon the road to that city, commanding the preparation of quarters for his whole army. On Wednesday morning, however, he suddenly gave out orders for a march towards the opposite extremity of the Border.

During his brief residence at Kelso, he sent a party of about thirty men down the Tweed, to the place, not far distant, where that river becomes the boundary of the two kingdoms, with orders there to cross the water, and proclaim his father upon English ground. The party, after doing so, immediately returned to Kelso.

The Prince lodged this night in Jedburgh, whence he set out early next morning,[1] and, crossing the high grounds to the south-west, led his men up Rule Water, famed of old for its hardy warriors, and over the *Knot o' the Gate* into Liddesdale, equally noted in former times for its predatory bands, as in more recent times for its primitive yeomen and romantic minstrelsy. After a march of at least twenty-five miles, he slept that night at Haggiehaugh, upon Liddel Water, his men lodging upon the ground, or in the houses, barns, and byres of the neighbouring peasantry. Before going to rest, he purchased a small flock of sheep for provisions to his men, and had a person sent for to kill and dress them. Charles Scott, a neighbouring farmer, more commonly called, in the fashion of that country, *Charlie o' Kirnton*, was the man employed for this purpose. He was up all night killing sheep, and the Prince next morning

---

[1] When the author was at Jedburgh, in November 1826, he saw an ancient lady who had been seven years of age when the Highlanders passed her native town, and who distinctly remembered all the circumstances of the memorable pageant. According to her report, they had a great number of horses, which it was said they had taken from the dragoons at Preston. She saw some of them dressing these animals in a stable, and could mimic the strange uncouth jabber which they used in performing the duties of hostlers. In particular, she remembers hearing them call to the beasts: 'Stand about, Cope!' &c. As at many other places, Charles was here saluted with marks of homage by many of the people as he passed, all the women running out to get a kiss of his hand, &c.

gave him half a guinea for his trouble. Two Highlanders, who had observed Charlie receive this guerdon, followed him as he was going home, and clapping their pistols to his breast, demanded an instant surrender of 'ta hauf keenie;' a command which the yeoman was obliged to obey, for fear of the pistols, though his strength and resolution, celebrated to this day as far surpassing those of modern men, would have enabled him to defy double the number of assailants unprovided with such weapons.[1]

Next day, Friday the 8th of November, Charles proceeded down Liddel Water; and the middle column, which had marched by Selkirk, Hawick, and down Ewesdale, came up to him at Gritmill Green, upon the banks of the Esk, four miles below Langholm. When the first division soon after entered England, they raised a loud shout, and unsheathed their swords; but some grew pale when informed that Locheil, in drawing his weapon, had cut his hand, this being looked on as an evil omen. The Prince took up his quarters for the night at Reddings, in Cumberland. On the succeeding day he was joined by the western column.

During this march the Highland army lost a great portion of its numbers by desertion. The eastern column, led by Charles himself, suffered most from this cause. The Lanarkshire and Stirlingshire roads are described as having for some days swarmed with the men who thus abandoned the standard;[2] and great quantities of arms were found lying in the fields adjacent to the line of march, which the deserters had flung away.[3]

On the 9th of November, Charles, having concentrated his forces, approached Carlisle—a city which could once boast of being the bulwark of England against the Scots in this direction, but whose fortifications were now antiquated, and not in the best order. Less pains had been taken on the present occasion to fortify the cities in the west of England than those upon the east; and while Newcastle and Hull had been for many weeks

---

[1] Tradition in Liddesdale. [2] *Edin. Courant* for the time. [3] Tradition at Peebles.

prepared to resist the insurgents, Carlisle was invested only four or five days after having first apprehended danger. It was protected by an ancient castle, in which there was a company of invalids; and the city itself was surrounded by an old and somewhat dilapidated wall, manned on the present occasion by the citizens, assisted by a considerable body of militia, which had been raised in the counties of Cumberland and Westmoreland.

On the 9th, a party of the Prince's hussars appeared on Stanwix Bank, and began to survey the city through glasses: but a few shots being fired at them from the walls, they were obliged to retire. Next day the insurgent army having passed the river Eden by several fords, invested the city on all sides; and the Prince sent a letter to the mayor, requiring him to surrender peaceably, in order to spare the effusion of blood, which must be the inevitable consequence of a refusal. The mayor, who was very confident, and had published an advertisement informing the world that he was not Paterson, a Scotchman, but Pattison, a loyal-hearted Englishman, answered by a discharge of cannon at the besiegers. Intelligence soon after reaching the Prince that Marshal Wade was marching from Newcastle to relieve Carlisle, he judged it proper to advance against that general, in order to engage the royal army in the mountainous country which intervenes betwixt the two towns. Leaving a small portion of his army to annoy Carlisle, he reached Warwick Castle at ten o'clock in the forenoon of the 11th, and quartered next night at Brampton and the adjacent villages.[1] He then learned that the information regarding Wade was false, and sent back the Duke of Perth, with several regiments of foot and some troops of horse, to prosecute the siege of Carlisle with all possible vigour.

Having prepared a quantity of ladders, fascines, and carriages out of the wood in Corby and Warwick parks, the besieging party reappeared in full force before the city on the afternoon

[1] Home's *History*.

of the 13th, and broke ground for a battery within forty fathoms of the walls, the Duke of Perth and Lord George Murray working in the trenches without their coats, in order to encourage the troops. The garrison of the city kept up a continual firing during these operations, but without doing much harm. Next day, intimidated by the formidable appearance of the enemy's works, and fatigued almost beyond their natural strength by several nights of ceaseless watching, they felt disposed to resign the city; and accordingly, on the first motion of the besiegers towards an assault, Pattison the Englishman was fain to display a white flag from the walls, and ask terms for the surrender of the town. A cessation of hostilities being then agreed upon, an express was sent to Brampton, to learn the Prince's pleasure; who, remembering the example of Edinburgh, would assign no terms for the city unless the castle were included. This being reported to the garrison, Colonel Durand, the commander of that fortress, consented to surrender his charge along with the city. At ten o'clock in the morning of the 15th the gates of Carlisle were thrown open, and many a brave man passed with a rejoicing heart beneath the arches over which his head was hereafter to be stationed in dismal sentinelship. The Duke of Perth, on receiving the submission of the garrison, shook them by the hands, told them they were brave fellows, and asked them to enlist in his service. He secured all the arms of the militia and garrison, besides about 1000 stand in the castle, with 200 good horses. A great quantity of valuables, which had been deposited there for safety by the neighbouring gentry, fell likewise into his hands; but these are said to have been returned to their owners. Next day the old Chevalier and his son were proclaimed at the cross, in presence of the mayor and aldermen, and a new document was at the same time read, under the title of a 'Declaration of the King's Majesty to his English Subjects.' Charles was not personally received with much favour in Carlisle, but his taking a town of such consequence, after so brief a siege, gave some lustre to his arms, and increased the fears of the government.

The short time spent by the army at Carlisle was marked by some rather important dissensions among the principal officers. According to Maxwell of Kirkconnel, the origin of these was with Secretary Murray, who aimed at exercising an exclusive influence over the Prince, and disliked Lord George Murray as the rival he had most reason to dread. He had gained over Sheridan, O'Sullivan, and the Duke of Perth (the last from easy-judging good nature) to support him. When Lord George, before the blockade of Carlisle, requested to be charged by the Prince with the terms he was inclined to grant to the town, Secretary Murray told him sharply that that was a matter within his province, and with which Lord George had no right to interfere. When Lord George afterwards saw the Duke of Perth take the chief command at the siege, the measure of his dissatisfaction was filled. He immediately (on the 15th) sent a resignation of his commission to the Prince, stating that he would henceforth act as a volunteer, and would that night take his place as such in the trenches. In a letter of the same date to his brother Tullibardine, he assigns the causes above stated for his resolution, adding, in the spirit of a true partisan and genuine Highlander: 'I shall shew as a volunteer that no man wishes more success to the cause; and I can be of more use charging in the first rank of your Athole men, than as a general, where I was constantly at a loss to know what was doing.' The Duke of Perth no sooner heard of the step taken by Lord George, than he also sent in his resignation as lieutenant-general, avowing his intention thenceforward to serve at the head of his own regiment. There might be fretfulness, or something worse, in Lord George's motives, but those of Perth, who was of prior appointment as a lieutenant-general, and therefore formally entitled to take the chief command at the siege, could not but be pure. Yet the army, while generally liking the Duke of Perth, had a higher opinion of the talents and experience of Lord George Murray as a commander, and when they heard of his resignation of his commission, a very general wish was expressed that he should resume it, while no such feeling was avowed with respect to the duke. Most of them had, in fact, another and strong reason for desiring that Perth should not be conspicuous either in command of the army or at the Prince's councils. His being a Catholic was already the subject of much unfavourable remark in the public journals, and seemed calculated to injure their prospects very seriously in England. There were even ante-revolution laws which made him ineligible as a councillor. They therefore presented a petition to the Prince, with one breath requesting him to reinstate Lord George Murray, and to dismiss Roman Catholics from his councils. Charles instantly complied with the first request, but, from the spirit of courtesy and gratitude, hesitated about the second. Some difficulty seemed likely to arise on that point, when the duke himself, learning what was the opinion of the army, put all to rights by informing the Prince that he was quite happy, for the sake of what was thought the good of the cause, to serve without a general's commission. Henceforth, Lord George Murray held the chief command in the army.

On the day after the reduction of Carlisle, Marshal Wade commenced a march from Newcastle; but hearing of the success of the insurgents, and being unable to cross the country on account of a great fall of snow, his excellency found it necessary to return to that city on the 22d.

More effectual means were now taken by the king to suppress what was generally styled 'the unnatural rebellion.' Before the Scottish army set foot on English ground, the mass of the British troops had landed at London from Flanders; and while the Prince was residing in Carlisle, an army of 10,000 troops, chiefly veteran and experienced, was rendezvoused in Staffordshire to oppose him. It seemed scarcely possible that he should either elude or vanquish so strong a force; and even the Highlanders themselves, with all their valour, real and adventitious, had little hope of doing so. In order, moreover, that the fate of the empire should not be perilled on such a chance, another army was raised for the protection of London, which the king was resolved to command in person. Charles himself was not intimidated by these great preparations, which he trusted to overcome by the vigour of his measures, and by the assistance which he expected in England. But the greater part of his council viewed the government proceedings with alarm.

At a council of war held a few days after the surrender of Carlisle, various movements were proposed and taken under consideration. It was proposed to march to Newcastle, and bring Wade's army to an action. It was proposed to march directly to London, by the Lancashire road, at the hazard of encountering the superior force mustered in Staffordshire. A third proposal urged an immediate retreat to Scotland, as there seemed no appearance of either a French invasion or an English insurrection. Charles declared his wish to march to London at all hazards, and desired Lord George Murray to give his opinion of the various proposals. Lord George spoke at some length, compared the advantages and disadvantages of each of the proposals, and concluded that, if his Royal Highness chose to make a trial of what could be done by a march to the southward, he was persuaded that his army, small as it was, would follow him. Charles instantly decided for the march.

Before proceeding, Charles sent Maclachlan of Maclachlan back to Scotland with a letter to Lord Strathallan, whom he had left at Perth commander-in-chief of his forces in Scotland, ordering him to march, with all the troops he might have collected, after the army into England. Meanwhile, he received some discouraging intelligence from the north. No sooner had he vacated Edinburgh, than it had returned under Whig domination; and even at Dundee and Perth, where he had considerable bodies of troops stationed, there had been outbreaks of popular feeling in behalf of the government.

Thirty baggage-wagons, in which were the tents for the army, had been left behind at Lockerby, through the eagerness of those in charge to get forward to the siege of Carlisle. These were seized on the 14th by a large party of people from Dumfries, and carried in triumph to that town. Charles sent Locheil to reclaim the property, or £2000 in lieu of it; but before either object could be accomplished, he had to recall the party to join the army on its march to the south. Owing to the want of tents and the severity of the weather (the 20th of November, old style, was in reality the 1st of December), it was necessary to arrange the march in such a way as to get the army accommodated in the towns along the road. It was determined that one portion of the army should march a day's journey ahead of the other, the latter always occupying at night the quarters which the former had vacated in the morning; but that, where the country would admit of it, there should be only half a day's march betwixt the two bodies.[1]

The army, on being mustered at Carlisle, was found to amount to about 4500, a full thousand having dropped away in the march from Edinburgh. Yet Charles had no doubt that it would soon be largely increased by the accession of his English friends. On the 21st, the first detachment of the army, consisting of five of the Low-country regiments, with Elcho's life-guards, under Lord George Murray, marched to Penrith. Next day, while these went forward to Kendal, the clan regiments, and the remainder of the horse, under the Prince in person, proceeded to Penrith, leaving 150 men as a garrison in Carlisle. The cannon followed the second division, under the care of the Duke of Perth's regiment.[2] In both divisions, each regiment had the van by turns. Thus they advanced by Shap, Kendal, Lancaster, and Garstang, to Preston, where the two divisions joined on the 27th. To encourage his men, Charles generally went on foot beside them. As he passed over the desolate tract between Penrith and Shap, he was so much overcome by fatigue and want of sleep, that he found it necessary to take hold of one of the clan Ogilvie by the shoulder-belt, to prevent him from falling; and he thus walked several miles half asleep.[3] As yet, they had observed nothing but marks of aversion and

---

[1] Maxwell's *Narrative*.   [2] Home's *History*.
[3] Information by a Scottish bishop, who has conversed with the proud Ogilvie whose shoulder was thus honoured.

suspicion amongst the English people. Their political object seemed to excite no sympathy; their uncouth dress, language, and habits spread terror before their march. It is credibly affirmed that many of the women hid their children at their approach, under an impression that they were cannibals, fond, in particular, of the flesh of infants.[1] Everywhere there was great surprise that these men, so far from acting like savage robbers, expressed a polite gratitude for what refreshments were given them. The Highlanders every day began their painful march before daybreak, with no provisions but what they carried in the shape of oatmeal, in a long bag by their sides, and which they never cooked, but merely mixed, before eating, with a canteen full of cold water—trusting for any variety in this simple cheer to the accident of a bullock killed for their use, or to the hospitality of their landlords at night. The English were amazed to find that men could, upon this fare, walk from twenty to thirty miles in a winter day, exposed to bitter cold and tempestuous weather, with what appeared to them imperfect clothing, or rather rags; and that, though generally housed some hours after sunset, they invariably rose very early to prosecute their march, taking advantage of the moonlight, which then shone in the mornings before daybreak.

At Preston, for the first time, did a slight gleam of approbation rest on the cause. The bells were rung at their

---

[1] 'The terror of the English was truly inconceivable, and in many cases they seemed bereft of their senses. One evening, as Mr Cameron of Locheil entered the lodgings assigned him, his landlady, an old woman, threw herself at his feet, and with uplifted hands, and tears in her eyes, supplicated him to take her life, but to spare her two little children. He asked her if she was in her senses, and told her to explain herself; when she answered, that *everybody said the Highlanders ate children, and made them their common food.* Mr Cameron having assured her that they would not injure either her or her little children, or any person whatever, she looked at him for some moments with an air of surprise, and then opened a press, calling out with a loud voice: " Come out, children; the gentleman will not eat you." The children immediately left the press, where she had concealed them, and threw themselves at his feet.'—*Johnstone's Memoirs*, p. 101.

In a letter from Derby, which made the round of the journals, the writer describes the ferocity and filthiness of the troop which was quartered upon him, with extravagant expressions of disgust. He allows, however, that he was amused a good deal to see them, before meat, take off their bonnets, assume a reverent air, and say grace, 'as if they had been Christians.'

entry, probably by the intervention of the Catholics, who abounded in the town. Some huzzas attended the reading of the proclamations, and a few recruits were obtained. Mr Townley, a Catholic gentleman, here joined the standard, being the first man of distinction who had done so in England. A council of war was held, at which the Prince, ever eager, like his ancestor Bruce, to 'go on,' renewed his assurances of English and French assistance, and thereby prevailed on the chiefs to continue their southward march. The clansmen had a superstitious dread, in consequence of the misfortunes of their party at Preston in 1715, that they would never get beyond this town: to dispel the illusion, Lord George Murray crossed the Ribble, and quartered a number of men on the other side.

On the 28th, the whole army left Preston, and, quartering for the night at Wigan, advanced on the ensuing day to Manchester. This town, now so remarkable for a reforming spirit, contained, in 1745, a larger proportion of the adherents of legitimacy than perhaps any other in England. Here, therefore, it might be expected that Charles would have a good reception, and obtain large reinforcements, if he was anywhere to be so fortunate in his southward march.

One Dickson, a sergeant enlisted into the Highland army from the prisoners taken at Prestonpans, having got more than a day's march ahead of the rest, entered Manchester on the morning of the 28th, attended by his mistress and a drummer. The adventure was entirely an idea of his own, and even contrary to the orders of his superior officer. Within an hour of his arrival he began to beat up for recruits. The populace did not at first interrupt him, conceiving that the whole army was near the town; but when they learned that no part of it could be expected till the evening, they surrounded him in a tumultuous manner, with the intention of taking him prisoner. Dickson presented his blunderbuss, which was charged with slugs, threatening to blow out the brains of those who first dared to lay hands on himself or the two who accompanied him; and by turning round continually, facing in all directions, and behaving like a lion, he soon enlarged the circle which a crowd of people had formed around him. Having continued for some time to manœuvre in this way, those of the inhabitants of Manchester who were attached to the house of Stuart took arms, and flew to the assistance of Dickson, to rescue him from the fury of the mob; so that he had soon 500 or 600 men to aid him, who dispersed the crowd in a very short time. He now triumphed in his turn, and, putting himself at the head of his followers, proudly paraded, undisturbed, the whole day with his drummer, enlisting all who offered themselves. The number of his levies has been differently stated. The Chevalier Johnstone says he obtained 180 recruits; but another authority says only thirty, 'to each of whom a white cockade was given, and a bounty of five guineas promised.'[1]

About nine o'clock that night, the vanguard, consisting of about 100 horsemen, arrived in Manchester; and next day the whole army came up. The Prince entered at two in the afternoon, walking in the midst of a select band of Highlanders; his dress a light tartan plaid, belted with a blue sash, a gray wig, and a blue velvet bonnet, topped by a rose of white ribbons, the badge of his house. He took up his quarters in a handsome house in Market Street, belonging to a gentleman named Dickenson—afterwards, from that circumstance, called 'The Palace,' and long after used as an inn.[2] A local writer has given a sufficiently minute account of what happened at Manchester on this and the following day. ' In the course of the day [the 29th], the public crier was sent round the town to require that all persons who had any duties to pay, or any public money in their hands, should pay the amount into the hands of Secretary Murray, at the palace, taking the receipt of this officer as their discharge. As evening approached, the bellman was again despatched to announce that there would that night be an illumination in honour of the arrival of the Prince. The illumination accordingly took place, bonfires were made, and the

[1] *Manchester Gazette*, January 19, 1828.
[2] The house has for some years been replaced by a new building.

bells rung joyfully; but the treasury was not much replenished, till a peremptory demand was made upon the inhabitants. Many of the communications at the headquarters were made with the intervention of a green silk curtain, which was suspended in the room of audience, and through which, it is said, even the master of the house, from prudential motives, communicated with his guest without seeing him. The borough-reeve, James Waller of Ridgefield, Esq., was made the reluctant organ for communicating the proclamations of the rebel army to the people; but the Rev. Mr Clayton celebrated, in strains of eloquence, the arrival of the Prince in the collegiate church, for which act of disaffection to the reigning sovereign he was afterwards degraded. A young clergyman, of the name of Coppoch, lately from the university, received the appointment of chaplain to the Prince.[1]

On the 30th, the whole of the rebel army, with the artillery and baggage, consisting of sixteen pieces of cannon, a number of covered wagons, and about one hundred laden horses, were assembled in the town and neighbourhood of Manchester. The recruiting service went on briskly, and from 200 to 300 young men, chiefly of the lower class, were dignified with the name of the Manchester regiment, of which Francis Townley, Esq., was appointed commander. Thomas Theodorus Deacon, Charles Deacon, and Robert Deacon, the sons of a nonjuring minister, catching the contagion of disloyalty, became officers in this corps; and George Fletcher, a linendraper in Salford; James Dawson, of St John's College, Cambridge, son of Mr Dawson of Manchester; and John Beswick, a linendraper in Manchester, were placed in the rank of captains. Thomas Chadwick, bred a tallow-chandler, was appointed lieutenant; and Thomas Syddall, the son of the peruke-maker who was executed for taking part in the rebellion of 1715, was appointed adjutant. Both officers and men wore white cockades, and the authority of the colonel was indicated by the addition of a tartan sash.

---

[1] Common rumour represented this young man as the rebel Bishop of Carlisle, as if the Prince had nominated him to that see. No such appointment ever took place.

The other officers had each a broadsword by his side, and a brace of pistols in his girdle. Before the Manchester regiment entered upon their campaign, they had the honour to be reviewed by their Prince the young Chevalier; and Colonel Townley, as if foreseeing their destiny, selected the churchyard for the field of review. The contributions levied upon the town amounted to £3000, and many of the horses within reach were put into requisition either to mount the cavalry or to convey the baggage. The conduct of the Highlanders was in some instances rapacious, wasteful, and offensive; but in general the troops conducted themselves with moderation, and the behaviour of their officers was conciliatory, and even courteous.[1]

An impression had prevailed that the Highland army might march into Wales, a country in which they could act with advantage as irregular troops, and where their cause was understood to have many friends. The bridges over the Mersey, on the way to Chester, had therefore been broken down, to impede their progress. This precaution proved unnecessary.

On the 1st of December, the army left Manchester in two divisions, one of which took the road to Stockport, the other that to Knottesford, thus shewing that London was their object. The bridges had been broken down in this direction also; the army had therefore to cross the Mersey by other means.[2] At Knottesford, a temporary bridge was made of the trunks of

[1] From a paper entitled 'The Highland Army in Manchester in 1745,' which appeared in the *Manchester Gazette*, January 19, 1828.

[2] While at Manchester, Charles published the following curious proclamation, for a copy of which I have been indebted to the kindness of an inhabitant of that town. The sneer at good old *Grandmother Wade*, who, according to the Jacobite punster, could not *wade* through the snow, will scarcely fail to be relished:

'TO THE INHABITANTS OF MANCHESTER.

'His Royal Highness being informed that several bridges have been pulled down in this country, he has given orders to repair them forthwith, particularly that at Crossford, which is to be done this night by his own troops, though his Royal Highness does not propose to make use of it for his own army, but believes it will be of service to the country; and if any forces that were with General Wade be coming this road, *they may have the benefit of it.*

'MANCHESTER, *Nov.* 30, 1745.'

poplar-trees, laid lengthwise, with planks across. The horse and artillery passed at Cheadleford. The Prince, with the other detachment, crossed at Stockport, having the water up to his middle. Here a romantic circumstance is said to have taken place. A few gentlemen of Cheshire had drawn up on the south bank of the river to welcome the Prince on his crossing the river, and among them was a Mrs Skyring, a lady in extreme old age. 'As a child, she had been lifted up in her mother's arms to view the happy landing at Dover of Charles II. Her father, an old cavalier, had afterwards to undergo not merely neglect, but oppression, from that thankless monarch; still, however, he and his wife continued devoted to the royal cause, and their daughter grew up as devoted as they. After the expulsion of the Stuarts, all her thoughts, her hopes, her prayers, were directed to another restoration. Ever afterwards she had, with rigid punctuality, laid aside one-half of her yearly income, to remit for the exiled family abroad; concealing only, what she said was of no importance to them, the name of the giver. She had now parted with her jewels, her plate, and every little article of value she possessed, the price of which, in a purse, she laid at the feet of Prince Charles, while, straining her dim eyes to gaze on his features, and pressing his hand to her shrivelled lips, she exclaimed with affectionate rapture, in the words of Simeon: " Lord, now lettest thou thy servant depart in peace!" It is added that she did not survive the shock, when, a few days afterwards, she was informed of the retreat. Such, even when misdirected in its object, or exaggerated in its force, was the old spirit of loyalty in England!'[1]

In the evening (December 1), the two divisions joined at Macclesfield, where Charles received intelligence that the Duke of Cumberland had taken command of the army mustered in Staffordshire,[2] which was now on its march, and quartered at

[1] *History of Great Britain*, by Lord Mahon, who states that he derived the anecdote from the late Lord Keith.
[2] The Duke of Cumberland left London on the 25th, and superseded Sir John Ligonier in the command of the army.

Lichfield, Coventry, Stafford, and Newcastle-under-Lyne. It was resolved that the Highland army should march to Derby. To deceive the enemy as to this design, Lord George Murray proceeded with a column to Congleton, on the straight road to Lichfield, while the rest advanced to Derby. It was calculated that the English commander, hearing of a body on the march towards his present position, would concentrate his forces and his attention there, and thus allow the main body of the Highland forces to pass beyond him uninterrupted. As Lord George advanced to Congleton, the Duke of Kingston, in command of a body of horse, retired from that town to Newcastle-under-Lyne. An advanced party of Lord George's men, under Colonel Ker, went forward at night (December 2) towards Newcastle-under-Lyne, whence the dragoons broke up with great precipitation, some of them escaping through windows. This party seized one Weir, a noted spy, who was only saved from hanging by the clemency of the Prince.[1] The effect of these movements, and of the false intelligence given out, was exactly what had been expected. The duke, at Stafford (December 2), received intelligence that a large body of the insurgents were at Congleton, and that the rest were to be there at night. He therefore proceeded that night *at eleven o'clock* to Stone, thus allowing the main body of the Highlanders to get past him. Early in the morning of the 3d, having effected his design, Lord George left Congleton, and passing through Leek, reached Ashbourne in the evening.

Some hours after he had passed Leek, the Prince, with the main body of the army, arrived there, being on the straight road to Derby. At midnight, the latter party set out from Leek, and reached Ashbourne early in the morning, in order that any sudden attack from the Duke of Cumberland might find them all together. Early on the 4th, a portion of the army proceeded to Derby, which they entered at eleven in the forenoon. About three, Lord Elcho came in with the life-guards and some of the

[1] Maxwell of Kirkconnel.

principal officers on horseback, 'making a very respectable appearance.' The main body of the army continued to enter in small detachments during all the latter part of the day (to convey, as was supposed, an impression of the greatness of their numbers), with bagpipes playing and colours unfurled;[1] and in the evening the Prince arrived on foot, and took up his quarters in the house of the Earl of Exeter. During the day the bells were rung, and bonfires lighted, and there was an illumination (how far voluntary is not stated) at night. The magistrates were ordered to attend the proclamations in their official gowns; but when it was known that they had sent these away beforehand, their attendance was excused, and the proclamations were made by the common crier.

Charles was now within 127 miles—to him less than a week's march—of the capital of England. In consequence of the dexterous manœuvre of Lord George Murray, he could have advanced thither without fighting with the Duke of Cumberland, who was, on the 4th, returning from Stone to Stafford, where he was nine miles farther from London than the Chevalier, whom he could have had no hope of overtaking with infantry, supposing that Charles had been pleased to proceed immediately.[2] Two armies in succession had thus been eluded by the Highlanders—that of Wade, in consequence of the weather or the old marshal's inactivity,[3] and that of Cumberland, through the ingenuity of their own leaders. There remained yet a third army at Finchley Common; but it was not formidable in character or numbers, and probably might have failed to meet the clans in battle, if they had marched still onward. No invading band, since the days of the Saxon kings, had ever been allowed to advance so far and so threateningly into England; for though the Duke of Hamilton, in 1648, had got to Uttoxeter,

---

[1] Boyse, 104. Their colours were mostly white, with red crosses.
[2] The duke employed the 5th in marching to Lichfield, where he would have had some chance of intercepting the Highlanders, who had spent that day at Derby.
[3] Wade's army had now advanced from Newcastle into Yorkshire. It was at Wetherby on the 4th, and on the 5th was marching to Doncaster, the commander having then heard of the advance of the Highlanders into Derbyshire.

it was only with a small portion of an army broken to pieces a good way farther north.[1]

Hitherto the English people had entertained a very inadequate idea of the insurrection. If we are to judge from the tenor of the public journals, where the Highland army is invariably spoken of with contempt, both on physical and moral grounds, the English generally had not the most faint apprehension of the bold and generous spirit of self-devotion which prompted these men to leave their homes, and thus expose themselves not only to the perils of war, but the pains of treason, for the sake of a cause which, however mistakenly, they conceived to be that of justice and patriotism. The whole expedition of the Chevalier and his attendant bands seems to have been regarded as only an odd piece of mob-procedure, which a proper exertion of regular military force would put down. There even seems to have been some disposition to look upon it as a novel kind of show. The poet Gray writes from Cambridge: 'Here we had no more sense of danger than if it were the battle of Cannæ. I heard three sensible middle-aged men, when the Scotch were said to be at Stamford, and actually were at Derby, talking of hiring a chaise to go to Caxton, a place on the high-road [on the high-road, be it recollected, from Derby to London, from which it is only distant fifty miles], to see the Pretender and the Highlanders as they passed.' Much of the apprehension was no doubt owing to a line of policy assumed by the government party. It was thought equivalent to a profession of Jacobitism to speak in respectful terms of the Chevalier, his followers, or the strength of his army. This of course was a sword that cut two ways, for while it tended to keep down popular feeling in behalf of Charles, it also

---

[1] Swarkeston Bridge, six miles beyond Derby, on the road to London, was, in reality, the extreme point of this singular invasion, because the insurgents posted an advanced guard there, which kept possession of the pass till the retreat was determined on. No former host from Scotland penetrated beyond the Tees, or overran more than the frontier counties; but this last, and, it may be added, *least*, of all the armies Scotland ever sent against the Southron, had thus reached the Trent, traversed five counties in succession, and insulted the very centre of England.

favoured a feeling of security in the highest degree useful to him.

Now, however, the metropolis at least became strongly impressed with a sense of danger. When intelligence reached it that the Highlanders were getting past the Duke of Cumberland's army, and had reached Derby, consternation took possession of the inhabitants. Fielding, in his *True Patriot*, describes the degree of terror which prevailed as beyond all belief. The Chevalier Johnstone, speaking from information which he procured a few months afterwards on the spot, says that the shops were shut, many people fled to the country, taking with them their most precious effects, and the Bank only escaped insolvency by paying in sixpences to persons in its confidence, who, going out at one door, and returning at another, received the same money over and over again, and thus kept back the *bonâ fide* holders of notes. The ministers were perplexed. It has been alleged that the Duke of Newcastle, then one of the secretaries of state, shut himself up in his house for a day, deliberating whether he should not at once declare for the Stuarts. King George was said to have ordered his yachts, in which he had embarked his most valuable effects, to remain at the Tower stairs, in readiness to sail at a moment's warning. Perhaps some of these allegations were mere popular rumour, but they shew at least a degree of fear which must have been thought sufficient to render them credible. And, in truth, the danger, if danger it is to be called, was by no means inconsiderable, for not only was the Highland army within a few days' march, with little to oppose its progress, but there was a party in the city, including, it now appears, one of the aldermen (a Mr Heathcote), who were expected to make a public appearance in the same cause, and a French army was expected to land on the coast. The day of all this consternation was afterwards remembered under the expressive appellation of *Black Friday*.

CHAPTER XVI.

RETREAT TO SCOTLAND.

'The games are done, and Cæsar is returning.'
Julius Cæsar.

INTELLIGENCE reached the Prince at Derby of the arrival of Lord John Drummond, brother of the Duke of Perth, at Montrose with a body of French troops. A treaty had been entered into at Fontainebleau, on the 23d of October, between the Marquis d'Argenson on the part of Louis XV., and Colonel O'Brien on the part of Charles, Prince Regent of Scotland, agreeing that there should be friendship and alliance between the parties; that the king should aid the Prince Regent in every practicable way against their common enemy the Elector of Hanover; and that the king should furnish the Prince with a body of troops from his Irish regiments, along with other troops, 'to defend the provinces which had submitted, or should submit, to the regency, to attack the common enemy, and to follow every movement which should be judged useful or necessary.'[1] In consequence of this agreement, Lord John Drummond, who was a subject of France, embarked 1000 men about the middle of November at Dunkirk, together with a considerable quantity of stores and ammunition. Excepting a few transports taken by English cruisers, containing one or two hundred of the men, this little armament arrived in good order at Montrose near the end of November; and Drummond, on the 2d of December, published the following manifesto: 'We, Lord John Drummond, commander-in-chief of his most Christian Majesty's forces in Scotland, do hereby declare that we are come to this kingdom with written orders to make war against

[1] The whole treaty is printed from the Stuart Papers in the Appendix to Browne's *History of the Highlands.*

the king of England, Elector of Hanover, and his adherents; and that the positive orders we have from his most Christian Majesty are, to attack all his enemies in this kingdom, whom he has declared to be those who will not immediately join and assist, as far as will lie in their power, the Prince of Wales, Regent in Scotland, &c., and his ally; and whom he is resolved, with the concurrence of the king of Spain, to support in taking possession of Scotland, England, and Ireland, if necessary, at the expense of all the men and money he is master of; to which three kingdoms the family of Stuart have so just and indisputable a title. And his most Christian Majesty's positive orders are, that his enemies should be used in this kingdom in proportion to the harm they do or intend to his Royal Highness's cause.' Lord John, according to instructions he had received, lost no time in sending a messenger to Count Nassau, commander of the Dutch auxiliaries called over into England, requiring him to observe a neutrality, agreeably to the capitulations of Tournay and Dendermonde, by which they had agreed for a certain time not to fight against the king of France and his allies.

Immediately after the departure of Lord John Drummond from France, the ministers made serious preparations for a much larger armament, which they designed to have landed on the south coast of England. Ten thousand troops were mustered for this purpose, and Prince Henry Stuart, Charles's younger brother, was brought to Paris to accompany the expedition. Every preparation had been made; the king had taken leave of the young Prince, telling him that he would 'dine quietly in London on the 9th of January' (meaning the 29th of December, old style); and the plan was only abandoned when intelligence came of the retreat of the Highland army from Derby.[1] Had that army gone on, the French invasion would have taken place in time to support Charles in London, supposing that he had

[1] The concentration of the English fleet to oppose the intended invasion, allowed the French privateers to be unusually active. In the months of November and December, these marauders were calculated to have taken a hundred and sixty British vessels, valued at £660,000.

seized the government; and the Stuart dynasty must have been reinstated on the throne.

The morning of the 5th saw the Prince at Derby, eager to go forward on his march at all hazards, but hopeful that succours from France, and a rising of his English friends, would make it less dangerous than it appeared. The men in general were in high spirits, and very anxious to come to an engagement with the Duke of Cumberland's army. The common expectation was, that a battle was about to take place; and with this view there was a general sharpening of broadswords at the cutlers' shops, and some took the sacrament in the churches. Little was it thought that their leaders were about to resolve upon quite a contrary movement.

At a council of war held on the morning of the 5th, Lord George Murray and the other members gave it as their unanimous opinion that the army ought to return to Scotland. Lord George pointed out that they were about to be environed by three armies, amounting collectively to about 30,000 men, while their own forces were not above 5000, if so many. Supposing an unsuccessful engagement with any of those armies, it could not be expected that one man would escape, for the militia would beset every road. The Prince, if not slain in the battle, must fall into the enemy's hands. The whole world would blame them as fools for running into such a risk. Charles answered that he regarded not his own danger. He 'pressed with all the force of argument to go forward. He did not doubt,' he said, 'that the justice of his cause would prevail. He was hopeful there might be a defection in the enemy's army, and that many would declare for him. He was so very bent on putting all to the risk, that the Duke of Perth was for it, since his Royal Highness was. At last he proposed going to Wales, instead of returning to Carlisle; but every other officer declared his opinion for a retreat.' These are nearly the words of Lord George Murray;[1] we are elsewhere told that the Prince

---

[1] Narrative, *Jacobite Memoirs.*

condescended to use entreaties to induce his adherents to alter their resolution. 'Rather than go back,' he said, 'I could wish to be twenty feet underground!'[1] His chagrin, when he found his councillors obdurate, was beyond all bounds. The council broke up, in the understanding that the retreat was to commence next morning, Lord George volunteering to take the post of honour in the rear, provided only that he should not be troubled with the baggage.

In the course of the day Charles spoke of the intended movement to various officers, in such terms, that a few, particularly Secretary Murray and Sir Thomas Sheridan (from a desire of ingratiating themselves with him, as Lord George Murray suspected), expressed their regret for the resolution, saying that they had approved of it in the morning only from an idea that the soldiers would not go heartily into a battle when they knew that their officers were otherwise inclined. In the evening, when the whole of the officers were once more together, and were given to understand what these gentlemen had said, they told the Prince 'that they valued their lives as little as brave men ought to do, and if he inclined to go forward, they would do their duty to the last; but they desired that those who had advised his Royal Highness to march forward would sign their opinion, which would be a satisfaction to them.'[2] Murray and Sheridan were not disposed to do this, and the retreat was therefore determined upon.

During the earlier part of the march of the Prince into England, the leading Jacobites of that country had kept back, under an impression that, with so small a force, he was not likely to produce a general mustering of the party in his favour. Charles had therefore little or no communication of any kind with the party during his march.[3] Yet it appears that the very boldness of his onward movement, especially taken in connection with the expected descent from France, at length disposed

---

[1] Memoirs of Captain Daniel, a volunteer, MS, *apud* Lord Mahon's *History*.
[2] Lord George Murray's Narrative, *Jacobite Memoirs*.
[3] Examination of Secretary Murray, Appendix to Lord Mahon's *History*.

them to come out; and many were just on the point of declaring themselves, and marching to join his army, when the retreat from Derby was determined on. A Mr Barry arrived in Derby two days after the Prince left it, with a message from Sir Watkin William Wynne and Lord Barrymore, to assure him, in the name of many friends of the cause, that they were ready to join him in what manner he pleased, either in the capital, or every one to rise in his own county.[1] I have likewise been assured that many of the Welsh gentry had actually left their homes, and were on their way to join Charles, when intelligence of his retreat at once sent them all back peaceably, convinced that it was now too late to contribute their assistance. These men, from the power they had over their tenantry, could have added materially to his military force.[2] In fact, from all that appears, we must conclude that the insurgents had a very considerable chance of success from an onward movement—also, no doubt, a chance of destruction, and yet not worse than what ultimately befell many of them—while a retreat broke in a moment the spell which their gallantry had conjured up, and gave the enemy a great advantage over them.

The resolution of the council not being made known that night to the army at large, the common men, and many of the officers, on commencing their march next morning before daybreak, thought they were going to fight the Duke of Cumberland, and displayed the utmost cheerfulness and alacrity. But as soon as daylight allowed them to see the surrounding objects, and they found, from marks they had taken of the road, that they were retracing their steps, nothing was to be heard throughout the army but expressions of rage and lamentation. 'If we had been beaten,' says the Chevalier Johnstone, 'our grief could not have been greater.'

[1] The Prince mentions this in a letter to his father, February 12, 1747. Stuart Papers; Lord Mahon's *History*.
[2] My informant adds, that the Jacobite squires of Wales used afterwards, in their cups, to boast how far each had travelled on his way to join the Chevalier; a man who had gone fifty miles looking upon himself as twice as good a partisan as one who had gone only five-and-twenty; and so on.

The vexation of the army on this account was nothing to the bitter disappointment of its unhappy leader. *Vestigia nulla retrorsum* had been his motto from the beginning; and so long as he was going forward, no danger, and far less any privation or fatigue, had given him the least concern. But now, when at length compelled to turn back from the glittering prize which had almost been within his grasp, he lost all his former spirit, and, from being the leader of his hardy bands, became in appearance, as he was in reality, their reluctant follower. In the march forward, he had always been first up in the morning, had the men in motion before break of day, and generally walked, in dress and arms similar to their own, at the head of their body; but now, all his alacrity gone, and with hopes nearly blighted, he permitted the whole army to march before him (except a rearguard, whom he often compelled to wait for him a long time); and on coming out of his lodgings, dejectedly mounted a horse, and then rode on, without intercourse with his men, to the quarters assigned for him in the van.

The retreat of the army was concerted with so much secrecy, and conducted with so much skill, that it was two days' march ahead of the royal forces ere the Duke of Cumberland could make himself certain of the fact, or take measures for a pursuit. When he at length ascertained that they were retiring, he changed the defensive system which he had hitherto pursued for one of active annoyance. Putting himself at the head of his dragoons, and having mounted 1000 foot on horses provided by the gentlemen of Staffordshire, he started from Meriden Common, a position he had taken near Coventry, and, passing by very bad roads through Uttoxeter and Cheadle, came to Macclesfield on the evening of the 10th, full two days after the insurgents had reached the same point. He here received intelligence that, after retreating with wonderful expedition through Ashbourne, Leek, and Macclesfield, the enemy had just that morning left Manchester, and set forward to Wigan.

The Highlanders managed their retreat in such a manner as to unite expedition with perfect coolness, and never to allow the enemy to obtain a single advantage. Though on foot, and pursued by cavalry, they kept distinctly ahead of all danger or annoyance for twelve days, two of which they had spent in undisturbed rest at Preston and Lancaster.[1] The troops of the duke were reinforced on the 12th by a body of horse, which General Wade, now with the army in the centre of Yorkshire, sent with haste over Blackstone Edge to intercept the retiring host, but who only reached Preston after it had been several hours evacuated, and in time to join the pursuing force of the Duke of Cumberland. After a halt of one day, occasioned by the false alarm of an invasion on the southern coast, the pursuing army, amounting to 3000 or 4000 horse, continued their course from Preston, through roads which had been rendered almost impassable, partly by the weather, and partly by the exertions of men. Orders had been communicated by the duke to the country-people to break down bridges, destroy the roads, and use all means in their power to retard the insurgent army.[2] But while the hardy mountaineers found little inconvenience from either storm in the air or ruts in the ground, these very

---

[1] At Wigan, some fanatic, intending to shoot the Prince, fired at O'Sullivan by mistake. Charles would not allow any harm to be done to the assassin. Captain Daniel, who mentions this fact, with a bitter comment on what he thought such injudicious clemency, also complains respecting a woman and her son who were brought before Charles, accused of murdering one of his volunteers at Manchester, and who confessed their crime, but whom he would not allow to be punished.

[2] 'The news of the retreat of the invading army had not reached Kendal, when, on the market-day, the Duke of Perth drove rapidly up the street, accompanied by an escort of horse. The town and country people instantly took it into their heads that the rebels had been defeated, and at once resolved on capturing the duke, in whose defence the escort fired on the populace, many of whom had armed themselves with guns. His Grace, putting his head out of the carriage window, with much humanity commanded his men to "fire high, it being useless to fire on a mob." This thoughtless procedure was not unattended with loss of life, and gave rise to a circumstance involved in future mystery. The duke's servant was knocked off his horse, upon which a countryman instantly leaped, and rode off. This was done in the heat of the rencontre, and no one had taken notice who the man was, nor was he ever discovered: on the horse was a portmanteau, containing a considerable sum of money. The servant died of his injuries, and was buried, along with some others of his countrymen, in that part of the churchyard next the river; a flat stone, with a suitable inscription, was laid down, commemorative of their fate.'—*Communication in the Edinburgh Advertiser (newspaper), Nov. 23, 1827.* See also *Scots Magazine*, 1745, p. 577.

The duke was on this occasion endeavouring to reach Scotland with orders, preparatory to the arrival of the army. The resistance he met with at Kendal shewed that he could not detach himself far from the army with safety, and he therefore proceeded no farther.

circumstances served materially to impede the English dragoons, and to place the two armies upon what might be considered a more equal footing than they could otherwise have been.

The Prince, with the main body of his troops, was at Penrith on the evening of the 17th; but his rearguard, under the command of Lord George Murray, owing to the breaking down of some ammunition wagons, was this night with great difficulty brought only to Shap. The delay thus occasioned allowed the lightest of the duke's horse to overtake the rear of the retiring army. Early in the morning of the 18th, soon after it had commenced its march from Shap, some of the English chasseurs were seen hovering on the adjoining heights; and about midday, as the Highlanders were approaching the enclosures around Clifton Hall, a body of light horse seemed to be forming for attack upon an eminence a little way in front. Against these, who were merely volunteer militia of the district, Lord George Murray ordered the Glengarry clan to go forward; but, without waiting for an engagement, they immediately retreated.

The rearguard consisted of John Roy Stuart's regiment of 200 men, of the Glengarry clan, and a few companies which attended the ammunition wagons; but it was reinforced on the present occasion by the Stuarts of Appin and Cluny Macpherson's regiment, being about 1000 men in all. Lord George, under a deep sense of the importance of his trust, was the last man in the line. Anxious to check the pursuit, he despatched Stuart forward to Penrith, requesting that 1000 men might be sent to him from the main body there stationed. With this force he intended to have gained the flank of the duke's army, now approaching obliquely from the left, and to have attacked them under favour of the approaching night. But Charles returned Stuart with an order, requiring him to march with all speed forward to Penrith, without taking any offensive measures against the duke. This order, proceeding upon a general view of what was proper, would have been attended, as Lord George well perceived, with injurious effects; for the men could not have retired in the face of the enemy without being much exposed. He therefore desired Colonel Stuart not to mention the Prince's wishes to any one; and proceeded to make arrangements for giving the enemy the necessary check. At the bridge, a little to the south of the village of Clifton, where the road passed between a high stone-wall surrounding Lord Lonsdale's park and the hedge enclosures of Clifton Hall, he placed the Glengarry regiment and John Roy Stuart's along the wall—the latter being nearest the village—and the Appin and Macpherson regiments within the opposite enclosures. Soon after sunset, the main body of the duke's army, composed exclusively of cavalry, and said to be about 4000 in number, came up and formed in two lines on the moor about a mile behind.

In order to deceive the enemy as to his numbers, Lord George made some men pass behind the hedges with the colours, and returning secretly, again pass, displaying the colours once more, and this several times over. Full of anxiety about his critical situation, he passed backwards and forwards amongst the men, encouraging them to behave with firmness. He then placed himself at the head of the Macphersons, with Cluny by his side. In a narrative by Cluny,[1] it is stated that he did not ultimately give orders for action till he had asked the opinion of the chief, and found him willing to make the attack, if ordered. Daylight passed away, succeeded by a dark and cloudy night, with occasional bursts of moonlight. By one of these transient gleams, Lord George saw a body of men—dismounted dragoons, or infantry who had resumed their proper mode of warfare—coming forward upon the enclosures beyond the road. He ordered the two regiments near him to advance, in doing which they received a fire from the enemy. At this Lord George exclaimed: 'Claymore!' an ordinary war-cry among the Highlanders, and rushed on sword in hand. The whole left wing, then making a direct and spirited attack, forced the dismounted dragoons back to their main body with considerable slaughter, and shouted to let the right wing know

[1] Of which an extract is given by Scott as a note to a chapter of *Waverley*, in the edition of 1829.

of their success. They then retired in order to their original position; while the Macdonalds, with equal intrepidity, repulsed the dragoons opposite to their body. A check having thus been given to the pursuing army, Lord George drew off his men towards Penrith, where they rested and refreshed themselves.[1] The English, in their accounts of this fight, allow that they had forty private men killed and wounded, and four officers wounded; they insinuate that the Highland army suffered a much greater loss; but a letter by a person present speaks of only five found dead on the field; while the gazette published by the Prince at Glasgow admits the loss of twelve men, who had gone too far forward on the moor, and who might have been taken prisoners. At an earlier period of the day, Lord George Murray had taken the Duke of Cumberland's footman, whom the Prince instantly sent back to his master. A Mr Hamilton, an officer in the Prince's hussars, had been taken, from want of caution, before the skirmish by a straggling party.[2]

The whole of the Highland army spent the night of the 19th of December at Carlisle, where it was thought necessary, on evacuating the town next morning, to leave a garrison, consisting of the Manchester regiment, some men from the Lowland regiments, and a few French and Irish; in all 300.[3] This small garrison, animated with a greater share of courage and fidelity to the cause they had embraced than of prudence or foresight, resolved obstinately to defend the city, and took every

[1] A very minute account of the affair at Clifton is given by Lord George himself. See *Jacobite Memoirs*, 64—72.

[2] 'An inhabitant of the village of Clifton, named Thomas Savage, was very serviceable in giving the English army timely notice of the disposition of the insurgents, who had hired all the lodges and outhouses. After the action, he joyfully entertained the Dukes of Cumberland, Richmond, and Kingston, besides 100 horse, in his own house.'—*Boyse*, 127. '. . . . At the skirmish on Clifton Moor, General Honeywood fell covered with wounds. On the retreat of the enemy, the general was carried in a mangled condition to Appleby, where, to the surprise of all, he recovered. He was afterwards so much respected there, from the foregoing circumstances, and became so attached to the place, that he was elected one of their members, and continued so to the day of his death. Having a vote for the county, it was there I had the honour of knowing him, of being shewn by him the scars of those mouthed wounds he had received, and of hearing from himself the foregoing particulars.'—*Jackson's History of the Scottish Stage*, p. 80.

[3] He also left ten out of his thirteen pieces of cannon.

measure for that purpose which the time and season would allow.

Charles left Carlisle on the morning of the 20th, after having publicly thanked the garrison for their devoted loyalty, and promised to relieve them as soon as he could. The men, drawn up to hear his address, saw him depart with acclamations, and gazing from the walls, soon beheld their comrades draw near the beloved land to which *they* were never to return. The army reached the Esk, which forms the boundary of the two kingdoms, about two o'clock in the afternoon. The river, usually shallow, was swollen, by an incessant rain of several days, to the depth of four feet. Yet it was resolved to cross immediately, lest a continuation of the rain during the night should render the passage totally impracticable. A skilful arrangement was made, which almost obviated the dangers of the flood. The cavalry were stationed in the river, a few paces above the ford, to break the force of the current; and the infantry formed themselves in ranks of ten or twelve abreast, with their arms locked in such a manner as to support one another against the rapidity of the river, leaving sufficient intervals between the successive lines for the water to flow through. The whole passed over in perfect safety. Cavalry were placed farther down the river, to pick up all who might be carried away by the violence of the stream. None were lost, except a few girls. The transit of the river occupied an hour, during which, from the close numbers of the men, it appeared to be crossed by a paved street of heads and shoulders. When they got to the other side, and began to dry themselves at the fires lighted upon the bank for that purpose, they were overjoyed at once more finding their feet upon their native ground, and for a moment forgot the chagrin which had attended their retreat, with all depressing anticipations of the future.

An expedition was thus completed which, for boldness and address, is entitled to rank high amongst the most celebrated in ancient and modern times. It lasted six weeks, and was directed through a country decidedly hostile to the adventurers; it was done in the face of two armies, each capable of utterly annihilating it; and the weather was such as to add a thousand personal miseries to the general evils of the campaign. Yet such was the success which will sometimes attend the most desperate case, if conducted with resolution, that from the moment the inimical country was entered, to that in which it was abandoned, only forty men were lost, out of nearly 5000, by sickness, marauding, or the sword of the enemy. A magnanimity was preserved even in retreat beyond that of ordinary soldiers; and instead of flying in wild disorder, a prey to their pursuers, these desultory bands had turned against and smitten the superior army of their enemy, with a vigour which effectually checked it. They had carried the standard of Glenfinnin a hundred and fifty miles into a country full of foes; and now they brought it back unscathed, through the accumulated dangers of storm and war.

In their descent upon England, when, in the height of their expectations, private rapine had few charms, the Highlanders conducted themselves with tolerable propriety; and as the public money was everywhere raised, they had been able to pay for food with some degree of regularity. But in their retreat, when their pay was more precarious, private property was less respected, though not invaded or injured to nearly so great an extent as might have been expected.

The unhappy garrison of Carlisle saw their fortifications invested by the whole force of the Duke of Cumberland on the very day following the departure of their fellow-soldiers. They fired upon all who came within reach of their guns, and shewed an intention of holding out to the last extremity. But the duke, having procured cannon from Whitehaven, erected a battery on the 28th, and began to play upon the crazy walls of the town and castle. On the morning of the 30th a white flag appeared upon the walls, and the governor signified a wish to enter into a capitulation. The cannon then ceased, and a message was sent by Governor Hamilton to the duke, desiring to know what terms he would be pleased to give them. His royal highness replied that the only terms he would or could grant were, 'that they should not be put to the sword, but reserved for his majesty's pleasure.' These terms were accepted, and the royal army immediately took possession of the city and castle, placing all the garrison under a strong guard in the cathedral. The fate meted out to them will be described in the sequel.

It was now judged proper that, as the more immediate danger from the Highland army was past, the Duke of Cumberland should return to London, in order to be of service in repelling the invasion which was still dreaded from France on the south coast. He accordingly proceeded thither, leaving his troops under the command of General Wade and Lieutenant-general Hawley, the last of whom was ordered to conduct a portion of the army into Scotland, while Wade remained at Newcastle.

The Chevalier meanwhile pursued his march towards the north. On crossing the Esk, he divided his army into two parties, one of which went by Ecclefechan and Moffat, with Lord George Murray and Lords Ogilvie and Nairn. He himself led the other, with the Duke of Perth, Lords Elcho and Pitsligo, Locheil, Clanranald, Glengarry, and Keppoch. He lodged the first night at Annan. Next day, Lord Elcho advanced with 400 or 500 men to take possession of Dumfries. The rest went forward with himself on the day following. Dumfries had reason, on this occasion, for alarm, on account of the seizure of the baggage-wagons at Lockerby. The clans marched into it as into a town where they expected resistance, or at least no kindly reception; and on an idiot being observed with a gun in his hand behind a grave-stone in the churchyard, which they supposed he was about to fire upon them, it was with the greatest difficulty that the poor creature's life was spared.[1] The Prince took up his lodging in what was then the best house in the town, being that which is now the Commercial Inn, near the centre of the market-place. He had ordered the citizens to contribute the sum of £2000 for his use, with 1000 pair of shoes; some of his men adding, that they might consider it well

[1] Tradition at Dumfries.

that their town was not laid in ashes. So lately as 1836, an aged female lived in Edinburgh who recollected the occupation of Dumfries by the Highland army, being then seventeen years of age.[1] She lived opposite to the Prince's lodging, and frequently saw him. In her father's house several of the men were quartered, and it was her recollection that they greatly lamented the course which they had taken, and feared the issue of the expedition. The proprietor of the house occupied by the Prince was Mr Richard Lowthian, a nonjuror, and proprietor of Staffold Hall, in Cumberland. Though well affected to the Prince's cause, he judged it prudent not to come into his presence, and yet neither did he wish to offend him by the appearance of deliberately going out of his way. The expedient he adopted in this dilemma was one highly characteristic of the time—he got himself filled so extremely drunk, that his being kept back from the company of his guest was only a matter of decency. His wife, who could not well be taxed with treason, did the honours of the house without scruple; and some other Jacobite ladies, particularly those of the attainted house of Carnwath,[2] came forward to grace his court. When the author was at Dumfries in 1838, he saw, in the possession of a private family, one of a set of table napkins, of the most beautiful damask, resembling the finest satin, which the ladies Dalzell of Carnwath had taken to grace the table of the Prince,[3] and which they had kept ever after with the care due to the most precious relics. The drawing-room in which Charles received company is a very handsome one, panelled all round with Corinthian pilasters, the capitals of which are touched with dim gold. He was sitting here at supper with his officers and other friends, when he was told that a messenger had arrived with intelligence respecting the enemy. One M'Ghie, a painter in Dumfries, and a friend of the insurgents, had been imposed upon at Annan with the

[1] Widow Blake was the name of this remarkable person, who died at fully the age of 108. She had been the wife of a dragoon in the reign of George II.

[2] Dalzell, Earl of Carnwath, attainted in 1716; restored in 1826, in the person of Robert Alexander Dalzell.

[3] It bore the initials J. D., and the date 1704.

false news that the Duke of Cumberland had already taken Carlisle, and was advancing to Dumfries. Charles received this intelligence in another room, and soon after returned to his friends with a countenance manifestly dejected. The consequence was, that he hurriedly left the town next day, with only £1100 of the £2000, but carrying the provost and another gentleman as security for the payment of the remainder. Mrs Lowthian received from him, as a token of regard, a pair of leather gloves, so extremely fine, that they could be drawn through her ring. These, as well as the bed he had slept on, were carefully preserved by the family, and are still in existence.[1]

On the morning of the 23d the Highland army directed its march up Nithsdale, and the Chevalier spent the night at Drumlanrig, the seat of the Duke of Queensberry. He occupied the state-bed, while a great number of his men lay upon straw in the great gallery. Before departing next day, it must be regretted that the Highlanders took that opportunity of expressing their love of King James by slashing with their swords a series of portraits representing King William, Queen Mary, and Queen Anne, which hung in the grand staircase—a present from the last of these sovereigns to James, Duke of Queensberry, in consideration of his services at the Union.

From Drumlanrig, Charles proceeded through the wild pass of Dalveen into Clydesdale, designing to march upon Glasgow, though still endeavouring to conceal his intentions from the members of government at Edinburgh. He spent the night in Douglas Castle, the residence of the Duke of Douglas. He next day proceeded along the uplands of Clydesdale towards the western capital, and halted at Hamilton, where he lodged in the palace of the Duke of Hamilton. He spent the next day in hunting through the princely parks attached to that house, shooting two pheasants, two partridges, and a deer. While there is ample evidence, from the account-book of his master-of-household,[2] that he was generally careful, during his march, to

[1] Information from Mr Lowthian Ross of Staffold Hall, and others.
[2] See *Jacobite Memoirs*.

make remuneration for his lodging and provision, it would appear that at Drumlanrig and Douglas, the proprietors of which were noted enemies of his family, he exacted free quarters. At Hamilton, the master of which was understood to be well affected, there were some small payments; but tradition avers that both there and at Douglas the custom of giving vails to the servants was neglected.

It was with great difficulty that, in this last day's march, his men were prevented from sacking and burning the village of Lesmahago. During the absence of the army in England, the people of this place, whose ancestors had distinguished themselves in resisting the house of Stuart when in power, committed an act of hostility to Charles's cause, which was calculated to excite the indignation of the whole army to no common degree. The circumstances, as gathered from tradition, were as follow: The youthful and gallant Kinlochmoidart, in a journey from the Highlands, on his return from making a last appeal to Macleod and Macdonald of Sleat, passed through Lesmahago on his way to England, and was recognised by a young student of divinity, named Linning, whose religious prepossessions led him to regard the Prince's adherents with no friendly eye. As the insurgent gentleman was attended by only a single servant, this zealot conceived a design of waylaying and capturing him, which he immediately proceeded to put in execution. Taking to himself arms, and having roused the country-people, he set out after the two travellers by a path which he knew would enable him to intercept them as they proceeded along the road. He came up with them upon a waste called Brokencross Moor, within two miles of the village, and shewing his arms, commanded them to surrender in the name of King George. Kinlochmoidart's servant, on first seeing the rabble at a distance, with their old guns and pitchforks, unslung his piece, and proposed to arrest their progress by a well-directed brace of bullets. But the generous youth resolved rather to surrender at discretion, than thus occasion an unnecessary effusion of blood. He accordingly gave himself up to the daring probationer, who immediately conducted him, under a strong guard, to Edinburgh Castle, from which he was only removed some months afterwards to the shambles of Carlisle.[1]

The city of Glasgow, upon which Charles was now in full march, had much greater reason than Dumfries, or even Lesmahago, to expect severe treatment from the insurgents; while its wealth gave additional cause for alarm, without in the least degree supplying better means of defence. This city, newly sprung into importance, had never required nor received the means of defence, but was now lying, with its wide-spread modern streets and well-stored warehouses, fully exposed to the license of the invaders. It had distinguished itself, ever since the expulsion of the house of Stuart, by its attachment to the new government; and, since the Highlanders entered England, had, with gratuitous loyalty, raised a regiment of 1200 men, to aid in suppressing the insurrection. Obnoxious by its principles, and affording such prospects of easy and ample plunder, it was eagerly approached by the predatory bands of the Chevalier. By one of their most rapid marches, the first body entered Glasgow on Christmas-day, and on the following the Prince came up with the rest of the army. It has been calculated that, from their leaving Edinburgh, they had marched about 580 miles in fifty-six days, many of these being days of rest.

The necessities of the army are described as having been at this time greater than at any other period of the campaign. It was now two months since they had left the land of tartan; their clothes were of course in a dilapidated condition. The length and precipitancy of their late march had destroyed their brogues; and many of them were not only barefooted, but barelegged. Their hair hung wildly over their eyes; their beards were overgrown; and the exposed parts of their limbs were, in the language of Dougal Graham, tanned red with the weather. Altogether, they had a wayworn, savage appearance, and looked rather like a band of outlandish vagrants than a body of efficient

[1] Kinlochmoidart's captor was afterwards rewarded by government with an appointment to the pulpit of his native parish.

soldiery. The pressure of want compelled them to take every practicable measure for supplying themselves; and, in passing towards Glasgow, they had stripped such natives as they met of their shoes and other articles of dress.

Immediately upon his arrival, Charles took measures for the complete refitting of his army, by ordering the magistrates to provide 12,000 shirts, 6000 cloth coats, 6000 pair of stockings, and 6000 pair of shoes.[1] He is also said to have sent for the provost (Buchanan), and sternly demanded the names of such as had subscribed for raising troops against him, threatening to hang the worthy magistrate in case of refusal. The provost is said to have answered that he would name no person but himself, and that he was not afraid to die in such a cause. He was forced to pay a fine of £500.[2] From the town of Paisley the sum of £500 was exacted, and contributions were also raised in Renfrew and other towns near Glasgow.

Charles took up his residence in what was then considered the best house in the city, one belonging to a wealthy merchant named Glassford, which stood at the west end of the Trongate, and was afterwards taken down for the extension of that noble street. At his arrival, he is said to have caused his men to enter this house by the front gate, go out by the back door, and then, making a circuit through some by-lanes, reappear in front of the mansion, as if they had been newly arrived. But this *ruse*, practised in order to magnify the appearance of his army, was detected by the citizens of Glasgow, whose acute eyes recognised the botanical badges of the various clans, as they successively reappeared. A careful estimate of his forces, made by the friends of government at Glasgow, represented them as about 3600 foot and 500 horse. Of the latter, which were all much jaded, sixty were employed in carrying the sick; whilst about

---

[1] Inclusive of £5500 paid in September, the exactions from Glasgow amounted to £10,000, of which reimbursement was made by parliament in 1749.

[2] *Gentleman's Magazine*, January 1746, p. 43. The various authentic anecdotes which shew the disinclination of the Prince to strong measures, throw a doubt on this tale of the day.

600 of the infantry neither had arms nor seemed able to use them.[1]

During his residence in Mr Glassford's house, Charles ate twice a day in public, though without ceremony, accompanied by a few of his officers, and waited upon by a small number of devoted Jacobite ladies. He also dressed much more elegantly here than he had done at any other place throughout the campaign.[2] But nothing could make the Whigs of Glasgow regard him with either respect or affection. Previously hostile to his cause, they were now incensed against him, by his severe exactions upon the public purse, and by the private depredations of his men. To such a height did this feeling arise, that an insane zealot snapped a pistol at him as he was riding along the Saltmarket.[3] He is said to have admired the regularity and beauty of the streets of Glasgow, but to have remarked, with bitterness, that nowhere had he found so few friends.[4] During the whole week he spent in the city, he procured no more than sixty recruits—a poor compensation for the numerous desertions which now began to take place, in consequence of the near approach of his men to their own country.

After having nearly succeeded in refitting his army, he held a grand review upon *the Green*. 'We marched out,' says Captain Daniel in his memoir of the campaign,[5] 'with drums beating, colours flying, bagpipes playing, and all the marks of a triumphant army, to the appointed ground, attended by multitudes of people, who had come from all parts to see us, and especially the ladies, who, though formerly much against us, were now charmed by the sight of the Prince into the most enthusiastic loyalty. I am somewhat at a loss,' continues this devoted cavalier, ' to give a description of the Prince as he appeared at the review. No object could be more charming, no personage more captivating, no deportment more agreeable, than his at

---

[1] *Scots Magazine*, viii. 29.
[2] James Gibb, in the Prince's Household Book, *Jacobite Memoirs*.
[3] Tradition. [4] Boyse, 132.
[5] Preserved in the archives of Drummond Castle.

that time was; for, being well mounted and princely attired, having all the best endowments of both body and mind, he appeared to bear a sway above any comparison with the heroes of the last age; and the majesty and grandeur he displayed were truly noble and divine.' It may be worth while to contrast with this flattering portraiture the description which has been given of Charles by a sober citizen of Glasgow. 'I managed,' says this person, quoting his memory after an interval of seventy years, 'to get so near him, as he passed homewards to his lodgings, that I could have touched him with my hand; and the impression which he made upon my mind shall never fade as long as I live. He had a princely aspect, and its interest was much heightened by the dejection which appeared in his pale, fair countenance and downcast eye. He evidently wanted confidence in his cause, and seemed to have a melancholy foreboding of that disaster which soon after ruined the hopes of his family for ever.'[1]

CHAPTER XVII.

PRELIMINARIES OF THE BATTLE OF FALKIRK.

> 'The Hielandmen cam owre the hill,
> And owre the knowe, wi' richt gude will,
> Now Geordie's men may brag their fill,
>   For wow but they were braw, man!
> They had three generals o' the best,
> Wi' lairds and lords, and a' the rest,
> Chiels that were bred to stand the test,
>   And couldna rin awa, man!'
>   *Jacobite Song.*

HAVING recruited the spirits of his men, and improved their appointments, by eight days' residence in Glasgow, the Prince departed on the 3d of January, and sent forward his troops in

[1] *Attic Stories,* 290.

two detachments, one to Kilsyth, and the other to Cumbernauld. The inhabitants of Edinburgh, who, on the return of the Highland army from England, had apprehended a second visit, and who had resolved, in such a case, to defend the city, now set seriously about preparations for a siege. After Charles had left Edinburgh in the beginning of November, the Whig part of the community had gradually regained courage; and on the 13th of the month, when the insurgents were at the safe distance of Carlisle, the state officers had returned in a triumphant procession to their courts and chambers, saluted by a round of cannon from the castle, and a most valiant performance of Whig tunes upon the music-bells of St Giles's. Next day, Hamilton's and Gardiner's dragoons, with Price's and Ligonier's regiments of foot, boldly took possession of the city, probably assured of the safety of the measure by their avant-couriers the judges. It had been for some weeks the duty of these men, and of the Glasgow regiment of volunteers, to form posts at Stirling and other passes of the Forth, in order to prevent troops and stores passing southward to the Prince; but on the arrival of the Highland army at Glasgow, they retreated with great precipitation to Edinburgh (December 26), when it was determined, with the assistance of a number of rustic volunteers,[1] and the wreck of the Edinburgh regiment, to hold out the city at all hazards against the approaching insurgents. Their courage fortunately did not require to be put to so severe a proof; for, ere the Highlanders had left Glasgow, the English army, beginning to arrive, strengthened the city beyond all danger.

The command of the army, in the absence of the Duke of Cumberland, had been bestowed upon Lieutenant-general Henry Hawley, an officer of some standing, but ordinary abilities; who, having charged in the right wing of the king's army at

---

[1] Of these the congregations which had recently seceded from the Kirk of Scotland, and who were afterwards known by the name of the Associate Synod, formed a conspicuous portion—carrying colours on which was painted: 'For Religion, the Covenants, King, Kingdoms.'

Sheriffmuir, where the insurgents were repulsed with ease by the cavalry, entertained a confident notion that he would beat the whole of Prince Charles's army with a trifling force, and did not scruple to stigmatise the conduct of those who had hitherto been worsted by the Highlanders as rank pusillanimity. It happened, in his approach to Edinburgh, that Hamilton's and Gardiner's dragoons, coming out to meet and congratulate him on his accession to the command, encountered him near Preston, the scene of their recent disgrace; which being pointed out to him, he sharply commanded the men to sheathe their swords, and see to use them better in the campaign about to ensue than they had hitherto done.[1] Little did Hawley anticipate what a short week was to bring about.

The march of the English army was facilitated by the people of the Merse, Teviotdale, and Lothian, who brought horses to transport the baggage, and provisions to entertain the men. At Dunbar, at Aberlady, and other places, they were feasted by the gentlemen of the district.[2] The loyal part of the inhabitants of Edinburgh beheld the arrival of this army with satisfaction, and entered into an association to provide them with blankets. The city was also illuminated in honour of the occasion; when a great number of windows belonging to recusant Jacobites, and to houses which happened to be unoccupied, were broken by the mob.

In his march from Glasgow, Prince Charles slept the first night at the mansion of Kilsyth, which belonged to a forfeited estate, and was now in the possession of Mr Campbell of Shawfield. The steward had been previously ordered to provide for the Prince's reception, and told that all his expenses would be accounted for. He had accordingly provided everything suitable for the entertainment of his Royal Highness and suite. Next morning, however, on presenting his bill, he was told that it should be allowed to him on his accounting (after the Restoration) for the rents of the estate, and that, in the meantime, he

[1] *Hist. Reb.* by an impartial hand, 134.   [2] *Scots Magazine*, viii. 32.

must be contented that the balance was not immediately struck and exacted.

On the succeeding day, Charles proceeded to Bannockburn House, where he was a welcome guest, this house being, as already mentioned, the residence of Sir Hugh Paterson, one of the most zealous of his friends. His troops lay this evening in the villages of Bannockburn, Denny, and St Ninians, while Lord George Murray occupied the town of Falkirk with the advanced guard of the army. In order to employ the time till he should be joined by his northern allies, Charles now resolved to reduce Stirling, which, commanding the principal avenue to the Highlands, had long been felt as an annoying barrier to his proceedings, and to subjugate which would have given an additional lustre to his arms.

Stirling, then a town of four or five thousand inhabitants, was imperfectly surrounded by a wall, and quite incapable of holding out against the insurgents; yet, by the instigation of the governor of the castle, who had resolved to die before surrendering his charge, an attempt was made to defend it. A small body of militia, consisting chiefly of the townsmen, was provided with arms from the castle; and the Reverend Ebenezer Erskine, founder of a well-known sect, and who was a clergyman in Stirling, did all he could to inspire them with courage, and even, it is said, assumed an active command in their ranks. By means of these men, the wretched defences of the town, which consisted on one entire side of only garden walls, were provided with a sort of guard, which Governor Blakeney endeavoured to animate by an assurance that, even in case of the worst, he would keep an open door for them in the castle.

On Sunday, the 5th of January, the town was invested by the insurgents, and about nine o'clock that evening a drummer approached the east gate, beating his instrument in the manner which indicates a message. The sentinels, ignorant of the forms of war, fired several shots at this messenger, upon which he found himself obliged to throw down his drum and take to his heels. The garrison then towed the deserted instrument in over the walls as a trophy.

On Monday, the insurgents having raised a battery within musket-shot of the town, and sent a more determined message to surrender, the magistrates implored a respite till next day at ten o'clock, which was granted. The whole of Tuesday was occupied in deliberations, and in adjusting the terms of surrender. The town, however, being stimulated that evening by the discharge of twenty-seven shots from the battery, a capitulation was concluded next morning, by which it was agreed to deliver up the town, under assurance of protection for the lives and property of the townsmen, whose arms, moreover, were permitted to be restored to the castle. The insurgents entered the town about three in the afternoon.

It now becomes necessary to advert to the transactions which had been taking place in the north of Scotland during the absence of the army in England. It will be recollected that Inverness was the point where President Forbes and the Earl of Loudoun proposed to rendezvous such of the Highlanders as they could induce to appear in arms for the government. Up to the middle of November, only five of the companies (which were to consist of 100 men each) had been mustered there. In the course of the few ensuing weeks, eighteen of the twenty which were contemplated had been assembled, four of them being the followers or tenants of the Laird of Macleod, two the Macdonalds of Sleat, two the Mackenzies of Kintail, two the Earl of Sutherland's men, two the Mackays, and of the Macleods of Assynt, the Rosses, the Grants, and Mackenzies of Lewis, one each, while one company had been raised in the town of Inverness. The primary cause of the mustering of these men for the government was simply that such was the will of their respective superiors. The men themselves, in general, were inclined to the other side, as indeed were the Highland people at large, with the exception only of a few chiefs, most of whom acted under reasons of mere policy. It was only by force of the clan-feeling of obedience to the chief, that the men in general were brought to serve King George. And even this powerful feeling did not in all instances prevail. For example, when the Laird of Macleod summoned his chief tacksmen or tenants to meet at Dunvegan, each with his quota of men, in order to go to the muster at Inverness, Macleod of Bernera, one of the principal men amongst them, wrote to him in the following, or similar terms: 'My dear laird, none of your clan would be more ready than I to attend your summons upon most occasions. I send you the men required, to whose service you are entitled; but, for myself, I go where a higher duty calls me.' And Bernera joined the Prince, with whom he continued to the end of the campaign, his own son being an officer in one of the laird's independent companies.[1]

As another illustration of the feeling which animated the dependants of the well-affected Highland proprietors, a body of Kintail Mackenzies were brought down by their chief, the Earl of Seaforth, to Brahan Castle, under pretence that his lordship's estates thereabouts were in danger from Lord Lovat, the real object being to draw them on to appear for the government, or at least to prevent them from joining the insurgent army. The men, at length penetrating the design, or at least thinking themselves deceived, went home, saying 'that they knew but one

---

[1] Information from Sir William Macleod Bannatyne, who, being cousin-german both to young Clanranald and Mr Macleod of Muiravonside (Charles's envoy to Skye), possessed much accurate knowledge respecting the transactions of this period, to which his own memory almost reached.* With reference to Bernera, Sir William added a curious anecdote, which was thus transcribed for me by my late amiable friend Mr Donald Gregory, author of a valuable historical work on the Highlands: 'Many years after the rebellion, an action was raised before the Court of Session, at the instance of the town of Paisley, against Secretary Murray, for the amount of a contribution imposed on the town, and received by the secretary on the Prince's behoof. While the judges were deliberating on this case, Bernera, in company with Sir W. M. B., entered the court. Lord Kames was speaking in his usual jocular way. "My lords," says he, "before proceeding to the merits of this cause, we should ascertain the proper designation of the defender. It appears to me that he should be styled Mr John Murray, secretary to Charles Edward Stuart, the leader of certain Highland banditti, who infested this country in 1745." It may be supposed that Bernera, who was himself one of the banditti, did not listen very patiently to this character of his comrades. Clenching his fist, he said to his companion: "If I had yon fellow anywhere than where he is now, I would teach him to call better men than himself banditti!"'

---

* Sir William died November 1833, aged above ninety

king, and if they were not at liberty to fight for him, they would do it for no other.'[1] It may thus be readily guessed that the troops gathered by Lord Loudoun were not likely, on a fair trial, to yield very hearty or effective service to the government. At the same time, it was of importance to the government that so many men should be engaged, however nominally, in its behalf, who might have otherwise been fighting under the insurgent standard.

The attention of Loudoun and the president was called chiefly to three points: the state of Fort Augustus under an investment by the Master of Lovat. the machinations of old Lovat himself, and some late proceedings in the counties of Aberdeen and Banff. The earl marched with a party (December 3) to Fort Augustus, which he easily relieved. He returned to Inverness on the 8th, after giving the people of Stratherrick (a district belonging to Lovat) a strong hint of what his troops would do to their country if they joined the insurgents. Allowing his men a single day's rest, he set out on the 10th for Castle Downie or Beaufort, the residence of Lord Lovat, to obtain the best satisfaction he could for the peaceable behaviour of such of the Frasers as had not yet risen. Lovat, still maintaining a fair face, promised to collect the arms of his clan for the earl, and, as a pledge for the fulfilment of his promise, agreed to accompany Lord Loudoun to Inverness. There the earl waited with patience till the appointed day, when, finding that the old chief was dallying with him, he clapped a guard upon his lodgings. Lovat nevertheless escaped by a back door during the night, being carried off upon men's shoulders. This was a perplexing event, for it obliged the earl to keep a large portion of his troops at Inverness, to watch the further proceedings of Lovat, while they were much needed in another quarter, to which our attention is now to be turned.

On the departure of the Highland army from Edinburgh,

---

[1] Paper by James Mackenzie, writer in Edinburgh (a native of Orkney), in Bishop Forbes's Papers (Lyon in Mourning, MS.), and attested by the bishop to be 'true and exact.'

Lord Lewis Gordon had returned to that district in Banff and Aberdeenshire over which his family had for centuries exercised almost unlimited control. There he busied himself for some weeks in raising men for the Prince's service, every landed proprietor being forced to furnish an able-bodied man, or £5 sterling, for every hundred Scots of his valued rent. He thus easily completed a regiment of two battalions, one of which he placed under the command of Gordon of Abbachy, the other under James Moir of Stoneywood. He also gathered a considerable sum of money. All this time his brother, the Duke of Gordon, kept up a fair appearance with the government. To put an end to the recruiting and exactions of Lord Lewis, the Laird of Macleod was despatched from Inverness on the 10th of December with his 500 clansmen, followed closely by 200 more under Major Monro of Culcairn, and soon after reinforced by 500 men under the Laird of Grant. An insurgent party, which had kept a post on the Spey, retired as he approached; and Lord Lewis, falling back on Aberdeen, called forward to that place a number of men who had been raised in the counties of Forfar and Kincardine, together with some of Lord John Drummond's French troops recently landed at Montrose, and 300 Farquharsons under Farquharson of Monaltrie. In all, his lordship had about 1200 men. Meanwhile, the Laird of Grant, under some apprehension of danger to his own country, went home with his men. Culcairn, with his two companies, took post at Old Meldrum; and Macleod, with only his 500 clansmen, advanced to Inverury, twelve miles from Aberdeen. Lord Lewis no sooner heard of this last incautious movement, than he marched from Aberdeen (December 23), and that afternoon, in the twilight, fell unexpectedly, with all his strength, upon the Macleods at Inverury. There being only 300 in the village against four times their number (for 200 were cantoned in the neighbourhood), and having had no preparation or warning, the Skye chief was in a situation of no small peril, more particularly as his men were not over-zealous in the cause. He quickly got them together, and, if we are to believe the government account, made a stand for about twenty minutes, fighting by moonlight. Their shot being at last expended, they retired with precipitation; nor did their retreat stop till they had got to Elgin.[1] Few were killed in this skirmish; but Lord Lewis took forty-one prisoners, among whom were Mr Gordon, younger of Ardoch, Forbes of Echt, Maitland of Pitrichie, and Mr John Chalmers, one of the professors of Aberdeen university, and remarkable as the first publisher of a newspaper north of the Forth.[2]

Lord Lewis thereafter conducted his forces to Perth, where Lord Strathallan already had a considerable body of troops assembled, including several hundreds of the Frasers, under the Master of Lovat, the Mackintoshes, 400 in number, a well-affected part of the clan Mackenzie, various recruits for the regiments in the south, some Low-country men, and the rest of the troops of Lord John Drummond. There was also a small party of Clanranald Macdonalds, who had come as a convoy with a considerable quantity of treasure, recently landed from a Spanish vessel in the island of Barra. The Mackintoshes had been raised under somewhat remarkable circumstances. The country of this clan was in Badenoch, not far from Inverness. The chief, or laird, usually called Mackintosh of Mackintosh, was, or affected to be, loyal to the existing sovereign, and personally appeared in arms on that side. At the same time his wife, a young woman of high spirit and resolution, raised the clan for the Chevalier, and adding to it the 300 Farquharsons just mentioned, formed a very good regiment, which was now ready for active service. The strange proceedings of this lady caused her to be distinguished by the jocular appellation of

---

[1] 'When he [Macleod] endeavoured to rally them at Elgin, they kept him in mind how he had already deceived them, by making them believe they were to serve the Young Man, when he first brought them out of the island; and afterwards how, to hold them together, at Inverness, he had dissembled with them, as if he always meant to let them follow their own inclinations; till at last, having led them to Inverury, a just dispersion (said they) had there befallen them for his perfidiousness to the Young Man. And yet (they told him), would he but still return to his duty, they would not so much as look home, for haste to go with him; whereas, if he continued obstinate, they would leave him to a man; which they did accordingly.'—*James Mackenzie's paper, as before quoted.*

[2] *The Aberdeen Journal*, which still exists under the charge of Mr Chalmers's descendant.

Colonel Anne. It is said that, at a subsequent part of the campaign, Mackintosh himself, being taken in the capacity of a loyal militia captain by a party of the insurgents, was actually brought as a prisoner into the presence of his wife, who was then acting a semi-military part in the Chevalier's army. She said, with military laconism: 'Your servant, captain!' to which he replied, with equal brevity: 'Your servant, colonel!'[1] Into such strange relations are the various parts of society apt to be thrown by a civil war.

It will be recollected that Charles had sent Maclachlan of Maclachlan from Carlisle, to urge Lord Strathallan to forward to him all the men he had assembled at Perth. His lordship, for what reason does not plainly appear, did not conceive it expedient to obey this order: perhaps he at first thought his forces too small, and afterwards the presence of a body of government troops at Stirling might seem a sufficient obstacle. The Highlanders, burning to be engaged in the active service of the Prince, urged him to allow them to march; but in vain. They would have gone without his permission; but they had no money, and many of those lately come down from the hills wanted arms. Lord Strathallan had possession of money, arms, ammunition, and stores of all kinds; and his views were supported by the Lowlanders and French. The Highland officers formed various projects for getting at the money and arms, in order to proceed to the south, for, under the sense of so high a duty, they were not disposed to be very scrupulous. Furious disputes had taken place between them and Lord Strathallan's supporters, and a battle seemed inevitable betwixt the two parties, when all was settled by the receipt of a letter from the Prince, dated at Dumfries, and conveyed by Rollo of Powhouse, commanding them to hold themselves in readiness to join the army, which was now marching to Glasgow, whence they should receive further orders.[2] Charles was now joined at Stirling by

---

[1] Letter of the late Bishop Mackintosh, MS., in possession of the author. Lady Mackintosh was a daughter of Farquharson of Invercauld, a friend of the government.
[2] Home, iii. 139.

these troops, who brought with them a great quantity of stores landed from France, and the Spanish money which had been debarked at the island of Barra.

The army, thus strengthened, broke ground before Stirling Castle on the 10th, and summoned Governor Blakeney to surrender. That officer gave for answer that he would defend his post to the last extremity, being determined to die, as he had lived, a man of honour. They first attempted to convert a large old building at the head of the town, called *Mar's Work*, into a battery; but finding themselves to be there peculiarly exposed to the fire of the garrison, they were soon obliged to look about for new ground.

On the day that Charles thus commenced the siege of Stirling, Hawley had been joined at Edinburgh by all the divisions of the army which he could immediately expect. As his force consisted of nearly eight thousand men, of whom thirteen hundred were cavalry, he considered himself fully a match for the insurgents, and now determined to offer them battle, though he knew that there were several other regiments on the march to Scotland, which would soon join him.[1] He was perhaps induced to take this step, partly by observing that the Highland force was every day increasing, and partly by a wish to relieve the garrison of Stirling; but a blind confidence in the powers of the army, especially the dragoons, and an ardent desire of distinguishing himself, must certainly be allowed to have chiefly instigated him to the measure. He had often been heard to reflect upon the misconduct of Cope (who, in his turn, had taken bets, it is said, to a large amount that this new commander would have no better success than himself). He therefore went on to battle under a kind of infatuation, of which the proper effects were soon seen.

On the morning of the 13th, five regiments, together with the Glasgow militia, and Hamilton's and Ligonier's (late Gardiner's)

---

[1] Six thousand Hessians, who were compelled to serve the king of Great Britain in terms of a recent treaty, and who had embarked at Williamstadt on the 1st of January, were also at this time hourly expected to enter the Firth of Forth.

dragoons, left Edinburgh, under the command of Major-general Huske, and reached Linlithgow that evening. A party of Highlanders under Lord George Murray, who had advanced thither, retired before them to Falkirk. Next day three other regiments marched westwards to Borrowstounness, to be ready to support General Huske in case of an engagement; on the following morning, the remainder of the army, with the artillery, pursued the same route. Hawley himself marched on the 16th, with Cobham's dragoons, who had just come up. The army was accompanied by a north-of-England squire named Thornton, whose zealous loyalty had induced him to raise a band called the Yorkshire Blues, who were maintained and commanded by himself.

The whole of this well-disciplined and well-appointed force encamped to the north-west of Falkirk, upon the same field where, four centuries before, Sir John de Graham and Sir John Stewart of Bonkill, the friends of Wallace, had testified their patriotism in the arms of death.

On the morning of the 17th, Lieutenant-colonel John Campbell (afterwards Duke of Argyll), who had been hitherto exerting himself to keep the West Highlands quiet, joined the English camp with upwards of a thousand of his clan.

General Hawley was this morning spared the necessity of marching forward to raise the siege of Stirling, by intelligence that the Highlanders were in motion; for Prince Charles, learning the near approach of the English general, had resolved, with his usual ardour, to meet him half-way, and was now drawing out his men, as for a review, upon the Plean Moor, two miles to the east of Bannockburn, and about seven from Falkirk. The English army did not, therefore, strike their camp, but judged it necessary to remain where they were till the intentions of the enemy should be revealed.

When the English lay upon the field of Falkirk, and the Highlanders were drawn up upon the Plean Moor, their respective camp lights were visible to each other over the level tract of country which intervened. Betwixt the two armies lay the straggling remains of the once extensive Torwood, in whose gloomy recesses Wallace used to find a refuge suited to his depressed fortunes.

On this occasion, as on almost all others throughout the campaign, Charles found himself able to outgeneral the old and experienced officers whom the British government had sent against him. Though he had drawn out his men, and seemed ready for an immediate encounter with Hawley's army, he kept his real intentions a secret from even his own officers, making the main body believe that the evolutions in which they were engaged were only those of an ordinary review;[1] and it was not till mid-day that, having suddenly called a council of war, he announced his determination to march in the direction of the enemy.

The conduct of Hawley displayed as much of negligence on this occasion as that of Charles displayed calculation and alacrity. He was inspired, as already said, with a lofty contempt for the Highlanders, or 'Highland militia,' as he himself was pleased to call them. Having come to drive the wretched rabble from Stirling, he could not conceive the possibility of their coming to attack him at Falkirk. Being apprised, on the 16th, by a Mr Roger, who had passed through the Highland army, and conversed with some of the officers, that there was a proposal amongst them to march next day against him, he treated the informant with rudeness, and contented himself with giving vent to a vain expression of defiance.[2] On the morning of the day of battle, such was his continued security, that he obeyed an insidious invitation from the Countess of Kilmarnock, by retiring from the camp to breakfast with her at Callander House, although quite aware of that lady's relationship to an insurgent chief, and even perhaps of her own notorious attachment to the cause of Prince Charles. The *ruse* of the countess was attended with success. She was a woman of fine person and manners; and Hawley, completely fascinated,

[1] Chevalier Johnstone's *Memoirs*.
[2] MS. in possession of Mr David Constable.

spent the whole of this important forenoon in her company, without casting a thought upon his army.

Charles, observing the wind to come from the south-west, directed the march of his men towards a piece of ground considerably to the right of Hawley's camp, in order that, in the ensuing encounter, his troops might have that powerful ally to support them in rear. He took care, at the same time, to despatch Lord John Drummond, with nearly all the horse, towards the other extremity of Hawley's lines, so as to distract and engage the attention of the enemy. In order to produce still further uncertainty among the English regarding his intentions, he caused a body to retire to Stirling, with colours displayed in their sight; and upon the Plean Moor, which was thus entirely deserted, he left his great standard flying, as if that had still been his headquarters.

Perplexed by the various objects which they saw dispersed over the country, the English army remained in their camp, not altogether unapprehensive of an attack, but yet strongly disposed, like their commander, to scout the idea that the Highlanders would venture upon so daring a measure. While they were still ignorant of the stealthy advance which Charles was making, a countryman, who had perceived it, came running into the camp, and exclaimed: 'Gentlemen, what are you about? The Highlanders will be immediately upon you!' Some of the officers cried out: 'Seize that rascal—he is spreading a false alarm!' But they were speedily assured of the truth of the report by two of their number, who had mounted a tree, and, through a telescope, discovered the Highlanders in motion. The alarm was immediately communicated to a commanding-officer, who, in his turn, lost no time in conveying it to Callander House. Hawley received the intelligence with the utmost coolness, and contented himself with ordering that the men might put on their accoutrements, but said that they need not get under arms. The troops obeyed the order, and proceeded to take their dinner.

It was between one and two o'clock that several gentlemen,

volunteer attendants on the camp, coming in upon the spur, gave final and decisive intelligence of the intention of the enemy. They reported that they had seen the lines of the Highland infantry evolve from behind the Torwood, and cross the Carron by the *Steps* of Dunipace. The drums instantly beat to arms; an urgent message was despatched for the recreant Hawley; and the lines were formed, in front of the camp, by officers on duty. The negligence of their general was now bitterly reflected on by the men, many of whom seemed impressed with the idea that he had sold them to the enemy.

The last message which had been despatched to Callander succeeded in bringing Hawley to a sense of the exigency of his affairs, and he now came galloping up to his troops, with his head uncovered, and the appearance of one who has abruptly left a hospitable table. The sky, which had hitherto been calm and cloudless, became at this moment overcast with heavy clouds, and a high wind beginning to blow from the south-west, foreboded a severe storm of rain.

While they stood in the position already mentioned, Charles was eagerly leading forward his desultory bands to a wild upland of irregular surface called Falkirk Muir, two miles south-west of the English camp. In crossing the Carron at Dunipace Steps, and thus making for a rising ground where he could overlook Hawley's position, he precisely acted over again the course he had pursued four months before, in crossing the Esk at Musselburgh, and ascending the heights above Cope's station at Preston; and it may be added, that there is a remarkable resemblance in the corresponding localities. Hawley, on learning the direction Charles was taking, seems to have suspected that he was in danger of becoming the victim of a similar course of measures to that which occasioned the defeat of Cope; and having the bad effect of that general's caution before his eyes, he appears to have immediately adopted the resolution of disputing the high ground. He therefore gave a hasty command to the dragoons to march towards the top of the hill, in order, if possible, to anticipate the Highlanders; the foot he commanded to follow at quick pace, with their bayonets inserted in the musket. To this precipitate measure, by which he placed his army on ground he had never seen, and which was extremely unfit for the movements of regular troops, while it was proportionately advantageous for the Highlanders, the disasters of the day are in a great measure to be attributed.

The dragoons galloped up a narrow way at the east end of Bantaskine Park; the foot followed, with a show of promptitude and courage; and the artillery, consisting of ten pieces, came last of all, driven by a band of Falkirk carters, who, with their horses, had been hastily pressed into King George's service that forenoon—for it was not till some time after this memorable campaign that the British artillery was drawn by horses and men regularly appointed for the purpose. Whether from accident, or from the design of the drivers, who were ill affected to their duty, the artillery stuck in a swampy place at the end of the loan, beyond all power of extrication; and the drivers then cut the traces of their horses, and scampered back to Falkirk. The sullen south-west, against which the army was marching, now let forth its fury full in their faces, blinding them with rain, and rendering the ascent of the hill doubly painful. Still they struggled on, encouraged by the voice and gesture of their general, whose white uncovered head was everywhere conspicuous as he rode about, and who seemed ardently desirous to recover the effects of his negligence.

Before Hawley commenced this unlucky march, Charles had entered Falkirk Muir at another side, and was already ascending the hill. His troops marched in two parallel columns, about two hundred paces asunder; that which was nearest the king's army consisting of the clans which had been in England, and the other comprising all the late accessions, with some Lowcountry regiments. The former was designed to become the front line in ranking up against the enemy.

A sort of race now commenced between the dragoons and clans towards the top of the moor; each apparently esteeming the preoccupation of that ground as of the most essential importance to the event. The clans attained the eminence first, and the dragoons were obliged to take up somewhat lower ground, where they were prevented from coming into direct opposition with the Highlanders by a morass on their left.

The three Macdonald regiments, according to the right of the great Clan Colla to that distinguished position, marched at the head of the first column, with the intention of forming eventually the right wing of the army in battle-array; but, on the present occasion, Glencairnaig's minor regiment of Macgregors, exerting greater speed in the race with Hawley's dragoons, and being therefore the first to reach the top of the hill, took that post of honour, which they retained throughout the ensuing conflict. The first line of the insurgent army was therefore formed by the following regiments, reckoning from right to left: Macgregor, Keppoch, Clanranald, Glengarry, Appin, Cameron, the Frasers under the Master of Lovat, and the Macphersons under Cluny their chief. At the right extremity, Lord George Murray had the chief command, fighting, as usual, on foot. On the left, there was no general commander, unless it was Lord John Drummond, whose attention, however, was chiefly directed to his French regiment in the rear. The second line was chiefly composed of Low-country regiments, which stood in the following order: Athole, Ogilvie, Gordon, Farquharson, Cromarty, and the French. The Prince stood on an eminence[1] behind the second line, with the horse; having been implored by the army not to hazard his person by that active collision with the enemy for which, as at Preston, he had expressed his ardent desire.

Opposite to the Highland army thus disposed, but rather inclining to the north, on account of the morass and the declivity, the English foot were drawn up also in two lines, with the horse in front, and a reserve in the rear. The first line comprised the following regiments from right to left: Wolfe, Cholmondley, the Scots Royals, Price, and Ligonier; the second, Blakeney, Monro, Fleming, Barrel, and Battereau. The

---

[1] Still popularly termed *Charlie's Hill*, and now covered with wood.

PRELIMINARIES OF THE BATTLE OF FALKIRK.   229

reserve was composed of the Glasgow regiment, Howard's, and the Argyle militia.

Falkirk Muir, an upland now covered with thriving farms, and intersected by the Union Canal and Edinburgh and Glasgow Railway, was then a rough tract, irregular in its surface, without rising into peaks, and bearing no vegetation but heath. It was upon its broad ridge, at the top, that the two armies were disposed, the Highlanders extending more to the south, and occupying, as already stated, somewhat higher ground. The country was not encumbered by enclosures of any kind; but a sort of hollow, or *dean*, as it is called in Scotland, commenced nearly opposite to the centre of the Highland lines, and ran down between the two armies, gradually widening towards the plain below, and opening up at one place into a spacious basin. By this ravine, which was too deep to be easily passed from either side, two-thirds of the English were separated from about one-half of the Highland army. Owing to the convexity of the ground, the wings of both armies were invisible to each other.

To conclude this account of the disposition of the English, the Argyle Highlanders and Ligonier's regiment were stationed in the hollow just mentioned; the Glasgow regiment was posted at a farm-house behind the other extremity; and the horse stood a little in advance of the foot, opposite to the right wing of the Highlanders, without any portion of the ravine intervening. General Hawley commanded in the centre, Brigadier Cholmondley on the left, and Major-general Huske on the right. The horse were immediately under the command of Lieutenant-colonel Ligonier, who, stationed on the left with his own regiment (lately Gardiner's), had Cobham's and Hamilton's on his right, and personally stood almost opposite to Lord George Murray.

In numbers, the two armies were nearly equal, both amounting to about 8000; and as they were alike unsupplied by artillery (for the Highlanders had also left theirs behind), there could scarcely have been a better match, so far as strength was concerned. But the English had disadvantages of another sort, such as the unfitness of the ground for their evolutions, the interruption given to so much of their lines by the ravine, the comparative lowness of their ground, and their having the wind and rain in their faces.

www.ingramcontent.com/pod-product-compliance
Lightning Source LLC
Chambersburg PA
CBHW020812230426
43666CB00007B/975